L

mer's®

Paris
& Disneyland® Resort Paris
with your Family

From captivating culture to the magic of Disneyland®

by Anna Brooke

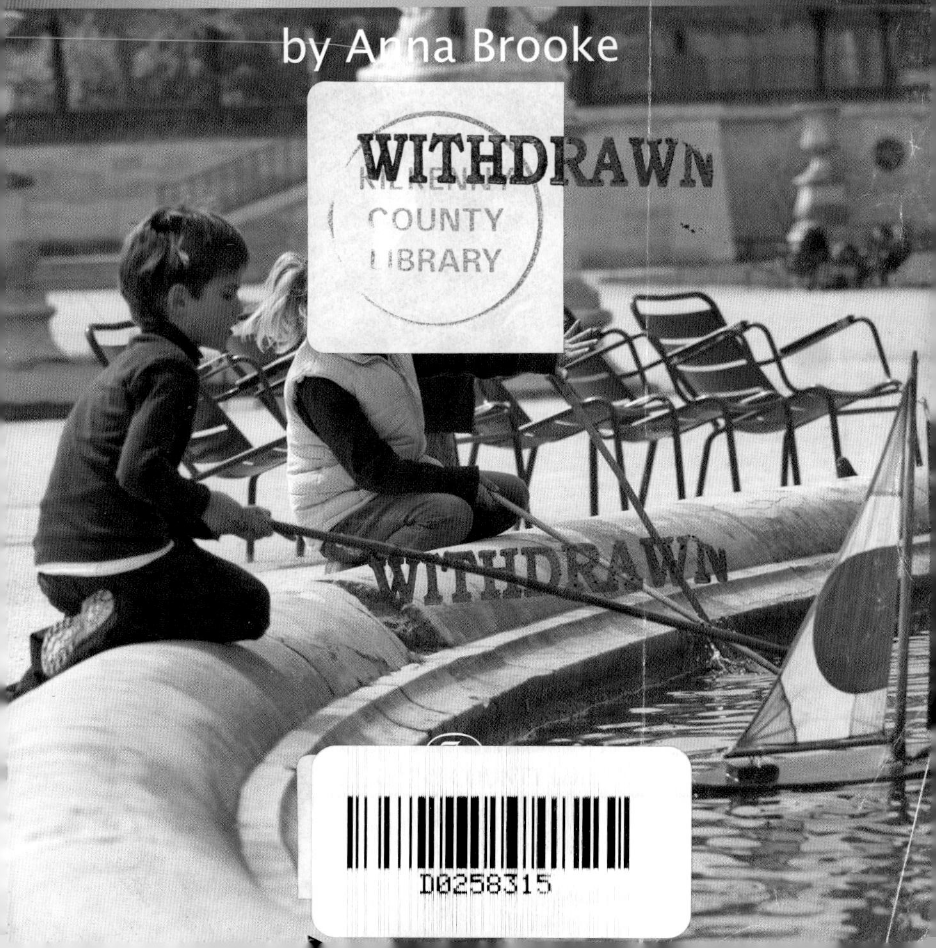

UK Publisher: Sally Smith
Executive Project Editor: Daniel Mersey (Frommer's UK)
Commissioning Editor: Mark Henshall (Frommer's UK)
Development Editor: Kate Calvert
Project Editor: Hannah Clement (Frommer's UK)
Cartographer: Jeremy Norton
Photo Research: Jill Emeny (Frommer's UK)

British Library Cataloguing in Publication Data
A catalogue record for this book is available from the British Library

ISBN: 978-0-470-51933-2

Typeset by Wiley Indianapolis Composition Services
Printed and bound in China by SNP Leefung Printers

5 4 3 2 1

Contents

METRO

About the Author

Anna Brooke began her love affair with France on a camping trip in Brittany aged 13. After studying French and European Studies at university, she moved to Paris in 2000 and has spent the last 8 years as a freelance travel writer for a variety of publications (*Time Out, Financial Times,* Alastair Sawdays, Dorling & Kindersley) and Frommer's, for whom she also wrote the Day by Day guide to Provence and the Riviera, the MTV Guide to France and updated the Day by Day guide to Paris. When she is not travel writing, she sings in an electro band called Monkey Anna (www.myspace.com/annaebrooke) and is an actress (three years performing in a cabaret, films, music videos and ads). She is currently looking to host her own TV travel programme. Any offers are welcome; contact her at annaebrooke@yahoo.fr.

Acknowledgements

To Perdy.

Dedication

Never-ending thanks to the love of my life, Pascal Chind, who has been a pillar of support throughout the writing of this book.

Immense gratitude also goes to everybody – friends, family and passers-by for your tips and constant stream of encouragement, particularly Kate Antcliff, Mike and Flora Baughan, Anne Bracconi, Jules-César Bréchet, Elodie and Etienne Cavard, Adam Christie, Maureen Clarke (Frommer's USA), Christelle and Pascal Cotin, Alison Culliford, Laurent Ferraro, Kate Gamble, Anna Goldrein (Wiley UK), Sandrine Hamon, Rosa Jackson, Sebastien Joly, Sebastien Lamisse, Rosie Lockley, Alexandre Markoff, Nicola Platts, Marc and Melly Poulain, Clothilde Redfern, Renaud Serniclay (the other half of Monkey Anna), Andrea Stemler, Juliette Vergez-Honta, Heather Whitehall, Nathalie Whittle, Sarah Worley and everybody at Agence Media Presse and at Woods TV.

A special thanks also goes to Constance Felix-Trubert, Pauline Vergez-Honta and Blandine, François and Armand Frechard, who all helped with research.

Un grand merci, for my wonderful editors Mark Henshall, Jill Emeny, Fiona Quinn and Kate Calvert, who have the patience of angels and have given a great deal of support.

And last but not least, thank you to Dawn Postans, the Horobin family, the Middleton family and Gail, Bill and Robin Brooke for their unconditional love and encouragement.

An Additional Note

Please be advised that travel information is subject to change at any time and this is especially true of prices. We therefore suggest that you write or call ahead for confirmation when making your travel plans. The authors, editors and publisher cannot be held responsible for experiences of readers while travelling. Your safety is important to us however, so we encourage you to stay alert and be aware of your surroundings.

Star Ratings, Icons & Abbreviations

Hotels, restaurants and attraction listings in this guide have been ranked for quality, value, service, amenities and special features using a star-rating system. Hotels, restaurants, attractions, shopping and nightlife are rated on a scale of zero stars (recommended) to three (exceptional). In addition to the star rating system, we also use 5 feature icons that point you to the great deals, in-the-know advice and unique experiences. Throughout the book, look for:

FIND	Special finds – those places only insiders know about
MOMENT	Special moments – those experiences that memories are made of
VALUE	Great values – where to get the best deals
OVERRATED	Places or experiences not worth your time or money
GREEN	Attractions employing responsible tourism policies

The following **abbreviations** are used for credit cards:

AE	American Express
MC	MasterCard
V	Visa

A Note on Prices

In the Family-friendly Accommodation sections of this book we have used a price category system.

An Invitation to the Reader

In researching this book, we discovered many wonderful places – hotels, restaurants, shops and more. We're sure you'll find others. Please tell us about them, so we can share the information with your fellow travellers in upcoming editions. If you were disappointed with a recommendation, we'd love to know that too. Please write to;

Frommer's Paris & Disneyland® Resort Paris with Your Family, 1st edition
John Wiley & Sons, Ltd
The Atrium
Southern Gate
Chichester
West Sussex, PO19 8SQ

Photo Credits

Cover Credits

Main Image: © Glenn Harper / Alamy
Small Images (L-R):
© Disney
© Frank Fell / TTL
© John Lawrence / TTL
© David Noton / TTL
Back Cover: © David Plummer / Alamy

Front Matter Credits

Pi: © Glenn Harper / Alamy; piii: © Disney; © Frank Fell / TTL; © John Lawrence / TTL; © David Noton / TTL; piv: © Disney; © Frank Fell / TTL; © John Lawrence / TTL; © David Noton / TTL.

Inside Images

© Anna Brooke: p. 5, p. 84, p. 108, p. 136, p. 140, p. 188, p. 191, p. 200, p. 247, p. 248, p. 251.

© David Carton / FotoLibra. All Rights Reserved: p. 243.

© Disney: p. 12, p. 201, p. 214, p. 217, p. 219, p. 224, p. 225, p. 228, p. 232, p. 237, p. 241.

© ELIOPHOT-Aix en Provence: p. 146.

© Elyane Prache – HJPP: p. 197.

© Hôtel Aviatic: p. 169.

© Lawrence Alemanno: p. 172.

© L'Hotel, Paris: p. 167.

© Pavillon de la Reine: p. 144.

© Relais du Louvre: p. 69.

Courtesy of Alamy: p. 13 (© Jon Arnold Images Ltd); p. 73 (© Andrew Sanger Photography); p. 82 (© Richard Wareham Fotografie); p. 105 (© Andrew Duke); p. 121 (© Neil McAllister); p. 138 (© Peter Horree); p. 149 (© Sam Gillespie); p. 160 (© photofrenetic); p. 173 (© Glenn Harper); p. 182 (© Cosmo Condina); p. 192 (© Tibor Bognar); p. 194 (© Cephas Picture Library).

Courtesy of Hôtel de Crillon: p. 4 (© Steve Murez); p. 68 (© C. Kicherer).

Courtesy of Les Etoiles du Rex: p. 97.

Courtesy of Paris Tourism Office: p. 3 (© Alain Potignon); p. 10, p. 55, p. 59, p. 101, p. 113, p. 131 (© Marc Bertrand); p. 50, p. 51, p. 62, p. 65, p. 81, p. 85, p. 86, p. 112, p. 129 (© Amélie Dupont); p. 57 (© David Lefranc); p. 63 (© Angélique Clément).

Courtesy of PCL: p. 1, p. 190 (© David Barnes); p. 47, p. 79, p. 158, p. 181 (© Bruce Yuan-Yue Bi); p. 104, p. 115 (© Brian Lawrence Images Ltd); p. 107 (© David Noble); p. 127, p. 154, p. 164, p. 177 (© Yann Guichaoua); p. 250 (© Oliver Benn).

Courtesy of Photolibrary Group: p. 93 (© Cephas Picture Library).

Courtesy of TTL: p. 7, p. 125 (© David Noton); p. 77 (© John Lawrence).

1 Family Highlights of Paris & Disneyland®

Few cities evoke as much promise and passion as the French capital. The mention of its name is enough for people to go starry-eyed as they dream of walking along the banks of the River Seine, stopping in café terraces, eating in some of Europe's finest restaurants, and introducing their children to the cultural attractions of one of the most beautiful capital cities in the world.

Paris has always been *the* city for me; first as a teenager, when my parents unexpectedly extended our holiday in Brittany to Paris and Disneyland (I remember walking across the gardens on the Champs-Elysées, dodging the sprinklers on the flowerbeds, and being wowed by Disney's fireworks display); then as a happy-go-lucky student on my year abroad; and now as an ex-pat who still hasn't seen everything there is to see – even after eight years.

I'm not alone in my enthusiasm. The French government reports that the world's most visited attractions last year were the Louvre (7.6 million), the Eiffel Tower (6.4 million), the Pompidou Centre (5.3 million), and Versailles (3.3 million) – proof that Paris and its suburbs are simply inexhaustible in their ability to charm.

For many families Paris is about discovery, the memories your family makes, and the broader history you, the children and the city are part of. But don't let yourself get stuck in the city centre for the whole of your trip – the **Île-de-France** (the region in which Paris lies) brims with activities for families, be it the parks and forests on the outer edges – Bois de Boulogne and Parc de la Villette; Versailles – the Sun King's Palace; Parc Astérix – a thoroughly French theme park; or **Disneyland® Resort Paris**, where the frivolous fun Walt Disney dedicated his life to bursts into action inside a fast-moving resort that you could easily spend two days in.

Placing both feet firmly on the ground again, visiting with children, especially babies and toddlers, can be frustrating in the city centre. Restaurants (unless you aim at the top end) rarely have high chairs or clean toilets, and the Métro with its narrow turnstiles and never-ending staircases is unsuitable for buggies. However, once you've accepted this and brought along the necessaries (wipes, baby-carriers, etc... see Children's Kit p. 20), you'll find Paris a delightful city – whatever the weather or the time of year.

BEST FAMILY EXPERIENCES

Strolling along the Seine is a highly enjoyable way to take in Paris's iconic, sweeping vistas, identify the main sights, and absorb the laid-back atmosphere as lovers walk hand in hand, anglers cast their lines, *bouquinistes* (secondhand-book dealers, see p. 163) peddle their old editions, and rollerbladers and cyclists dodge passers-by—especially on Sundays during the summer months when stretches of the quaysides are closed to cars, and the river's edge becomes a beach with activities for youngsters. See Paris Plage, p. 24.

Ambling around the open-air or covered markets (*marchés*) to buy fresh food – perhaps a ripe 'n' creamy Camembert, some *saucisson*, or a pumpkin-gold melon for a picnic. For market listings see each chapter.

Meeting Mickey and Friends can be the highlight of any young child's trip to Disneyland Paris. To make the magic last longer, book a Disneyland Resort® hotel where the characters make regular appearances, and sometimes join you for breakfast. See p. 234.

Watching a movie in the open air in July and August at **Parc de la Villette**. Parisians turn up in their thousands, picnic basket and blankets in hand, to watch films projected onto Europe's largest inflatable screens. This is the ultimate way for your family to soak up the easy-going atmosphere that reigns in Paris during the summer months. See p. 140.

Enjoy the bustling markets

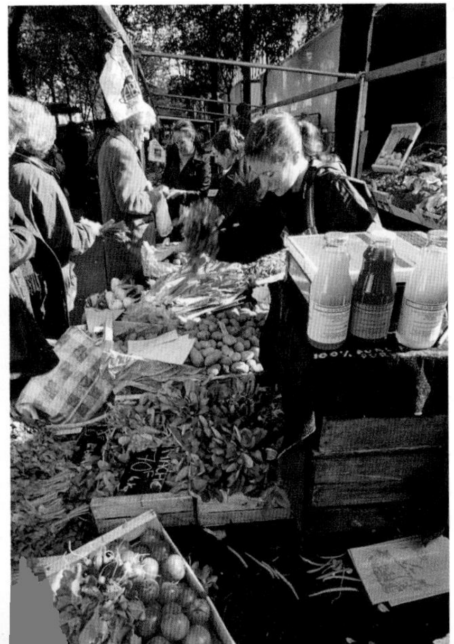

Cheering on the jockeys in the famous and classy **Hippodrome de Longchamp**, in the Bois de Boulogne (the site of the Prix de l'Arc de Triomphe Grand Prix) or the **Hippodrome d'Auteuil** (see p. 22) is fun throughout the year, but even better on Sundays in April and May when huge picnic areas are set up between the tracks, with candyfloss, games and attractions for children. See Les Dimanches au Galop, p. 22.

Pulling faces at the gargoyles on top of Notre-Dame – taking photos of family members impersonating one, then deciding who was most convincing. See p. 186.

Getting to the top of the Eiffel Tower never fails to impress and is something everybody should do at least once in their lives. At night, the tower sparkles like a giant Christmas tree, every hour on the hour for 10 minutes. See p. 77.

Immortalising your children with a portrait painted at Place du Tertre is cheesy but fun. The café-lined square in Montmartre, once frequented by painters like Toulouse Lautrec, is jam-packed with modern artists ready to caricature your youngsters and give you something fun to look back on. See p. 112.

Taking the boat along the Canal St-Martin from Bastille to the Villette quarter, past tree-lined quays and old working-class areas – now gentrified and rather hip. Canauxrama, see p. 139.

Feeling sombre in the Mémorial des Martyrs Français de la Déportation de 1945 (Deportation Memorial) on the tip of Île de la Cité. It movingly brings home the fact that the Nazi genocide took millions of lives, many from Paris. See p. 188.

Walking up the Champs-Elysées past chic shops, cinemas, car showrooms, and cafés towards the Arc de Triomphe where you can see the grave of the unknown soldier and climb the arch for spectacular views across Paris. See p. 60.

Getting dressed up for a gourmet family treat in the Crillon palace hotel's restaurant Les Ambassadeurs (or their lower-key and less expensive brasserie L'Obélisque). See p. 70.

Blanc à Manger at Les Ambassadeurs

Catching a puppet show in the Théâtre des Marionnettes, smack-bang in the heart of the Luxembourg gardens makes for a wonderful Gallic giggle, whether your children speak French or not. See p. 161.

Taking the funicular to the top of the Butte de Montmartre from where you can visit the Sacré Coeur basilica, take in sweeping vistas of the whole of Paris, and watch talented street performers. See p. 104.

Bike riding along the Canal St-Martin, lined with cafés and shops, up to the Canal de l'Ourcq and Parc de la Villette with its open spaces and fabulous children's science museum, or beyond to the Marne river. See p. 140.

Strolling on top of a converted viaduct on the Promenade Plantée. Pack a picnic or some games for the Jardin de Reuilly (see p. 140) or further on in the Bois de Vincennes (see p. 140), or come down to ground level near Bastille and look in the interesting shops under the viaduct arcades. See p. 140.

Riding the transparent escalator tubes on the side of the Pompidou Centre is almost as fun as seeing the works of art inside. Watch in wonder as the rooftops get closer and closer, and look to see which lucky devils have rooftop gardens. See p. 124.

Tucking into Oriental pâtisseries and couscous inside the Paris Mosque (Mosquée de

Enjoy the open space at Parc de la Villette

Paris). On a sunny day opt for a table in the white-and-blue tiled courtyard where cheeky sparrows fly down to beg for crumbs. See p. 184.

Taking a boat trip along the Seine is a relaxing way to admire Paris's beautiful quays and monuments. It's also the best way to see the sculptures and underbellies of the bridges. Both **Bateaux Parisiens** (see p. 87) and **Bateaux Mouches** (see p. 87) companies offer commentated tours. You can also use the **Batobus** boats like a bus service along the river. See p. 49.

BEST CHILDREN'S PLAYGROUNDS & PARKS

Jardin d'Acclimatation in the Bois de Boulogne is one of the best parks in Paris for families with children of all ages: you can pet animals, get soaking wet under sprinklers, test the rollercoasters, take a relaxing boat ride, swing off climbing frames, and navigate remote-controlled boats. Take time too to go boating on the lake and laugh at your funny forms in front of the distorting mirrors. A handy mini-train transports families from Porte Maillot to the Jardin. See p. 245.

Jardin de Luxembourg
Youngsters love riding on the backs of ponies and donkeys, and playing in the enclosed play area and sandpits. Older children can try their hand at a game of chess if they're brave enough to take on the ageing regulars. See p. 160.

Jardin du Palais Royal
Cardinal Richelieu's former gardens are exceedingly pretty, surrounded by covered arcades, and shaded by trees. Young children will enjoy climbing on the modernist black-and-white pillar-sculptures near the front entrance. If you have older ones into photography, get them to take some arty shots of the sculptures and shadows cast between the arcade railings. See p. 65.

Jardin Tino Rossi With the Institut du Monde Arabe (see p. 176) on one side and the Seine in the other, this picturesque park is a skateboarders' paradise. See p. 194.

Parc de la Villette This is a must-see for families with children of any age. The park area is made up of wide open lawns, perfect for kicking a ball around in, and enclosed parts surrounded by plants for a secluded read or picnic. Different play areas target children from babies to 12-year-olds, featuring climbing frames, swings, and carousels. See p. 246.

Pocahontas Village in Disney This is a tranquil spot for your little ones to run around in away from the queues and hype of Disneyland Park®'s big attractions. (It's also a secluded spot to breast-feed a baby.) See p. 216.

TOP ATTRACTIONS FOR TEENS

Autour de Midi-Minuit This hip Montmartre jazz institution is a cool place to be seen, with or without parents in tow. Dine in the upstairs restaurant before heading down to the vaulted cellar for some serious foot-tapping, and music played by both confirmed and up-and-coming artists. See p. 115.

Catacombs See if your teenagers are as intrepid as they say they are by taking them 18m underground to these fascinating quarry tunnels, filled with the remains of millions of Parisians, whose bones had to be moved in the 18th century when Paris's communal graves burst. See p. 162.

Jeu de Paume At the bottom of the Tuileries gardens, this museum is devoted to experimental film and photography – a must-see for teenagers interested in image. See p. 196.

Palais de Tokyo If your teenagers are into modern, experimental art, they'll love the weird and wacky installations on show in this 1930s' Art Deco palace. Take a break in the funky restaurant, Tokyo Eat, where lights look like giant floating eggs. See p. 85.

The Twilight Zone Tower of Terror in Disneyland's Walt Disney Studios® Park is their brand new thrillseekers' ride that plunges the brave straight down a 13-floor lift-shaft. See p. 226.

Tonnère de Zeus In the Parc Astérix Gallois theme-park, this is the ultimate stomach-churner: a 30m vertical drop on Europe's biggest wooden rollercoaster. See p. 246.

BEST MUSEUMS

Cité des Sciences In Parc de la Villette, the science museum has been specially designed with children in mind and interactive displays allow children to manipulate the exhibits. See p. 247.

Musée Carnavalet This museum is not only free to get into, it's set in two of Paris's most lovely mansions and documents the history of the city in an interesting and understandable manner for children. See p. 127.

Musée de Cluny If your youngsters love history, this medieval museum will teach them about how people lived in the Middle Ages, and show them the old Roman baths built by Parisian boatmen. See p. 182.

Musée d'Orsay This former railway station houses one of the world's best collections of Impressionist art. Treat your children to lunch in the Café des Hauteurs – a relaxed table-service restaurant that looks out over the city from behind a giant, transparent clock-face. See p. 154.

Musée du Quai Branly This neo-cubist building by the Eiffel Tower is a new museum dedicated to non-European cultures. The views from the rooftop restaurant to the Eiffel Tower are particularly good – a special treat for well-behaved children. See p. 82.

Musée Rodin Easily the most charming museum in Paris, this stately home with its sumptuous statue-studded gardens makes Rodin's statues accessible to children. If you don't want to go around the house, come to enjoy an ice cream in the gardens – free entry for parents with buggies. See p. 84.

The Louvre This world-famous museum is so big there's always more to see, even if you've been before. Children particularly love the mummies in the Egyptology department and the castle remains in the Medieval Louvre. See p. 48.

Explore the Louvre

BEST ART SITES

Centre Pompidou The avant-garde building is as much a piece of art as the works inside – the most important and comprehensive multi-disciplinary art collection in Europe. The art spans from 1905 to today, with a separate section for post-1960s works and a temporary exhibition floor. See p. 124.

Cité de l'Architecture Architecture as an art form is given pride of place in this vast museum where ceilings are tall enough to house portions of cathedrals and a recreation of the Le Corbusier house. See p. 76.

Musée d'Art Moderne de la Ville de Paris The Pompidou doesn't have it all; this excellent museum, opposite the Palais de Tokyo, has a good selection of Cubist and Fauvist art. See p. 80.

Musée Gustave Moreau For older children looking for something different from Impressionism, Fauvism, and Cubism, Moreau's fantasist style

Parisian History in a Nutshell for Children

2000 B.C. Lutétia thrives along a strategic crossing of the Seine, the headquarters of the Parisii tribe.

52 B.C. Julius Caesar conquers Lutétia during the Gallic Wars.

200 A.D. Barbarian Gauls force the Romans to retreat to the fortifications on Ile de la Cité.

300 Lutétia is renamed Paris; Roman power weakens in northern France.

350 Paris's Christianisation begins.

400s The Franks invade Paris, and there is social transformation from the Roman to the Gallo-Roman culture.

466 Clovis, founder of the Merovingian dynasty and first non-Roman ruler of Paris since the Parisii, is born.

800 Charlemagne, founder of the Carolingian dynasty, is crowned Holy Roman Emperor and rules from Aachen in modern Germany.

987 Hugh Capet, founder of France's foremost early medieval dynasty, rises to power; his family rules from Paris.

1100s The Sorbonne University is founded and attracts scholars from across Europe.

1422 England invades Paris during the Hundred Years' War.

1429 Joan of Arc tries to regain Paris for the French. The Burgundians later capture and sell her to the English, who burn her at the stake in Rouen.

1500s François I, first of the French Renaissance kings, embellishes Paris but chooses to maintain his court in the Loire Valley.

1549 Henri II rules from Paris; construction of public and private residences begins, many in the Marais.

1572 The Wars of Religion reach their climax with the St. Bartholomew's Day massacre of Protestants.

1615 Construction begins on the Palais du Luxembourg for Henri IV's widow, Marie de Médicis.

1636 The Palais Royal is launched by Cardinal Richelieu.

1643 Louis XIV, the "Sun King" and the most powerful ruler since the Caesars, rises to power. He moves his court to the newly built Versailles.

1789 The French Revolution begins.

1793 Louis XVI and his Austrian-born queen, Marie Antoinette, are publicly guillotined.

1799 Napoleon Bonaparte crowns himself Emperor of France.

1803 Napoleon abandons French overseas expansion and sells Louisiana to America.

1812 Napoleon is defeated in the Russian winter campaign.

1814 Aided by a coalition of France's enemies, especially England, the Bourbon monarchy under Louis XVIII is restored.

1821 Napoleon Bonaparte dies.

1824 Louis XVIII dies, and Charles X succeeds him.

1830 The more liberal Louis-Philippe is elected king. Paris industrialises.

1848 A violent working-class revolution deposes Louis-Philippe, who's replaced by autocratic Napoleon III.

1853–70 On Napoleon III's orders, Baron Haussmann redesigns Paris's landscapes.

1860s The Impressionist style of painting emerges.

1870 The Franco–Prussian War ends in the defeat of France; a revolution rises and the Third Republic elects its president, Marshal MacMahon.

1878–1937 Several World Fairs and redevelopment add monuments to Paris's skyline, including the Tour Eiffel (1889) and the Sacré Coeur.

1895 Capt. Alfred Dreyfus, a Jew, is wrongfully charged with treason and sentenced to life on Devil's Island. The incident becomes the biggest political scandal of 19th century France.

1898 Emile Zola publishes *J'Accuse* in defence of Dreyfus and flees to exile in England.

1906 Dreyfus is finally exonerated, and his rank is restored.

1914–18 World War I rips apart Europe. The Germans are defeated.

1940 German troops invade Paris. The French government, under Marshal Pétain, evacuates to Vichy, while the French Resistance under General Charles de Gaulle maintains symbolic headquarters in London.

1944 Allied troops liberate Paris; de Gaulle returns in triumph.

1952 The creation, with Germany, of the ECSC (European Coal and Steel Community), the precursor of the modern European Union.

1954–62 War begins in Algeria and is eventually lost. Refugees flood Paris, and the nation becomes divided over its North African policies.

1958 France's Fourth Republic collapses; General de Gaulle is called out of retirement to head the Fifth Republic.

1968 Paris's students and factory workers engage in a general revolt; the French government is overhauled in the aftermath.

1981 François Mitterrand is elected France's first Socialist president since the 1940s; he's re-elected in 1988.

1989 Paris celebrates the bicentenary of the French Revolution.

1992 Euro Disney (Disneyland Resort® Paris) opens.

1994 François Mitterrand and Queen Elizabeth II ride under the English Channel in the new Channel Tunnel.

2002 France replaces the Franc with the Euro, the new European currency.

The Orangerie is a must for Monet fans

and choice of subject never fails to impress. See p. 100.

Orangerie Monet fans should flock to this lovely museum, which showcases the Impressionist's famed lilies. See p. 55.

BEST SHOPS

Christian Constant Try the delicious ganaches at this award-winning chef's chocolate shop. See p. 165.

Grands Magasins Galeries Lafayette and Printemps department stores behind the Opéra Garnier are still winners for one-stop shopping with children in tow, selling men's, women's and children's fashion, homeware, jewellery, make-up, and toys. See p. 114.

Joué Club Village Inside the 19th-century covered Passage des Princes, this toy mega-store sells everything from cowboy and Indian miniatures to modelling kits for aeroplanes, Lego, dolls, party costumes, and cuddly toys. See p. 114.

Nature & Découvertes This child-friendly and environmentally friendly chain sells all sorts of interesting objects, games, and gifts linked to nature and science. See p. 66.

Place de la Madeleine All around the Madeleine church, gourmet food shops stimulate hunger with truffles from La Maison de la Truffe, biscuits and foie gras from Fauchon, caviar from Caviar Kaspia, and exotic foods from Hédiard. See p. 64.

Poilâne Breadmakers since before World War II, Poilâne makes delicious organic loaves and biscuits in a traditional oven in the cellar. A small ball of dough is taken from one batch and put into the next, creating an un-interrupted link from the first Poilâne loaf to the one your family can buy today. See p. 164.

BEST FAMILY ENTERTAINMENT

Attending a ballet or opera Let your family rub shoulders with the Paris literati at the **Opéra Bastille** (see p. 136) or *grande dame* of the music scene, the 19th-century rococo **Opéra Garnier** (see p. 100) Whether for a performance of Bizet or a men-only Swan Lake, dress with pomp and circumstance.

Going to the circus All things circus are lapped up big time in Paris. From lions, tigers, and bears (oh-my!) in the traditional Big Top (Cirque Pinder, see p. 248) to avant garde acrobatics in the Grande Céleste Cirque (see p. 248) or pioneering acts in the Cirque d'Hiver (see p. 135) – there's something for all the family.

Jazz clubs Paris and jazz go hand in hand. Try Autour de Midi-Minuit in Montmartre (see p. 115) or mosey on down to the Latin quarter where the golden age of jazz lives on in a handful of clubs. See p. 196.

BEST ACCOMMODATION

Aviatic Just off the beaten track near Montparnasse, this small, family-run hotel will pack you a picnic – ideal for lunch in the nearby Luxembourg gardens. See p. 168.

Hotel Valadon Right by Les Invalides and the Eiffel Tower, this hotel is used to welcoming families with children of all ages. Budget travellers can store food in a communal fridge. See p. 90.

Le Crillon It was good enough for Ernest Hemingway, Pierce Brosnan, and Zinedine Zidane, and it's good enough for you. If you fancy a splurge, this place comes up trumps with excellent family facilities and a gourmet restaurant to die for. See p. 67.

Paris Oasis If you would like a self-catering apartment in the heart of Montmartre, these small but fully equipped flats even have a heated swimming pool you can use. See p. 117.

Résidence des Arts This family favourite is in a great location on the Left Bank and offers apartments with a kitchenette and space for three to four people. The next-door café also serves decent food should you decide to eat out. See p. 168.

BEST EATING OPTIONS

Breakfast in America Fine crispy bacon, pancakes in maple syrup, perfect burgers, fries, and milkshakes make this a sought-after address in the Marais, and one worth queuing at, for week-end brunch or all-day-breakfast. See p. 147.

Coco & Co Eggs in every shape, size and form are the

Sleeping Beauty Castle, Disneyland

only foodstuffs served in this hip café. Opt for a boiled egg, an omelette, or *oeuf-en-cocotte* (egg baked with wine and cream), but expect perf'egg'-tion! See p. 172.

Le Potager du Marais If you or your children are vegetarians (and even if you're not) taste reigns supreme in this restaurant that does things with vegetables unlike anywhere else in the capital. See p. 147.

Memère Paulette Large portions prevail in this reasonably priced local's haunt, which feels like its décor (as well as the menus) haven't changed since the 1940s. See p. 120.

Nos Ancêtres les Gaulois Pretend you're Astérix or Obélix in this fun restaurant where meat is cooked as in medieval times and wine is poured straight from the barrel. See p. 199.

BEST DAYS OUT

Disneyland Mickey Mouse and the cartoon legends created by Walt Disney make this theme park one of the most fun things to do in Île-de-France. See p. 201.

Parc Astérix For a truly French theme park, Astérix the Gaul's hangout won't disappoint children of any age. Watch the fabulous dolphin shows, get wet on the log-flumes, and shake with fear and anticipation on the rickety-looking wooden rollercoasters – some of the biggest in Europe. See p. 245.

Versailles The Sun King's palace is not only an architectural wonder; its grounds are big enough to spend several hours in and are particularly atmospheric when the fountains spring to life and classical music is played. Les Grandes Eaux Musicales, see p. 249.

2 Planning a Family Trip to Paris

PARIS & ARRONDISSEMENTS

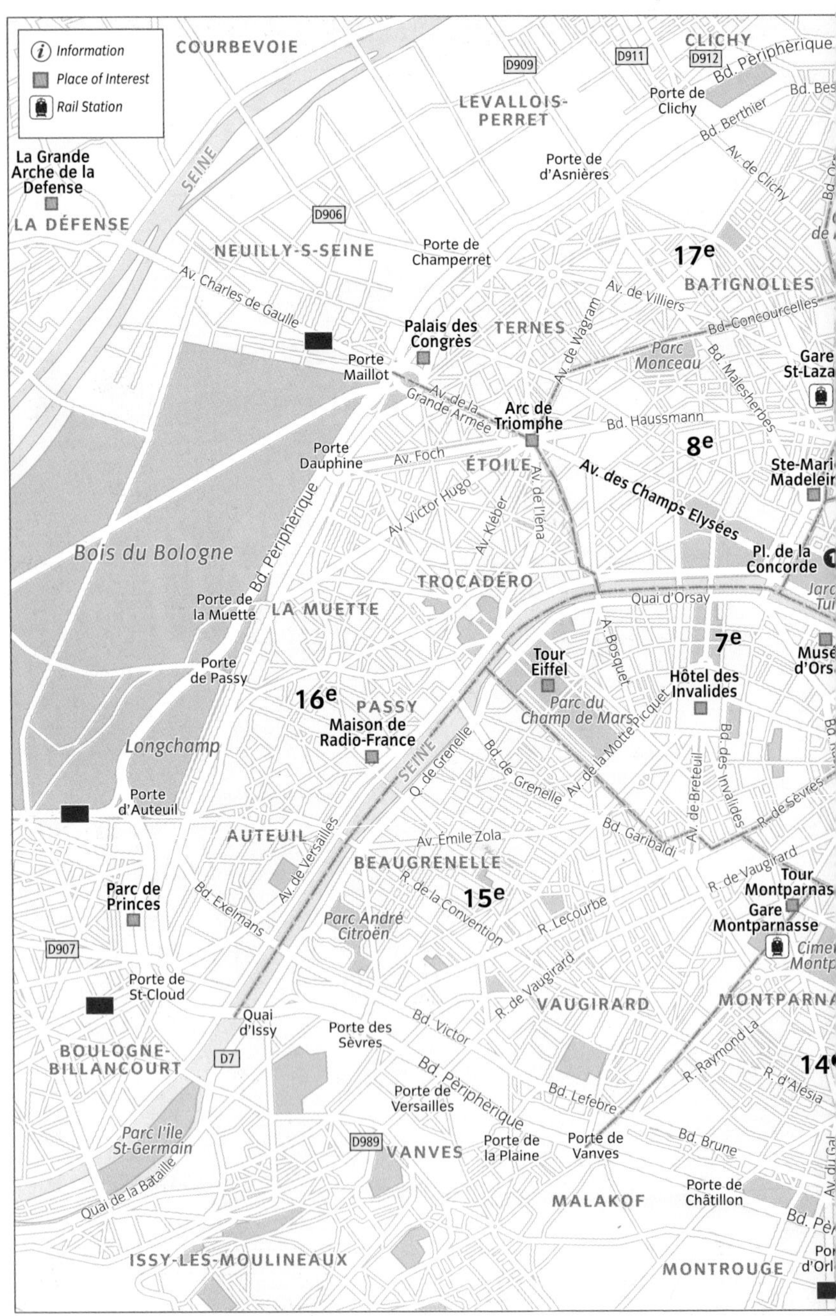

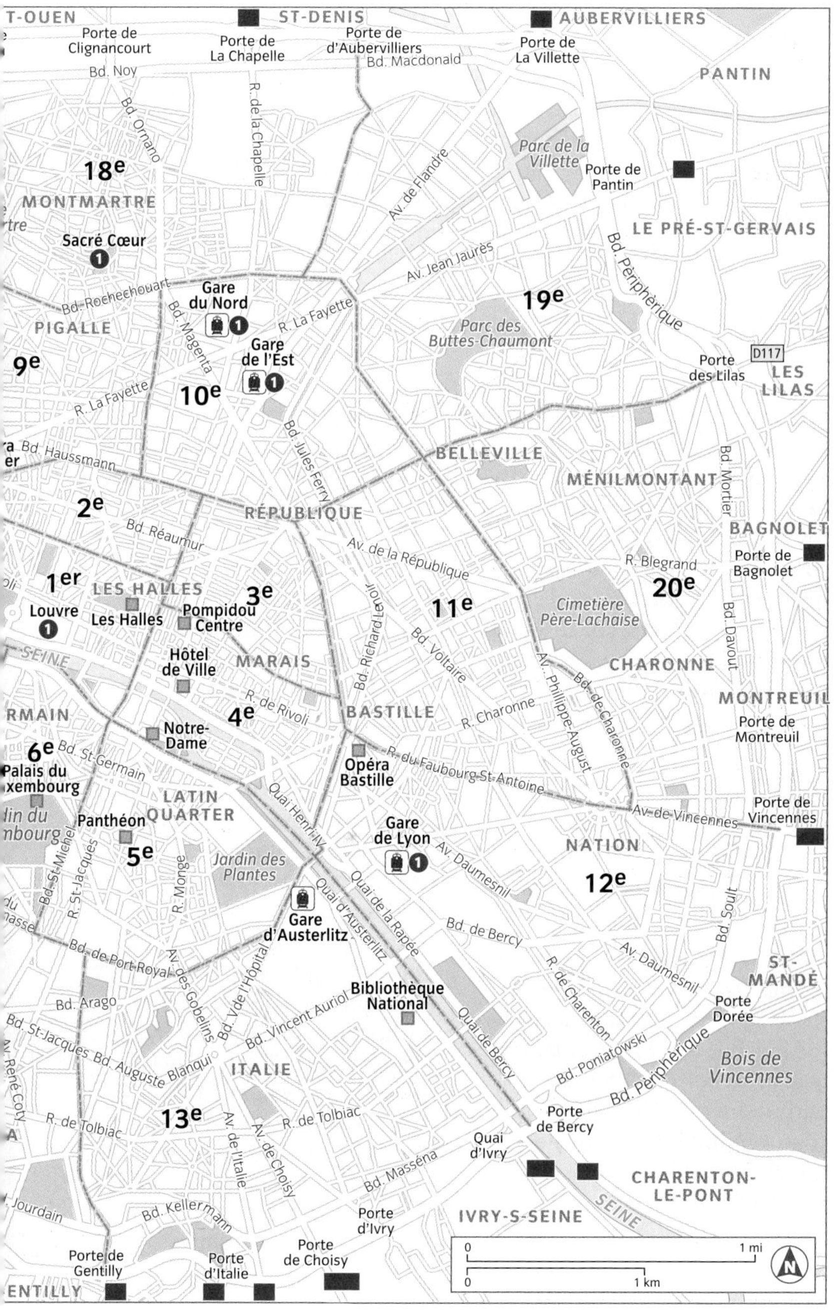
ST-DENIS
AUBERVILLIERS
Porte de Clignancourt
Porte de La Chapelle
Porte de d'Aubervilliers
Porte de La Villette
PANTIN
18e
MONTMARTRE
Sacré Cœur
Parc de la Villette
Porte de Pantin
LE PRÉ-ST-GERVAIS
Gare du Nord
Gare de l'Est
19e
PIGALLE
9e
10e
Parc des Buttes-Chaumont
Porte des Lilas
LES LILAS
BELLEVILLE
MÉNILMONTANT
2e
RÉPUBLIQUE
BAGNOLET
Porte de Bagnolet
1er
LES HALLES
3e
11e
20e
Louvre
Les Halles
Pompidou Centre
Cimetière Père-Lachaise
Hôtel de Ville
MARAIS
CHARONNE
4e
BASTILLE
MONTREUIL
Porte de Montreuil
Notre-Dame
6e
Palais du Luxembourg
Opéra Bastille
LATIN QUARTER
Porte de Vincennes
Panthéon
Gare de Lyon
NATION
5e
Jardin des Plantes
12e
Gare d'Austerlitz
ST-MANDÉ
Bibliothèque National
Porte Dorée
Bois de Vincennes
ITALIE
13e
Porte de Bercy
Quai d'Ivry
CHARENTON-LE-PONT
IVRY-S-SEINE
Porte de Gentilly
Porte d'Italie
Porte de Choisy
Porte d'Ivry
SEINE
0 1 mi
0 1 km

The key to a successful family holiday is to involve the youngsters. When children and teenagers have worked to gather information – and voiced their opinions – they are much more likely to feel excited, and will have far fewer grounds for grumbles.

Forward planning is equally important. Paris and Disneyland® Resort Paris are two of the world's most popular tourist destinations, and hotels, especially the budget ones, fill up quickly. Beware, however, of over-planning. While last-minute organising could leave you disappointed or out-of-pocket, inflexible timetabling could turn your relaxing break into a military expedition. Part of Paris's beauty comes from its unpredictability: a hidden passage here, a concealed garden there, an impromptu conversation with a stranger in a café. It's these unforeseen events and encounters that create the most magical holiday memories for all the family.

This guide covers Paris's centre, must-sees in the outskirts and suburbs, and Disneyland® Resort Paris. Central Paris is split into districts called *arrondissements*, which spiral out from the centre like a snail, in a clockwise direction, and are numbered from 1 to 20. Large monuments and important streets, however, also lend their name to parts of town – areas known as *quartiers* (quarters). These *quartiers* usually straddle several *arrondissements* (arr.). For example, the Eiffel Tower quarters cover the 7th and 15th arr.; Montparnasse covers the 6th, 14th, and 15th arr. For this guide the chapters are arranged by *quartiers*, with the relevant arrondissement and its nearest Métro (M°) mentioned in the address of each attraction.

VISITOR INFORMATION

France's official tourist board, the **Maison de France**'s website, ***www.franceguide.com***, has links to ***http://uk.franceguide.com*** for the UK, ***http://ie.franceguide.com*** for Ireland, and ***http://us.franceguide.com*** for the USA, along with more than 30 other countries. Online services include a travel shop offering booking for accommodation, events, and sports activities.

In the UK, the Maison de France's headquarters are at 178 Piccadilly, **London** W1 (✆ *09068 244 123*); in the USA, there are offices in **New York** at 825 Third Avenue, 29th floor (entrance on 50th Street), NY 100 22 (✆ *01 514 288 1904*); and in France, they can be found at 23 place de Catalogne, 14th arr., **Paris** (✆ *01 42 96 70 00*).

English-language websites for tourism in Paris and in the Île-de-France (its suburbs) are ***www.parisinfo.com*** (L'Office de Tourisme de Paris – Paris Tourist Office) and ***www.pidf.com*** (Paris Ile-de-France's regional tourist board). Information on Disneyland® Resort Paris can be found on both the aforementioned sites and at ***www.tourisme77.com***, the Seine and Marne regional tourist office (where the park is located ***www.disneyland paris.co.uk***).

For route planning or street finding before your journey, or even just for fun, ***http://maps.google.com*** has zoomable maps of just about anywhere, directions to and from places, and even detailed satellite images. If you will be using public transport to get to your accommodation from the airports or Eurostar terminal, the webite ***www.ratp.fr*** shows Métro, bus and RER routes.

Child-Specific Websites

www.france4families.com is a very useful resource, with lots of general information about France from a family perspective plus guides to all regions including a section on Paris.

More general family-oriented sites are ***www.takethefamily.com***, with tips, destination guides (including hotel and serviced apartment accommodation in Paris), and a discussion board; ***www.babygoes2.com***, with general tips and location reports; ***www.family-travel.co.uk*** covering all aspects of travel with children; ***www.travellingwithchildren.co.uk***, which sells tried and tested baby-travel products online; and ***www.deabirkett.com***, a handy family travel forum for exchanging tips and views, run by a former *Guardian* journalist and children's travel specialist.

The books *Family Travel* (Lanier Publishing International) and *How to Take Great Trips with Your Kids* (The Harvard Common Press) are full of good, general advice that can apply to family travel anywhere.

If you read French, ***www.cityjunior.com*** is a goldmine of ideas with information on children-oriented shows, exhibitions, workshops, and outings in Paris and Île-de-France; ***www.commeundimanche.com*** also lists children's attractions in Paris; ***www.paris.fr*** is the Paris council's official site with a section on children's activities; and ***www.lamuse.net*** is an online magazine that lists children's activities according to their age.

Entry Requirements, Customs & Bringing Pets

Passports & Visas

Citizens of European Union (EU) countries need an **identity card** to enter France. For the time being, this means a **passport for UK nationals**. Non-EU citizens also need a passport, and some nationalities, including South Africans, require a visa. Stays of more than three months by all non-EU citizens also require a visa. For French embassies/consulates around the world see ***www.diplomatie.gouv.fr***.

Taking Your Pet

Under the **Pet Travel Scheme** (PETS), UK-resident dogs and cats can now travel to many other EU countries and return to the UK without being quarantined. Dogs and cats are issued with a **passport** (by a vet) after being fitted with a microchip and vaccinated against rabies at least **six months** prior to travel. On re-entry to the UK, you need to get your pet treated for ticks and tapeworm (by an EU vet 24–48 hrs before being checked in with an approved transport company). For full details see ***www.defra.gov.uk/animalh/quarantine/index.htm.***

Most Parisian **hotels** and some self-catering properties permit small animals, often for an extra fee (10–20€). The commercial website ***www.visitfrance.co.uk*** is a good source of pet-friendly self-catering options. ***www.petfriendlyholidays.com*** and ***www.dogfriendly.com*** both also list hotels that openly accept pets.

Money

The Euro

France, in common with 15 other countries at the time of writing, has the **euro** € as its currency. There are 100 **cents** in a euro, with **notes** for 5 to 500€ and coins for 1 cent to 2€. As of writing, the **euro-sterling exchange rate** is hovering around the 1.23€ to £1 (approximately 79p to 1€), making mental calculations relatively easy (drop about a fifth to get a rough figure in pounds). For current rates and a currency converter, see ***www.xe.com.***

Credit & Debit Cards

Most French shops, restaurants and hotels take credit or debit cards, at least **Visa** and **MasterCard** (American Express and Diner's Club are only usually accepted in expensive establishments). There is often a minimum spending limit of 10–15€.

Although times are changing, some small businesses still **refuse to accept cards,** so it's always wise to check in advance. Also, watch out for **charges** when you use cards abroad. For further information about the best credit cards to use abroad see ***www.moneysupermarket.com***

You now use your **PIN** when making a purchase with your card as well as using it at ATMs in many shops, restaurants, hotels, and petrol stations.

Before you leave, tell your credit card company you're going abroad, as they sometimes put a block on cards that deviate from their normal spending pattern. For **lost or stolen cards,** see p. 45.

Travellers' Cheques

You probably won't need travellers' cheques in Paris where ATMs are abundant, but if you do take some as back-up (available in UK banks, building societies, travel agents, and at the Post Office), keep a record of their serial numbers in case of loss or theft and carry them separately from money and cards. You'll need to show ID when you cash one.

Cash Points

There are 24-hour cashpoint machines or ATMs outside all French banks in Paris and many Post Offices (*La Poste*). Disneyland® Resort Paris also has plenty inside and outside the parks. You usually get a better rate at an ATM than an exchange booth (which may also take a commission). However, your bank will probably charge a fee for using a foreign ATM, so avoid drawing small sums every day.

Bring some cash (either pounds or euros) into France as a back-up, and have two or more cards to use in case of a hiccup.

When to Go & What to Pack

Paris's weather is a little like London's (cold and wet in winter, warm and humid in summer), although global warming has recently made the weather unpredictable; for instance summer 2007 was grey, wet, and cold, whereas summer 2005 was an abnormal scorcher. Spring and autumn are still good times to come, with relatively long days, and weather warm enough to sit outside.

To be on the safe side, it's best to **pack** winter clothes if visiting between November and April. However, it's also useful to take T-shirts just in case. Whatever the time of year, you'll need comfortable **walking shoes** (much of Paris is walkable), some **going-out shoes and clothes** for those swish Parisian nights (including shirts and trousers for the boys), as well as **sunglasses** and **sun-hats** for sensitive-skinned little ones, especially babies. If you forget anything, Monoprix supermarkets are dotted around the capital (see relevant chapters' Fast Facts) and can cater to all your everyday needs, selling food and drink, clothes, accessories, and baby items.

A helpful tool for planning what to take is ***www.meteofrance.com;*** even with only basic French (you need to know the days of the week) you get a general idea of what weather to expect from the click-on maps. Good English-language sites are ***http://weather.uk.msn.com*** and ***www.freemeteo.com***.

Paris and Disneyland® are popular year round, but they're at their **busiest** and most **expensive** at **Easter**, during the French **May Bank Holiday** (1st to 8th) and **October half-term school holidays.** Parisians usually desert the capital en masse in **July** and **August**, which means parking spaces are easily found in the centre (unheard of at any other time of year) and many

Average Minimum and Maximum Daily Temperatures in °C

	Jan	Feb	Mar	Apr	May	Jun	Jul	Aug	Sep	Oct	Nov	Dec
	1–6	1–7	4–12	6–16	10–20	13–23	15–25	14–24	12–21	8–16	5–10	2–7
Record	15	21	26	30	33	38	40	35	33	28	21	17

Children's Kit

The following items can be bought before you leave and can make travelling with babies or young children easier or more relaxing:

Bébétel Baby Monitor: Unlike battery-powered listening devices, this is not limited by range and suffers no interference, so you can use it in all hotel restaurants. You plug it into a standard phone line (there are foreign adapter sets) and program in your mobile phone number (you may have to add the international code). If your child gets up or cries, the monitor calls you. It costs a hefty £180 or so from ***www.bebetel.co.uk***, but your hotel may have its own you can use.

Littlelife Baby Carriers: These backpacks in which to carry children are a great idea if you're doing a lot of walking or plan to use the Métro (Paris's subway with its hundreds of steps is difficult to navigate with a buggy). 'Voyager' has a zip-off bag for drinks, snacks, and wipes. It's about £170 but lighter models start at half that. You can get hold of them at ***www.johnlewis.com*** and outdoor pursuits shops. The same firm's compact, super-absorbent travel towels are also very handy for travelling.

Portable Highchairs: Most Parisian restaurants don't provide high-chairs; and even when they do, they are often old and without a front bar, leaving you trying to eat with one hand and holding a squirming baby or toddler with the other. Lightweight options you can carry around include the supremely compact 'Handbag Highchair' (a loop of fabric that secures your baby to the chair), the foldable Handysitt toddler seat, and the Early Years inflatable booster seat. All are sold at ***www.bloomingmarvellous.co.uk***, priced from £15 to £75.

Boardbug Baby & Toddler Monitor: Great for shopping (and Disneyland®), this wristwatch-style monitor alerts you to whenever your little one (or ones – the parent monitor can be paired with up to three child units) strays from you, with adjustable distances from 2m to 150m. It costs about £55 from ***www.travellingwithchildren.co.uk.***

Baby Equipment Rental in France: French-based **Les Petits Voyageurs** (☎ *02 40 05 58 48*, ***www.petitsvoyageurs.com***) hires children's equipment that can be delivered to your holiday accommodation. Deals include 'Pack Malin' (buggy, bed, and baby seat) for 85€ per week and 'Pack Randonnée' (buggy and baby sling) for 55€ per week. All equipment conforms to safety standards and is cleaned after each rental.

hotels offer special **summer promotions**. While the prospect of having a Parisian-free Paris may seduce some families, bear in mind that some (but not all) restaurants and bars also close for two weeks (usually the first two in August). On the up side, summer in Paris is also synonymous with **Paris Plage** (an artificial beach along the Seine and Canal de l'Ourcq packed with family activities, see p. 24) and **open-air cinema** and **music festivals**. You'll find details of these on tourist office websites and in this book under 'Special Events', below.

Public & School Holidays

French **national holidays** are called *jours fériés*. Banks and small shops close. However, larger supermarkets and department stores increasingly open in the morning. Some museums close but many other visitor sites (including Disneyland® Resort Paris) stay open, as do the majority of restaurants. If there's a public holiday on a Thursday or Tuesday, many people take the Friday or Monday off as well – this is called *faire le pont* ('making a bridge').

The main public holidays are **New Year's Day** (1st January), **Easter Monday** (March or April), **Labour Day** (*Fête du Travail*; 1st May), **VE Day** (8th May), **Whit Monday** (late May), **Ascension Thursday** (late May/40 days after Easter), **Bastille Day** (14th July), **Assumption of the Blessed Virgin** (15th August), **All Saints' Day** (1st November), **Armistice Day** (11th November), and **Christmas Day** (25th December).

There are five **school holidays** a year in France: two weeks in February, two weeks at Easter, all of July and August, one week at the end of October and two weeks at Christmas. As in the UK, holidays are staggered throughout the country. Most museums in Paris offer **children's activities** during the Parisian school holidays, though you will need to check if there are English-speaking supervisors. For further details see ***www.frenchentree.com***, then click on 'Living in France' followed by 'Education' then 'School Calendar.'

Special Events

Paris offers year-round family events, the main ones are listed below, month by month. For more information on these and others buy the weekly **Pariscope** and **Official de Spectacles** events guides from newspaper kiosks and supermarkets:

January

Chinese New Year South of the Latin Quarter, lions, dragons, and live martial arts demonstrations fill the streets around Avenue d'Ivry (13th arr.) and Avenue de Choisy (13th arr.). Some parades also go along the Champs-Elysées (8th arr.).

Fête des Rois Epiphany is celebrated in France (6th Jan.) by eating a delicious sweet, puff-pastry pie (filled with almond paste) called a *Gallette du Roi*. They are sold in bakeries throughout the month. Watch out for the *fève* (a porcelain figurine): whoever gets it in their slice is king (*roi*) for the day and has to wear a paper crown.

February

Salon de l'Agriculture ★★ A must for any animal and food-loving family, this two-week festival brings the countryside to Paris, with prize-winning bulls, cows, horses, sheep, and Billy Goats Gruff for your little ones to pet. Cheese and fois gras makers are joined by wine-makers and bakers for one giant celebration of France's *terroirs* (agricultural lands).

Mid-Feb to early Mar daily 9am–7pm. Porte de Versailles exhibition centre (Paris Expo), 15th arr. M° Porte de Versailles. ***www.salon-agriculture.com***

March

Foire du Trône A mammoth amusement park, the Foire du Trône originated in 957 AD, when merchants met with farmers to exchange grain and wine. This hi-tech continuation of that tradition, held on the lawns of the Pelouse de Reuilly, has a Ferris wheel, carousels, acrobats, fire eaters, and other fun diversions.

Bois de Vincennes, 12th arr., ***www.foiredutrone.com****. End of March to end of May, daily 2pm to midnight. M° Porte Dorée or Porte de Charenton. Also free shuttle buses from Nation (12th arr.) and Cour St-Emilion (12th arr.).*

April

Horseracing and picnicking at Longchamp and Auteuil Races ★★ During *Les Dimanches au Galop* (galloping Sundays), the legendary races' lawns become a picnicker's Eldorado with pony rides, candy floss, outdoor games, and, of course, top-notch horseracing.

End Apr–early May. ☎ 08 21 21 32 13; ***www.dimanchesaugalop.com****,* ***Hippodrome d'Auteuil****, Bois de Boulogne, Route des Lacs, 16th arr. M° Porte d'Auteuil.* ***Hippodrome de Longchamp****, Bois de Boulogne, Route des Tribunes, 16th arr.. M° Porte Maillot then Bus No. 244.*

Les Grandes Eaux Musicales ★★ To re-create the atmosphere of the aristocratic past, the fountains around the Palace of Versailles pump and spurt to music by French composers (Couperin, Charpentier, and Lully) and others (Mozart or Haydn) of the period.

☎ 01 30 83 78 89; ***www.chateauversailles-spectacles.fr****. Saturday and Sunday from 11am–noon and 3:30pm–5.30pm between April and early September.*

Musique Côté Jardins From April to October, look out for free concerts in bandstands across the city's parks including at Les Buttes-Chaumonts, 19th arr. and the Jardin du Luxembourg, see p. 160. *☎ 39 75* (special number); ***www.paris.fr***

May

L'Esprit Jazz Festival in Saint-Germain-des-Prés Let the whole family swing to the rhythm of jazz concerts and street performances around the Saint-Germain quarters.

First two weeks in May. ☎ 01 56 24 35 50; ***www.espritjazz.com****. St-Germain-des-Prés quarters, M° St-Germain-des-Prés.*

La Fête du Pain (Bread festival) Show your children how the

French make their bread during this annual festival where some *boulangers* offer bread-making demonstrations and tastings, usually in front of the Hôtel de Ville, 4th arr., M° Hôtel de Ville; and in front of Notre-Dame cathedral, 4th arr., M° Cité, and in their bakeries.

01 43 25 43 50; ***www.fetedupain.com****. 3rd week in May.*

Nuit des Musées ★★ More than 40 museums stay open from sundown to midnight, often offering visits by torch-light. The Galerie de l'Evolution in the Natural History Museum (see p. 180), Musée Rodin (see p. 84), and the Grand Palais (see p. 56) are particularly impressive for children.

www.nuitdesmusees.culture.fr. *One night mid-May.*

June

Fête de la Musique ★ This celebration at the summer solstice is the only day noise laws don't apply in Paris. Musicians and wannabes pour into the streets to both make and listen to music. Musical parties pop up in virtually all the open spaces, with more organised concerts at Place de la Bastille (see p. 136), Place de la République, in La Villette (see p. 246), and the Latin Quarter (see p. 175).

www.fetedelamusique.culture.fr*. 21 June.*

Fêtes du Bassin de la Villette For two days the Canal de l'Ourcq (in the up-and-coming Villette district, see p. 246) comes alive with pedal-boats, *boules* (French open-air bowling also known as *pétanque*), open-air concerts, and fireworks on the Saturday night.

01 44 52 29 12; ***www.mairie19.paris.fr****, 19th arr., M° Jaurès or Stalingrad. One weekend early June.*

Les Pestacles Festival ★★ 'Pestacle' is a children's nickname for 'spectacle' (show), and fittingly, this summer festival in the Parc Floral near the Château de Vincennes and Vincennes Zoo is devoted to entertaining children every Wednesday from early June to late September (from 10.30am) with theatre, music, puppet shows, clowns, and children's games.

Parc Floral de Paris, Esplanade du Château de Vincennes, Vincennes, M° Château-de-Vincennes and RER A Vincennes. 39 75; ***www.pestacles.fr*** *and* ***www.paris.fr***

Paris Jazz Festival ★ The stunning Parc Floral in Vincennes is the setting for this annual jazz jamboree, with names big and small on the stages. Pack a picnic and be entertained.

Bois de Vincennes, Esplanade du Château, M° Château-de-Vincennes. Early Jun to end Jul. Concerts on Sat and Sun (3pm and 4.30pm), musical parades at 1pm and 3pm

July

Bastille Day This celebration of the 1789 storming of the Bastille is the birth date of modern France, and festivities reach their peak in Paris with street fairs, pageants, fireworks, an air show over the centre, and feasts. The day begins with a parade down the Champs-Elysées and ends with fireworks in Montmartre.

July 14.

Paris Plage ★★ On the initiative of Bertrand Delanoë (mayor of Paris since 2001), the quays along the river Seine between the Hôtel de Ville (4th arr.) and Quai de Gare (13th arr.) are turned into beaches where families can stroll, relax, sun-bathe, and play water games. Since 2007, Paris Plage has extended on to the Canal de l'Ourcq (19th arr., M° Jaurès and Stalingrad).

*39 75; **www.paris.fr**. Mid-July–mid-Aug, 7am–midnight.*

Paris Quartier d'Eté ★ For four weeks, places around the capital (including the Arènes de Lutèce, see p. 191, and the Sorbonne's Cour d'Honneur, see p. 190) host pop and orchestral concerts. There are also films, plays, jazz, and parades in the Jardin de Tuileries (see p. 62) and Parc André Citroën parks.

*Various locations, 01 44 94 98 00 or see **www.quartierdete.com**. Mid-July–early Aug.*

Paris Slide ★ If your children are into skateboards and rollerblading, don't miss this annual extravaganza where under-16s can get free lessons and experts show off.

*Pelouse de Reuilly, 12th arr., M° Porte Dorée. **http://mairie12.paris.fr**. Mid-July–early Sept*

Tour de France The most over-abundantly televised bicycle race in the world is decided at a finish line drawn across the Champs-Elysées, 8th arr.

*01 41 33 14 00; **www.letour.fr**. In July.*

August

Le Cinema en Plein Air ★★ Every August the Parc de la Villette becomes a giant open-air cinema with the biggest inflatable screen in the world, showing everything from cartoons for the children to old classics and recent releases. Deckchairs can be hired and don't forget your blankets or picnic.

*Check dates and films at **www.villette.com**.*

September

Famillathlon Grannies, grandpas, mums, dads, and children alike get their running shoes out for a family sports day at the foot of the Eiffel Tower. You can try aerobics, combat sports, table tennis, boules, and volleyball.

*Champ de Mars, 7th arr., M° Ecole Militaire. **www.famillathlon.org**. One Sunday at the end of Sept.*

Fête d'Automne (Autumn Festival) ★ Paris welcomes the return of its residents from their August holidays with an ongoing and eclectic festival of modern music, ballet, theatre, cinema and contemporary art in venues throughout Paris.

*Fête d'Automne, 156 rue de Rivoli, 1st arr., 01 53 45 17 00; **www.festival-automne.com**. Mid-Sept–late Dec.*

Journées du Patrimoine ★★ For two days only, national heritage buildings and private institutions open their doors to the public – a great time to explore the hidden parts of town.

*Programme at **www.journeesdu patrimoine.culture.fr**. 2nd/3rd weekend Sept.*

La Villette Jazz Festival ★★ This homage to the art of jazz incorporates dozens of concerts in Parc de la Villette's Cité de la Musique (see p. 247) as well as other venues around town. Past festivals have welcomed Herbie Hancock, Shirley Horn, and Michel Portal.

*La Villette, 19th arr., M° Porte de Pantin or Porte de la Villette. 01 44 84 44 84; **www.villette.com** and **www.cite-musique.fr**. Early Sept.*

October

Nuit Blanche ★ If you're here with teenagers this is a fun way to sightsee, with Paris's museums and otherwise private buildings staying open until dawn. Some cafés offer food throughout the evening and others open early to serve breakfast.

***www.paris.fr**. 1st weekend in Oct.*

Vignes de Montmartre Every year there's a celebration in honour of the harvest at this last remaining vineyard in Paris. It's a party for the whole family with a parade, a concert, and fireworks above the Sacré Coeur, and food stands in Place du Tertre cooking up regional specialities.

*01 30 21 48 62 or 08 20 30 01 11. **www.fetedesvendangesdemont martre.com**. 1st Saturday in Oct.*

Health, Insurance & Safety

Travel Insurance

Travellers to France from the EU should carry a **European Health Insurance Card** (EHIC) as proof of entitlement to free or reduced-cost medical treatment abroad. Each family member should have their own card. Apply online (***www.ehic.org.uk***), call (from the UK) *0845 606 2030*, or get a form from the Post Office. You still pay up front for treatment and related expenses; the doctor will give you a form to reclaim most of the money (about 70% of doctor's fees and 35–65% of medicine/prescription charge costs), which you should send off while still in France (see the EHIC website for details).

Note that the EHIC only covers 'necessary medical treatment', not repatriation costs, lost money, baggage, or cancellation, so is not a replacement for **travel insurance**. Before you buy the latter, check whether your existing insurance policies and credit cards cover you for lost luggage, cancelled tickets, or medical expenses. Also, make sure your package includes **trip-cancellation insurance** to help get your money back if you have to back out of a trip or go home early (more likely if you're travelling with children), or your travel supplier goes bust.

Other **non-EU nationals** – with the exception of Canadians, who have the same rights as EU citizens to medical treatment in France – need comprehensive travel insurance that covers medical treatment overseas. Even then, you pay bills up front and apply for a refund.

Staying Healthy

There are no real health risks when travelling in France – you don't need vaccinations and you can drink tap water. For general advice on travelling with children, read *Your Child Abroad: A Travel Health Guide*, by Dr Jane Wilson-Howarth and Dr Matthew Ellis (Bradt, £10.95).

If You Fall Ill

If any family member uses medicine regularly, bring copies of **prescriptions** in case you lose it or run out. Also carry the generic name of prescription medicines in case a local pharmacist is unfamiliar with the brand name, and bring an extra pair of contact lenses or prescription glasses.

When flying, pack any **prescription medicines** you'll need while in the air in your hand luggage in their original containers, with pharmacist's labels. At the time of writing, anti-terrorism precautions require some medicines to be verified by airport chemists. For details, see your departure airport and/or airline website.

For any family member requiring it, the charity **MedicAlert** (***www.medicalert.org.uk***) provides body-worn bracelets or necklets for those needing swift and accurate treatment for, say, epilepsy, diabetes, asthma, or a food allergy. The items are engraved with the wearer's medical condition(s), along with ID number and a 24-hour emergency telephone number that accepts reverse charge calls to access your medical information in more than 100 languages.

Here's a quick **Health SOS list for Paris**. For Disneyland see p. 211.

Fire Brigade and Paramedics ☎ *18* (usually arrive faster than the SAMU).

Hospitals with English-speaking staff
Hôpital Americain, 63 boulevard Victor Hugo, Neuilly-sur-Seine (92), ☎ *01 46 41 25 25*
Hôpital Franco Britannique, 3 rue Barbès, Levallois Perret (92) ☎ *01 46 39 22 22*

Pharmacies open 24 hours a day
Pharmacie des Champs-Elysées, 84 avenue des Champs-Elysées, 8th arr., ☎ *01 45 62 02 41*, M° Georges V.
Pharmacie Européenne, Place de Clichy, 9th arr., ☎ *01 48 74 65 18*, M° Place de Clichy.

Police ☎ *17*

SAMU (ambulance) ☎ *15*

SOS dental emergencies ☎ *01 43 36 36 00*

SOS doctors ☎ *01 47 07 77 77* (if your illness isn't bad enough for casualty, but you need to see a doctor out of consulting hours).

Travelling Safely with Children

The centre of Paris is generally safe for families; the main worry is being targeted by **pickpockets or petty thieves.** Always keep your bags closed (with a zip) when travelling around town and, if driving, don't leave **valuables** in a car.

As a parent, be wary of Parisian drivers who often jump traffic lights and drive aggressively. Practically no one stops at **pedestrian crossings**, so tell your child to wait until vehicles have stopped before proceeding especially at some junctions; cars can legally cross onto pedestrian crossings even when the green man is lit.

As everywhere, **hold hands with young children** and don't let them out of your sight unless they are being supervised by someone you trust. Avoid situations where young children could get swept away in a **crowd**, and with older children, agree on a **place to meet** should you get parted. Make sure they have your mobile number and accommodation address on them, and give them instructions to ask for a member of the police (*agent de police* or *gendarme*) should they become lost. Their name should never be visible on their bag/clothing and tell them the importance of **never divulging their name to a stranger** (other than the police).

For peace of mind, especially if you have more than one child to keep an eye on, you could invest in **Boardbug** wrist-worn monitors (see p. 20). You could also try a set of reins if you have a toddler who likes to go walkabout, but be prepared for strange looks from passers-by as the French think reins are for dogs, not children.

Specialised Resources

For Single Parents

For a good holiday page with contact details of useful UK associations and operators, see ***www.singleparents.org.uk***. The US-based ***www.singleparenttravel.net*** is also good for general travel advice for single parents.

One Parent Families (*0800 018 5026*, ***www.oneparentfamilies.org.uk***) is a British charity offering information and advice for lone parents. **Gingerbread** (*0800 018 4318*, ***www.gingerbread.org.uk***) is similar, with members getting regular emails with discounts and holiday ideas. **Lone fathers** should check out ***www.onlydads.org***.

For Grandparents

Grandparents travelling with children are a rapidly growing market but specialist tour operators tend to be US-based. **Grand Travel** (*1 800 247 7651*, ***www.grandtrvl.com***), for instance, runs a trip to Paris. If you take your grandchildren on outings, remember that over-60s generally get **discounts** on travel tickets, museum and zoo entry.

For Families with Special Needs

Many of Paris's historic buildings, whether museums or hotels, have limited or non-existent **wheelchair access**. That said, things are changing and some Parisian hotels have at least one accessible or ground-floor room.

A wheelchair (and even a buggy) can be a real hindrance on public transport and though certain stations (all of Métro line 14, some parts of line 1, and the RER) have lifts, it is still very difficult to move around without a car.

Les Compagnons du Voyage provide escort services on all transport (☎ *01 53 11 11 12*; ***www.compagnons.com***); **Association des Paralysées de France** (☎ *01 53 80 92 97*; ***www.apf.asso.fr***) supplies useful reading material and recommendations, as does **GHIP** (☎ *01 43 95 66 36*; ***www.gihpnational.org***). Finally, ***http://www.jaccede.com/*** is a useful site (French only) that lists venues (concerts, theatres, etc.) with disabled access in Paris.

Because you stay in your car when travelling on **Eurotunnel** (see p. 32), this is easier than the ferry for wheelchair users, and **Eurostar** (see p. 33) offers first-class travel at second-class fares for disabled people.

The 21st-Century Traveller

Mobile Phones

Luckily, these days a British mobile phone will simply switch to a **French network** when you reach France, but you'll usually need to put in the relevant country code (see p. 46) to dial numbers both in France and abroad. It's wise to **check in advance with your provider** that your phone is set up for **international roaming** and have them explain the procedure for accessing voicemail while abroad (this is usually trouble-free but do check). For **pay-as-you-go phones** you'll need to check the situation with your network provider.

Call charges to the UK from France using a UK mobile will be higher than calls made within the UK, and you will also pay for any incoming calls you receive. If you're going to be making or receiving a lot of calls, or go abroad often, it might be worth buying an **international SIM card** to temporarily replace your UK one (see ***www.0044.co.uk*** or ***www.globalsim.co.uk***). This will give you a local number and **lower calling rates.**

If you're staying more than a few weeks or come to France regularly, you could just buy a pay-as-you-go ('*sans abonnement*') phone on a French high street or from a larger supermarket. The French networks include Orange, Bouygtel, and SFR.

For those from further afield, such as the **USA**, the situation is basically the same provided you have a world-capable multiband phone on a **GSM** (Global System for Mobiles) system, with 'international roaming' activated. Installing an international SIM card can save you money if you are using the phone frequently.

Remember to bring an adaptor plug to **recharge your phone.**

Other Phones

For information about **area** and **international dialling codes** and public phones see p. 46.

The Internet

Paris has surprisingly few cyber-cafés (see each chapter's Fast Facts for some addresses and ***www.cybercafe.fr***). Most **hotels**, however offer Internet access either for free or at a charge, but **French keyboards** are laid out on the AZERTY rather than QWERTY principle and may slow you down.

If you come with your own computer, more than **400 free WiFi** points have been set up across the city in public parks and outside monuments (***www.paris.fr*** lists the spots). ***www.cafes-wifi.com*** also lists cafés where you can get WiFi connections.

Essentials

Getting There

By Plane Paris is an international hub with both **low-cost airlines** and **major airlines** flying to its two main airports: **Aeroport Roissy CDG** (Charles de Gaulle) 23km north of the city and **Aeroport d'Orly**, 14km to the south. A third airport, **L'Aeroport de Beauvais**, lies a 1¼-hr (80km) drive from Paris and is used by the low-cost airlines **Ryanair** (see below) and **Blue Islands** (also see below).

Blue Islands (UK ☎ *08456 20 21 22*/ France ☎ *08 92 68 20 89* ***www.blueislands.com***) links Guernsey and Jersey to Paris Beauvais airport.

Bmibaby (UK ☎ *0871 224 0224*/ France ☎ *0890 710 081*, ***www.bmibaby.com***) flies to Paris CDG from East Midlands Airport.

EasyJet (***www.easyjet.com***) flies to Paris CDG from Belfast, Bristol, Edinburgh, Glasgow, Liverpool, London Luton, and Newcastle.

Flybe (UK ☎ *0871 700 0535*/ outside UK ☎ *00 44 13 922 685 29*, ***www.flybe.com***) flies to Paris CDG from Belfast, Birmingham, Cardiff, Exeter, Glasgow, Manchester, Norwich, and Southampton.

Jet 2 (UK ☎ *0871 226 1737*/ France ☎ *08 21 23 02 03*, ***www.jet2.com***) flies to Paris CDG from Leeds-Bradford and Manchester.

Ryanair (UK ☎ *0871 246 0000*/ France ☎ *0892 68 20 73*, ***www.ryanair.com***) flies from Dublin and Shannon in Ireland and Glasgow in the UK to Paris Beauvais (***www.aeroportbeauvais.com***).

You can also fly to **Paris** from the UK and Ireland with **British Airways** (UK ☎ *0870 850 9850*/ France ☎ *0825 825 4400*, ***www.ba.com***), **Air France** (UK ☎ *0870 142 4343*/ France ☎ *0820 820 820*, *www.airfrance.com*), **Aer Lingus** (UK ✆ *0870 876 5000*/ Ireland ✆ *0818 365 000*, ***www.aerlingus.com***) and **British Midland** (✆ UK *0870 607 0555*; ***www.flybmi.com***).

Among airlines that fly regularly between the USA and Paris are **American Airlines** (✆ *1 800 433 7300*, ***www.aa.com***), **British Airways** (✆ *1 800 AIRWAYS*, ***www.ba.com***), **Continental Airlines** (✆ *1 800 525 0280*, ***www.continental.com***) and **Delta Air Lines** (✆ *1 800 241 4141*, ***www.delta.com***). **Air France** flies to **Paris from the USA and Canada** and **Air Canada** (✆ *888 247 2262*, ***www.aircanada.com***) and **Zoom Airlines** (✆ *866 359 9666*, ***www.flyzoom.com***) fly from **Toronto and Montreal.**

There are currently no direct flights from **Australia to Paris**; most people fly to London and take a connecting flight or Eurostar. **South African Airways** (✆ *0861 359 722*, ***www.flysaa.com***) fly to Paris from **Cape Town** and other cities in South Africa.

As a general rule, **under-twos fly free** if they sit on your knee; older than that, they pay the same fare as you. **Fares** can start from as little as £0.01, depending on your destination and when you book. However, these don't include **airport taxes and other charges**, which can add up to about £60–80 for a family of four. Also, some airlines, including Ryanair and Jet 2, might charge for checked-in baggage, so it's good to do your research into what you're paying for before you book in order to keep costs down.

What you can take on flights: passengers are currently allowed to take one **bag** as hand luggage, although check with both the airport and airline for more information. If you are carrying **liquids** in your hand luggage, they must be in individual containers with a maximum capacity of 100 millilitres (ml). You must pack these containers in one transparent, re-sealable plastic bag of not more than one-litre capacity. **Medicines, baby food, and milk** over 100ml must be presented for **inspection** at X-ray. It's wise to check the current security status with your airline or departure airport before packing.

INSIDER TIP

If possible, keep children with colds grounded, as ascent and descent can be especially painful – and even dangerous – when they have congested sinuses. If that's not an option, give them an oral child's decongestant an hour before ascent and descent, or administer a spray decongestant before and during take-off and landing. When travelling with a baby, you might want to invest in a Baby B'Air Flight Safety Vest, which attaches to your seatbelt to protect lap-held little ones during turbulence and allows you to sleep knowing your baby can't fall from your arms. It costs about £27 from ***www.babybair.com***. Check first that your airline doesn't already have babyholders to loan you.

Getting into Town from the Airport

From Roissy CDG, a **free shuttle bus** (*navette*) links the terminals to each other and also transports passengers to the **Roissy rail station (CDG T1)** and **RER T2**, from which fast RER trains (Line B) leave every 15 minutes daily between 5am to midnight for Métro and RER stations such as Gare du Nord, Châtelet, Luxembourg, Port Royal, and Denfert-Rochereau (it continues to Orly airport too). From any of those points within central Paris, Métro lines can carry you on to most parts of the city. The cost is 8.20€ adult single and 5.80€ for 4–10s.

If you land at Terminal 3, you can walk to the rail CDG T1 Roissy rail station.

Air France also runs **shuttle buses** from Roissy and Orly for points within central Paris and between the airports. They depart at 15–20 minute intervals every day between 6am and 11pm. The journey to the centre from CDG lasts about 40 mins (50 min–1 hr for CDG to Orly, Line 3); and from Orly about 30 mins.

Line 1 runs between Orly, Montparnasse and Les Invalides (9€ single, 14€ return, 4.50€ 2–11s, free for under 2s).

Line 2 runs between CDG and the Arc de Triomphe, with a stop en route at Porte Maillot (13€ single, 20€ return, 6.50€ 2–11s, free under 2s)

Line 3 runs between the airports (16€ single (no returns), 8€ 2–11s, free under 2s).

Line 4 runs between CDG and the Gare de Lyon and Montparnasse (14€ single, 22€ return, 7€ 2–11s, free under 2).

Another option, the **Roissybus** (***www.ratp.fr***), departs from a point near the corner of the Rue Scribe and Place de l'Opéra (9th arr., M° Opéra or RER B Auber) every 15–20 minutes from 6am to 11pm to Roissy CDG (covers all 3 terminals). The cost for the 50-minute ride is 8.60€.

Taxis from Roissy into the city run for about 50€ on the meter. At night (8pm–7am) fares are about 30% higher, and luggage can cost extra. Long queues of both taxis and passengers form outside each of the airport's terminals in a surprisingly orderly fashion.

Orly has two terminals: Orly Sud (south) for international flights and Orly Ouest (west) for domestic flights. A free shuttle bus links them.

Air France buses leave from Exit E of Orly Ouest and from Exit K, Platform 5, of Orly Sud (see above **Line 1**).

An alternative method for reaching central Paris involves taking a monorail (Orly Val) to the RER station of Anthony and then the RER train into central Paris. The Orly Val makes stops at the north and south terminals, and continues at eight-minute intervals for the 10-minute ride to the Anthony RER station. At Anthony, you'll board an RER train (Line B) for the 30-minute ride into the city. The cost of the Orly Val monorail is 7.20€

adult, 3.60€ 4–10s. The RER (Line B) transit into Paris is 9.30€ adult and 4.65€ 4–10s, a fare that might seem a bit high but that offsets the horrendous construction costs of a monorail that sails above the congested roadways encircling the airport.

A **taxi** from Orly to the centre of Paris costs about 35€ (more at night and on weekends).

Caution: Don't take a meterless taxi from either airport as they can be unsafe. Choose instead a metered cab (marked Taxi Parisien) from the taxi queues, which are supervised by a police officer.

To and from **Beauvais** airport **Transport Paris Beauvais** runs a shuttle service from Porte Maillot (17th arr., M° Porte Maillot, at the bus park on Boulevard Pershing near the James Joyce pub). Show up at least 3 1/4 hours before your flight. A one-way ticket costs 13€ and can be bought on the bus. The journey takes just over an hour. ✆ *08 92 68 20 64*; ***www.paris-beauvais.fr***.

By Car

Ferries: The shortest way across the Channel is **Dover to Calais**. Then it's about a three-hour non-stop drive to Paris (along the A1), around 290km (180mi). A good resource to plan your route is ***www.drive-alive.co.uk*** (click on 'route planner'), which will also tell you how much you'll pay in toll charges.

P&O Ferries (UK ✆ *08705 980 333*/ France ✆ *08 25 12 01 56*, ***www.poferries.com***) sails from Dover to Calais in just over an hour. All vessels have children's play areas and entertainment, including films and video games. There are also inexpensive children's meals and free baby food. Another operator on the route is **Seafrance** (UK ✆ *0871 663 2546*/ France ✆ *08 25 08 25 05*, ***www.seafrance.com***), which has similar onboard facilities.

The major ferry operator between Britain and northern France is **Brittany Ferries** (UK ✆ *0870 907 6103*/ France ✆ *08 25 82 88 28*, ***www.brittanyferries.com***), which sails from **Poole to Cherbourg** and from **Portsmouth to Caen, Cherbourg, and St Malo** and is possibly **more convenient** for holidaymakers from the **south west of England**. Bear in mind that these are overnight crossings, but four-bed cabins are available. Again, the ferries have children's areas and entertainment. The distances you'll need to drive to Paris are: 400km (250mi) from St Malo, 360km (225mi) from Cherbourg, and 240km (150mi) from Caen.

Eurotunnel: This shuttle train taking cars through the Channel Tunnel (UK ✆ *08705 353 535*, ***www.eurotunnel.com***), between Folkestone and Calais takes just **35 minutes** and you don't even need to get out of your car. Sample prices in late Aug–mid-Sept range from £49 to £141 each way per car, with lower fares early in the morning or late at night. These are standard fares rather than the more expensive Flexiplus fares, but you can still take a different train from the one you're booked on (at no extra cost) provided you arrive within two hours of your scheduled departure time.

By Train You can travel from **London** (St Pancras) or **Ashford International** and **Ebbsfleet International** in Kent (there is extra parking space in Ebbsfleet) to Paris and Marne-la-Vallée (Disneyland® Resort Paris) on **Eurostar** (UK ☎ *0870 530 0003*/ France ☎ *08 92 35 35 39*; ***www.eurostar.com***). Fares vary according to how far in advance you book and the degree of flexibility you require for exchanges or refunds. They can be as low as £109 per adult and £94 per child aged 4–11 for a return ticket in standard class. **Rail Europe** (☎ *08708 371 371*, ***www.raileurope.co.uk***) is a good place to book, as you can save money booking online. Check out ***www.seat61.com*** for timetables and booking tips that will help you get the best deals and navigate the pitfalls. The best deals and promotions are sometimes found in the national press. Direct Eurostars to Disney usually include a free children's games pack and visits by Disney characters. There are also baby-changing facilities on all Eurostar trains, and the whole experience can often be less stressful than airport queues.

If travelling by train from elsewhere in France, Paris has six major train stations: **Gare d'Austerlitz,** 55 quai d'Austerlitz, 13th arr. (serving the southwest, with trains from the Loire Valley, the Bordeaux area, and the Pyrenees); **Gare de l'Est,** Place du 11 Novembre 1918, 10th arr. (serving the east, with trains from Strasbourg, Nancy, Reims, and beyond to Zurich, Basel, Luxembourg, and Austria); **Gare de Lyon,** 20 boulevard Diderot, 12th arr. (serving the southeast with trains from the Côte d'Azur and Provence to Geneva, Lausanne, and Italy); **Gare Montparnasse,** 17 boulevard Vaugirard, 15th arr. (serving the west, with trains from Brittany and the TGV from Bordeaux and the Southwest); **Gare du Nord,** 18 rue de Dunkerque, 10th arr. (serving the north, with trains from the Netherlands, Denmark, and Germany as well as Eurostar from the UK and Thalys from Belgium); and **Gare St-Lazare,** 13 rue d'Amsterdam, 8th arr. (serving the northwest, with trains from Normandy).

For general train information and to make reservations, call ☎ *36 35* (special number). Buses operate between rail stations and each of these stations has a Métro stop, making the whole city easily accessible. Taxis are also available from designated stands at every station.

By Bus This is your cheapest but slowest and least comfortable means of getting to the Continent, and, with little ones in tow, you might be asking for one long headache of a journey. It might be bearable with older children if you bring the required mp3 players, games, and books. However, it is one of the greenest ways to travel.

Eurolines (☎ *08705 808 080*, ***www.nationalexpress.co.uk***) runs services (10hr journey) from London Victoria to **Paris,** arriving just out of the centre at Porte de Bagnolet, the terminus of M° line 3 (Gallieni), from where you can get to any other part of Paris (in under 30 mins) or La Défense, Paris's out-of-centre business district (RER and M° La Défense). Some buses have extra legroom; all have air-conditioning, toilets, and stop at mealtimes for rest and refreshment. Return prices start at £40 for adults and £20 for children.

Packages & Deals

Package deals let you buy your aeroplane, ferry, or train ticket, accommodation and, where appropriate, Disneyland tickets, as well as other elements of your trip (e.g. car hire or airport transfers) at the same time, often at a discount. However, they may include hidden charges that you would avoid by booking direct with a hotel or carrier. The obvious appeal for parents is that package deals save you time researching and booking.

The following are a few of the best package holiday companies to Paris and Disneyland. You will find many more on the Internet and advertised in local and national papers. Again, check that your travel insurance (see p. 25) covers you if your operator goes bust.

In the UK

One good city-break specialist is **Leisure Direction** (UK ☎ *0871 423 5519*; ***www.leisuredirection.co.uk***) which offers packages to both Paris and Disneyland. **Lastminute.com** (UK ☎ *0871 222 5969*; ***www.lastminute.com***) is, as its name implies, good for some last-minute deals. **Thomson Holidays** (UK ☎ *0871 231 4138*; ***www.thomson.co.uk***) also run package holidays to Paris and Disney, as do **Thomas Cook** (UK ☎ *0870 750 5711*; ***www.thomascook.com***). **British Airways Holidays** is ideal for combining hotels, car rental, and sightseeing offers (UK ☎ *0870 850 9850*; ***www.baholidays.com***). **Expedia** (UK ☎ *0871 226 0808*; ***www.expedia.co.uk***) finds deals for Eurostar holidays and city breaks to Paris. **Anderson Tours** offers 'tailor-made' packages (including car hire) to Paris (UK ☎ *0870 1111 400*; ***www.andersontours.co.uk***).

In the States

Most major airlines offer air/land packages, including **American Airlines Vacations** (☎ *800/321 2121*; ***www.aavacations.com***), **Continental Airlines Vacations** (☎ *800/301 3800*; ***www.covacations.com***), and **Delta Vacations** (☎ *800/654 6559*; ***www.deltavacations.com***). Several big **online travel agencies** – Expedia, Travelocity, Orbitz, Site59, and Lastminute.com – also do brisk business in packages.

The French Experience, 370 Lexington Ave., Room 511,

New York, NY 10017 (☎ *800/283 7262* or ☎ *212/986 3800*, ***www.frenchexperience.com***), offers inexpensive tickets to Paris on most scheduled airlines and tours can be adapted to suit individual needs.

Getting Around

By Car Parking is difficult, traffic is dense, and networks of one-way streets make navigation, even with the best of maps, a problem. Few hotels, except the luxury ones, have garages (I've included some hotels with private parking), although staff will usually be able to direct you to one nearby. If you do drive, remember that Paris is encircled by a ring road called the *périphérique*. Always obtain detailed directions to your destination, including the name of the exit on the *périphérique* you're looking for (exits aren't numbered). Once you arrive in the centre you probably won't need to use your car, unless you drive to Disneyland or other parts of the region. Underground car parks are indicated on signposts by a large 'P' with a blue background. If you park on the street, you may need to get a ticket (look for a sign marked '*parking payant*'). Display the ticket in the front window.

By Métro & RER When you're in Paris, the **Métro** (or subway) efficiently covers the centre; the **RER** (part-subway, part outside train line) covers the centre and some of Île-de-France including Disneyland Paris. Information on both can be found at ***www.ratp.fr*** (☎ *32-46*). Métro lines are numbered from 1 to 14, RER lines from A to E. Both run daily from around 5.30am to 1.15am (depending upon the line, and an hour later on Fridays, Saturdays, and the night before public holidays). Keep your children close by, especially during rush hour (7.30am–9.30am and 5pm–7.30pm), but all lines are reasonably safe at any hour. Just beware of pickpockets and pay special attention at crossover stations like Châtelet, Gare du Nord, and Montparnasse (especially at night), where several TGV lines, Métro, and RER lines run out to the suburbs, attracting the odd unsavoury group of youths.

Central Paris is classed as zones 1 and 2 and a standard ticket (see Which Ticket p. 36) is valid in these two zones. For zones further afield (Versailles, Parc Astérix, the airports, and Disneyland), separate tickets should be purchased, unless yours already includes outer zones (look on the ticket – some special passes, like *Paris Visite* and *Carte Orange*, can include outer zones). To get through the turnstiles to the Métro and RER, put your ticket in the slot then take it with you on the train. Don't lose it whatever you do; you may need it to get out, and mean-spirited *contrôleurs* (inspectors) dressed in uniform can stop you at any time on the trains or in the station. If you're ticketless you'll be fined.

Which Ticket?

Single-journey tickets or packs of 10 tickets (*un carnet*, pron. '*car-nay*') can be bought from a machine in the Métro station with cash or a credit card, or from a ticket window. Individual tickets cost 1.50€ and a pack of ten is 11.10€ (5.55€ 4–10s, under-4s free). These are valid on the Métro, RER, and buses in the centre, and while you can use one ticket for an uninterrupted journey on the Métro and RER, you'll have to use a separate one for buses.

If you plan to ride the Métro a lot, the **Paris Visite** pass (☎ *32 46*; ***www.parisvisite.com*** available from all RATP desks in the Métro and from Tourist Offices) may be worthwhile. You get unlimited rides for one, two, three, or five days for access to zones 1 to 3, which includes central Paris and its nearby suburbs, or zones 1 to 6, which includes Disneyland (zone 5), Versailles (zone 4), and the CDG (zone 5) and Orly (zone 4) airports. It's valid only from the first time you use it so you can buy it in advance. Remember to fill in your name (and your children's names) as well as the series number on the card and the date of its first use. **Adults Zone 1–3:** 8.50€ – 1-day, 14€ – 2-day, 19€ – 3-day, 27.50€ – 5-day; **4-11s Zone 1–3:** 4.25€ – 1-day, 7€ – 2-day, 9.50€ – 3-day, 13.75€ – 5-day: **Adults Zone 1–6:** 18€ – 1-day, 27.50€ – 2-day, 38.50€ – 3-day, 47€ – 5-day. **4–11s Zone 1–6:** 9€ – 1-day, 13.75€ – 2-day, 19.25€ – 3-day, 23.50€ – 5-day. Under-4s free.

If you're staying in Paris for a week, arriving early in the week, the cheapest option is a **Carte Orange,** which allows unlimited access on the Métro, RER, and buses from Monday–Sunday. It's sold at large Métro and RER stations and requires a passport-size photo. Cost for zones 1–2 is 16.30€ (no child reduction but under-4s free)

Another discount pass is **Carte Mobilis,** which allows unlimited travel on bus, subway, and RER lines for one day for 5.60€ to 15.90€, depending on the zone. Ask for it at any Métro station. You will need passport photos.

Most stations display a map of the Métro at the entrance. To work out the line you need, find where you are on the map, locate your destination (or station to change), follow the line to the end of its route, and note the name of the final stop in that direction. In the station, follow the signs for the final stop in your direction along the passageways until you reach the platform. Just before you get to the platform, a panel will list the stops served by the train, so you can double-check you're in the right place. Many larger stations have maps with push-button indicators that light up your route when you press the button for your destination, and others have help points where you can ask directions. The route is also always marked inside the train cars.

The Métro, RER, & Buggies Some underground stations (usually in the RER) have doors separate from the turnstiles that can be opened on request for buggies to go through. Otherwise, you'll have to take your child out and open and close the buggy every time you cross the subway's turnstiles (don't expect help from the RATP staff). Both the Métro and RER feature multiple steps which are also difficult to navigate. Line 14 is the only one fully equipped with lifts, as are some stations on line 1 and RER A. You'll also be confronted with gaps between the platform and the train. A baby-carrier (back-pack – see Children's Kit p. 20) will make life easier with little ones.

By Bus Getting around by bus is fairly easy and, although slower than the Métro, buses allow you and the children to see where you're going and there are designated areas for buggies. The majority run from 7am to 8.30pm, a few operate until 12.30am, and several night-time buses (**Noctilien**) operate 12.30am–5.30am. Most start at train stations Châtelet, Gare de Lyon, Gare du Nord, Montparnasse, and Gare St-Lazare. All bus services are limited on Sundays and holidays. Bus and Métro fares are the same, and you can use the same tickets on both.

At certain stops, signs list destinations and bus numbers serving that point. Most stops are also posted on the sides of the buses and inside them. If you intend to use the buses a lot, pick up an RATP bus map at any Métro station, or print one off from ***www.ratp.fr***.

The RATP also operates the **Balabus,** tourist buses that run on Sunday afternoons between April and September. Itineraries run in both directions between Gare de Lyon and the Grande Arche de La Défense, passing some of the city's most beautiful views. Two Métro tickets, just 1.50€ each, will carry you and the children the entire route (look out for the *Bb* symbol emblazoned on each bus's side and on bus stops, ✆ *32 46* or consult ***www.ratp.fr***).

L'Open Tour is another practical sightseeing bus offering four routes (*lignes*) operating seven days a week year round. On a fine day your children can run upstairs to grab a seat on the top deck and listen to commentary in English. Passes can be bought for one or two days. **Prices:** 26€ 1-day adult (4€ reduction with a valid Paris Visite, Carte Orange, or Batobus pass), 29€ 2-day adult; 13€ one and two day passes for 4–11s. Under-4s free.

By Taxi Taxi **fares** in Paris are metered and, for safety and to avoid rip-offs, you should only use taxis marked ***Taxi Parisien***. If the entire light on top of the car is on, the taxi is available; if a small bulb is lit under the light, it is busy. The cost on the meter when you get in is 2.10€. The minimum fare is 5.60€, an extra 1€ is charged for more than one piece of luggage in the boot, and 2.75€ for a fourth person. Most taxis take cash only, but some companies accept credit cards (min. 15€). You can request a credit-card equipped car if you order a taxi by telephone or use the special yellow taxi-call booth at Taxi stations.

Reputable companies to use are:

Paris accredited taxis ☎ *01 45 30 30 30*

Taxis Bleu ☎ *01 49 36 10 10*

Taxi G7 ☎ *01 47 39 47 39*

Your hotel can also call you a taxi.

By Bike Although Paris does have cycle paths, they are not everywhere and children not used to riding on the 'wrong' (right) side of the road may be perturbed by traffic. However, organised bike tours are a good way to sightsee on two wheels. **Fat Tire Bike Tours** next to the south leg of the Eiffel Tower offer children's bikes, child seats, child tandems, and trailers, and outings including a day tour, which covers everywhere from the Eiffel Tower to the Louvre, a night tour that combines a river cruise, a trip to Versailles, and a day trip to Giverny to see Monet's garden. ☎ *01 56 58 10 54*; ***www.fattirebiketoursparis.com***. Day Hire: 24€ adult, 22€ students and children. Night Hire: 28€ adult, 26€ students and children. If you brave it with older children and teenagers, you can rent bikes from a number of places in town. **Maison Roue Libre** rents bicycles for 10€ (mid-week) to 15€ (weekends) for one day in several locations in Paris: Les Halles (1 passage Mondétour, 1st arr., corner of Rue Rambuteau, M° Les Halles) and at Bastille (37 boulevard Bourdon, 4th arr., M° Bastille) are the most central hire shops. You'll need photo ID and a deposit to hire the bikes. ☎ *08 10 44 15 34*; ***www.rouelibre.fr***.

The best deal, however, is the **Vélib**: Paris's excellent self-service bike scheme. More than 20,000 bikes can be hired for just 1€ per day or night, seven days a week, during which you can take a bike from any stand and use it for 30 minutes free of charge. At the end of your 30 minutes, return it to any bike-stand (if it's full, check the map on the service point for the nearest stand). Tickets can be bought with your credit card in a service point. You'll have to authorise a 150€ deposit to be taken from your card only if the bike is not returned and type in a PIN of your choice. The machine will give you a ticket, with a code, that you use to unlock the bikes. A separate ticket is needed for each bike, but one credit card can hire bikes for all the family.

If bikes seem a little too much effort, **Segway Tours** (part of Fat Tires Bike Tours (see left)) have a solution: two-wheeled cruisers (motorised platforms that you stand on and guide using handlebars) that move you effortlessly around the city. They offer guided tours in English (70€) and hire them out by the hour (25€/hr, minimum 2 hours). 01 56 58 10 54; **www.citysegwaytours.com**. Over-12s only.

By Boat The **Batobus** (08 25 05 01 01; **www.batobus.com**) is a 150-passenger ferry that operates daily along the Seine from end May to end Aug 10am–9.30pm; Sept to mid-Nov and mid-Mar to end May 10am–7pm; mid-Dec to early Jan 10.30am–5pm: early Feb to mid-Mar 10.30am–4.30pm (closed late Jan and early Feb). Boats stop at all the main points of interest: Eiffel Tower, Musée d'Orsay, St-Germain-des-Prés, the Louvre, Notre-Dame, Jardin des Plantes, Hôtel de Ville, and Champs-Elysées. Unlike the Bateaux-Mouches and Bateaux Parisiens (see p. 87), the Batobus does not provide recorded commentary, and the only fare option is a pass valid for either one, two, or five days, each allowing unlimited use. A one-day pass costs 12€ adults, 6€ under-16s; a two-day pass is 14€ adults, 7€ under-16s; a five-day pass costs 17€ adults, 8€ under-16s. Boats operate daily (closed most of Jan) every 15 to 30 minutes, starting between 10 and 10.30am and ending between 4.30 and 10.30pm, depending on the season. I have included useful Batobus stops in each chapter.

Museums & Attractions

Not all museum staff speak English, however if museums don't provide an audio-guide in English or offer English-speaking guided tours, there will always be an English leaflet outlining the museum's collections. Ask when you buy your tickets.

Many museums offer children's workshops. These are often excellent but generally only in French. However if you reserve far enough in advance, some organisations are willing to provide an English speaker.

If your family plans to visit several museums you can save money buying the **Paris Museum Pass**. It gives free and quick access to more than 60 museums and monuments (including the Louvre, Musée d'Orsay, Pompidou Centre, Versailles, Quai Branly, Arc de Triomphe, and the Rodin museum). You can choose between a two-, four- or six-day pass. Most museums are free for under-18s, so the pass is targeted at adults: 30€ – 2-day, 45€ – 4-day, 60€ – 6-day. 01 44 61 96 60; **www.parismuseumpass.fr**.

Accommodation & Eating Out

Accommodation

There are accommodation options all over the city centre and over the last five years hotel standards have improved as '70s wallpaper and creaking stairs have, more often than not, been replaced with modern décor and lifts. Some smaller hotels, however, particularly in old, classified buildings, still don't have lifts. This may be a problem with small children, but could add to the fun with older ones. All the hotels in this guide can cater for families, either with family-sized rooms or extra beds and cots for children and babies. The official star ratings haven't been included as they generally don't take into account décor, staff, or family facilities.

We have based the accommodation **price categories** on the following, based on price per room. Extras (such as parking, extra beds, etc.) are mentioned separately. With few exceptions prices are without breakfast.

Very expensive: More than 350€

Expensive: 220–350€

Moderate: 150–220€

Inexpensive: Less than 150€

Hotels

For family trips it makes more sense to deal directly with individual hotels and other accommodation suppliers than book them through a website or booking agency. Doing it by email (or the old-fashioned way, by fax) lets you explain your needs and make sure that the hotel provides the services and facilities you require, from bottle warmers and cot linen to games consoles and DVD players. It also means you have the details in writing in case of queries or misunderstandings when you get there (in the worst-case scenario, you have proof if the hotel doesn't deliver what was promised). Hotels often offer special low-season deals or last-minute prices on their websites, though these are rarely available at peak family holiday times. Still, for late-booking deals, some of France's **centralised booking services** can turn up trumps – for smaller hotels in Paris and all over France, check out ***www.guidesdecharme.com***, ***www.guide-hotels-charme.com*** and ***www.logisdefrance.com***.

B&Bs & Apartments

B&Bs and apartments in Paris are less common than hotels, however they do exist and can be excellent for families looking for self-catering or reasonably priced rooms. Some have been included in this book. To find others **Alcove & Agapes** *01 44 85 06 14*; ***www.bed-and-breakfast-in-paris.com*** is a wonderful resource with a list of B&Bs and some unhosted studios and apartments (minimum stay four or five nights). **Good Morning Paris** (*01 47 07 28 29*; ***www.goodmorningparis.fr***) has more than 100 rooms in the city, plus apartments for two to four people (from 99€–125€). **Citadines Apart'hotel** (*01 41 05 78 87*, ***www.citadines.com***) has 16 modern, serviced apartment complexes in the city. All have a kitchenette and in-room facilities for children. ***www.frenchconnections.co.uk***, is another good site, with a selection of furnished apartments for four or more people; as is ***www.apartmentservice.com***, which provides a wide selection of serviced apartments in the city centre.

Eating Out

Some people come to Paris for the cuisine alone, in the belief that it is still the capital of *haute gastronomie*. The city has its share of world-famous, Michelin-starred restaurants, patronised by the rich and famous, but there are also plenty of tourist traps where food is mediocre, the service surly and indifferent, and the prices inflated. That said, most restaurants and cafés (with the odd notoriously rude exception) are welcoming to children. Despite the traffic, Paris still enjoys al fresco eating, and many restaurants have **children's menus** (generally about 10€), though the standard choice is *steak haché* (a burger by any other name) and chips, pizza, or pasta as a main course, followed by ice cream.

Vegetarians may find Paris difficult. Vegetarianism in France is not widespread and many people still think that vegetarians eat chicken or fish. Some trendier restaurants offer 'real' vegetarian options, and bistros will sometimes serve a plate of vegetables in place of a meat dish. However, to get tasty vegetarian or vegan food, you'll have to go to a handful of specialised restaurants. Some such addresses are:

Vegan

La Victoire Suprême du Coeur 31 rue du Bourg Tibourg, 4th arr., M° Hôtel de Ville. *01 40 41 95 03*.

Les 5 Saveurs d'Ananda 72 rue Cardinel-Lemoine, 5th arr., M° Cardinel-Lemoine. *01 43 29 58 54*; ***www.anada5saveurs.com***

Vegetarian

Au Grain de Folie 24 rue de la Vieuville, 18th arr., M° Abbesses. *01 42 58 15 57*.

Le Grenier de Notre Dame 18 rue de la Bûcherie, 5th arr., M° Cité. *01 43 29 98 29*.

Le Potager du Marais 22 rue Rambuteau, 3rd arr., M° Rambuteau, *01 42 74 24 66* (possibly the best vegetarian in Paris).

The **Pain Quotidien** chain (18–20 rue des Archives, 4th arr., M° St-Paul. *01 44 54 03 07*; ***www.lepainquotidien.com***) is not exclusively vegetarian but has good options.

Restaurants and cafés occasionally have one **highchair,** but these are available on a first-come first-served basis, so a portable highchair (one that can double as a child's car seat) or a blow-up travelling booster seat or foldable fabric one is almost a must (see p. 20 for some recommendations).

Mealtimes in Paris are less rigid than in much of France, but restaurants usually serve from noon–2.30pm and again from 7pm–10.30pm. However, many *brasseries* are often open all day, providing parents with an opportunity to get family blood-sugar levels back up to normal with *croque monsieurs* (cheese on toast), *tarte aux pommes* (apple pie) and *sandwich jambon* (ham baguette sandwich) or *sandwich fromage* (cheese baguette sandwich). These bar-restaurants and other French eating and drinking spots are even more family-friendly since the ban on smoking in bars and restaurants, although it is still permitted on outdoor terraces.

Two handy restaurants that serve food all day and into the wee hours are:

Au Pied du Cochon 6 rue Coquillière, 1st arr., M° Les Halles. *01 40 13 77 00*

Le Tambour 41 rue Montmartre, 2nd arr., M° Etienne Marcel, Sentier or Les Halles. *01 42 33 06 90*; ***http://restaurantletambour.com/index.htm***

INSIDER TIP

Always take a portable changing mat and wipes with you to restaurants as very few places in Paris have a baby-changing area.

In the 'Eating Out' sections of the sightseeing chapters in this book, I've tried to cover as wide a range of eating options as possible. Virtually every restaurant offers set menus *(menu)* for lunch and dinner, which are a lot more budget-friendly than ordering *à la carte.* I've based the **price categories** on the price of an average meal for one adult, without drinks:

Expensive: More than 60€

Moderate: 30–60€

Inexpensive: Less than 30€

Getting Children Interested in Paris

Bonjour France! (Rebecca Welby, Beautiful Books) offers games, maps, puzzles, and activities for 7–12 year olds, who can register their scores on the Young Travellers' Club website (***www.youngtravellersclub.co.uk***). If your children are learning French at school, ***www.1001contes.com*** is a fabulous French website with original fairy-stories they can listen to online and download for a small fee. Most of the well-loved Madeline books by Ludwig Bemelmans, about the escapades of a French schoolgirl, are set in Paris and the **Madeline Says Merci: The Always Be Polite Book** (republished in 2006) is a good way of getting youngsters aged 4 to10 interested in France and French ways, and learning some essential French phrases. Albert Lamorisse's **The Red Balloon** and Kay Thompson's **Eloise in Paris** are great for children under eight.

Astérix, the cunning little Gaul, and his lumbering side-kick Obélix are good comic-book companions, the books are available in English as well as French. Most bookshops also have long shelves packed with other graphic books (*bandes dessinnées)* for all ages (some of them perhaps a little *too* graphic for younger readers).

Disneyland rarely needs an introduction to children, but if they've not seen **Ratatouille**, set in Paris, the DVD is a must.

Older children and early teens may enjoy Maurice Leblanc's sagas on **Arsène Lupin**, the notorious gentleman thief (translated into English). Older teens may appreciate selected **Stories** by the master of short stories, Guy de Maupassant, Ernest Hemingway's **A Moveable Feast** (recollections of Paris during the 1920s), Victor Hugo's **Les Misérables,** a classic tale of social oppression and human courage set in the era of Napoleon I, Mark Twain's **Innocents Abroad**, and **The Autobiography of Alice B. Toklas**, by Gertrude Stein, which is her account of 30 years in Paris. For a more contemporary read try **Me Talk Pretty One Day** by David Sedaris, an entertaining summing-up of French culture as seen by an American tourist. Or check out Steven Clarke's **A Year in the Merde** (and sequels), a funny account about cultural differences between the Anglo-Saxons and the Gauls.

Lastly, *The Da Vinci Code* offers a (schlocky) chance to read about places you'll be visiting.

And if it's food you think will get them excited, ***www.edible-paris.com*** is run by Rosa Jackson, who offers families a tailor-made, gastronomy-themed day out visiting key shops and markets in Paris. Themes include chocolate, bread, pastry, cheese – anything edible.

FAST FACTS: PARIS

Area codes See 'Telephone', p. 46.

Baby equipment Most hotels, B&Bs, and apartments can provide cots, either free or for a charge (around 15€ on average), and some offer other equipment such as bottle warmers and changing mats. Some places do not provide linen for their cots because of allergy risks. For equipment rental, see p. 20.

Supermarkets, especially larger ones such as Monoprix, are good for baby equipment from nappies and jarred food to baths and creams. Paris also has two baby and toddler-specific supermarkets called Bébé 9 at 4 rue Saint Ferdinand, 17th arr., M° Ternes. ☎ *01 45 74 48 41* (open Tues–Sat 10am–7pm) and 54 avenue Jean Jaurès, 19th arr., M° Jaurès or Laumière. ☎ *01 42 38 95 44*; ***www.bebe9.com***.

Babysitters Most expensive and some mid-range hotels offer babysitting services, usually subcontracted to local agencies and requiring at least 24 hours' notice. You usually pay the sitter directly and rates average 8–13€ per hour. One good agency is **Baby Sitting Services** (1 place Paul Verlaine, 92100 Boulogne Billancourt, ☎ *01 46 21 33 16*; ***www.babysittingservices.com***). Specify when calling that you need a sitter who speaks English.

Banks are normally open 9.30am–5.30pm Monday–Saturday. Most have 24-hour **ATMs** (p. 19).

Public **museums** close on Monday or Tuesday and on some public holidays, but most tourist sights open on public holidays and always during school holidays.

Some shops and restaurants close for two weeks during August (the first two weeks) and sometimes between Christmas and New Year.

Breastfeeding Breastfeeding in public is much less common in France than in the UK, and you may get stared at, especially if you're feeding an older infant. You can brazen it out, since breastfeeding is your right, or you may prefer to find a secluded spot.

Business hours In Paris shops generally open at 9 or 10am (7 or 8am for bakeries) and close at 7 or 8pm. Some still take a two-hour lunch break from 12.30 to 2.30pm. Some Monoprix **supermarkets** stay open all day till 9 or 10pm, and a few boutiques in the Marais, Bercy Village and on the Champs-Elysées open on Sunday. In most districts, *epiceries arabes* (corner shops) sell basics and stay open after hours.

Climate See 'When to Go', p. 19.

Currency See 'Money', p. 18.

Doctors Some hotels have an expensive private doctor on call, and most accommodation providers will be happy to help you contact a doctor in a minor emergency. See p. 26.

Electricity Electricity runs on 220-volt, 50-cycle AC and is adequate for UK appliances, but you will need an adapter (easily available from French supermarkets) to use the two-pin sockets. Most hotels will be able to lend you an adapter.

Embassies & Consulates
British Embassy 35 rue du Faubourg St-Honoré, 8th arr., ☎ *01 44 51 31 00*, ***www.britishembassy.gov.uk***; US Embassy, 2 avenue Gabriel, 8th arr., ☎ *01 43 12 22 22*, ***http://france.usembassy.gov***; Canadian Embassy, 35 avenue Montaigne, 8th arr., ☎ *01 44 43 29 00*, ***www.international.gc.ca/canada-europa/france/***.

Emergencies Hotel staff are trained to deal with emergencies so call the front desk before you do anything else. Otherwise, for an ambulance ☎ *15*, for police ☎ *17*, and for the fire service ☎ *18*. You will be expected to pay for ambulance service and claim reimbursement from your insurer, so adequate travel insurance is essential.

Hospitals Note that hospitals are sometimes signposted *Hôtel de Dieu* rather than *Hôpital* or *Centre Hospitalier*. See p. 26.

Internet access See p. 29.

Legal aid Contact your embassy, consulate, or insurance company.

Lost property Go to the nearest police station. For lost passports, contact your embassy or consulate (see above). For lost credit cards, see p. 45. If you think your car may have been towed away for being illegally parked, ask at the local police station.

Paris's general **Lost Property Bureau** (Service des Objets Trouvés de la Préfecture de Police) is at 36 rue des Morillons, 15th arr., M° Convention. If you have lost something with your name on it, you can call ☎ *08 21 00 25 25* to see if anyone has handed it in.

Mail Post offices are generally open Mon–Fri 8am–7pm and Sat 8am–noon. One post office, La Poste du Louvre (52 rue du Louvre, 1st arr., M° Louvre Rivoli) is open 24/7. Postcards or letters to the UK weighing less than 20g cost 0.55€ and take one to five days. Stamps are sold at tobacconists (*tabacs*) as well as post offices.

Money & Credit Cards See also 'Money', p. 18. For lost/stolen cards, call the relevant company immediately – for Amex call ☎ *01 47 77 72 00*, for Visa ☎ *08 92 70 57 05*, for Diners ☎ *08 10 31 41 59*, and for Mastercard ☎ *01 45 67 84 84*. In emergencies, you can have money wired to you online, by phone, or from an agent's office through Western Union (☎ *0800 833833*; ***www.westernunion.com***).

Newspapers & Magazines British newspapers (often available on the day of publication) are sold at many newsagents and news-stands in Paris. They are also available in WH Smith (248 rue de Rivoli, 1st arr., M° Concorde – also see p. 65) and Brentanos (37 avenue de l'Opéra, 2nd arr., M° Opéra or RER Auber). Also look out for **Pariscope** and **Officiel du Spectacle**, two cheap magazines that list current exhibitions, concerts, and plays as well as café-théâtres and circuses.

Pharmacies Pharmacies are signposted by a prominent green cross; staff can provide **first aid** in minor emergencies and dispense a range of remedies including homeopathic, and some antibiotics that would require a doctor's prescription in the UK. Rotas of pharmacies operating outside normal hours (9am–8pm Mon–Sat) are posted in every pharmacist's window, and some are open 24 hours a day (see p. 26).

Police In emergencies ☎ *17*. For thefts, file a report at the nearest police station to receive a claim number for insurance.

Post Offices See 'Mail', above.

Public holidays See p. 21.

Safety See also p. 25. The same commonsense tips apply as would at home: don't leave money or valuables where they can be seen (theft from cars is very common) and be wary of pickpockets and bag snatchers; do not walk alone at night in unlit public spaces.

Taxes Value added tax (TVA) of 19.6% is included in the price of most goods and hotel and restaurant services.

Taxis There are taxi ranks at all airports, in the centre of Paris, and at main railway stations and bus terminals. Taxis can also be flagged down on the street, or called from the reception desk of hotels, restaurants, and bars. Check that your taxi has a meter and that it is switched on, and ask the driver for an estimated fare before setting out. Also see p. 31 and p. 37.

Telephone All phone numbers are 10 digits, including a two-digit **area code** (01 for Paris) that you must dial even when calling from within the area. Numbers starting with 06 are mobile numbers and will cost more to call. 0800 and 0805 prefixed numbers are toll-free within France. Other numbers with a 08 prefix have differing rates.

To call a French number from abroad (or when using a British mobile phone in France), drop the initial 0 of the area code after dialling the international code (00 33 from the UK). To call the UK from France, dial 00 44 then the British number minus the initial 0. International mobile phone charges can be high, as can those from hotel phones. To save money, buy a phonecard (*télécarte)* from a post office, tobacconist, or newsagent and use public phone boxes. *Télécartes* start at 7.40€ for 50 units. Phone boxes with a blue bell sign can take incoming calls.

Time Zone France is one hour ahead of UK time and six hours ahead of New York.

Tipping *Service compris* means a service charge has been added to your bill. However, an extra tip (10%) may be added if you wish.

Toilets & Baby changing Public toilets can be found in most larger towns in railway stations and bus terminals, but can be less than pristine. Bars, cafés, and large supermarkets and department stores are a better bet. Few places except large family-oriented tourist attractions, such as theme parks, aquariums, museums, and airports, have baby-changing facilities, so be armed with a portable folding mat.

Water French tap water is safe to drink. Many restaurants automatically serve you a carafe of chilled tap water (*eau de robinet*), though most waiters will enthusiastically try to persuade you to buy expensive *eau minerale* (bottled mineral water), either *sans gaz* (still), *gazeuse* (sparkling) or *pétillante* (mildly fizzy).

Weather See 'When to Go.'

3 From the Louvre to the Champs-Elysées

LOUVRE TO CHAMPS-ELYSEES

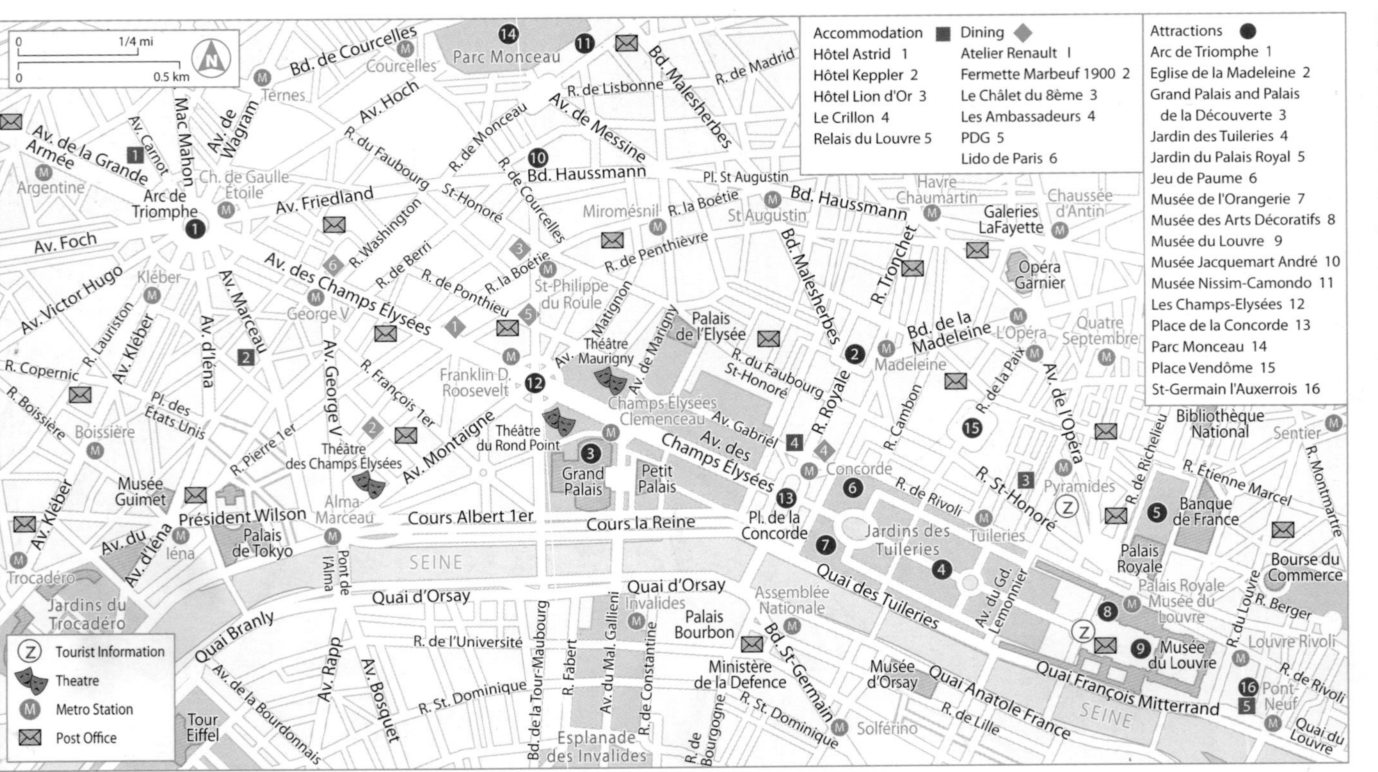

Lined with Haussmann-style fronted buildings are the hidden parks, narrow streets, and old palaces that make historic Paris – the Paris of the Louvre palace and the Champs-Elysées, once the Sun King's private gardens. Today it's an area of contrasts; elegant squares and arcades turn into wide, traffic-filled boulevards; vast teeming crossroads merge into peaceful parks and gardens; prominent museums give way to smaller, converted townhouses. And then there's the symmetry: climb to the top of the Arc de Triomphe and you'll be struck by the way the Louvre, the Champs-Elysées, and the Arch of La Défense sit perfectly in line. It all embodies the best and the worst of Paris – a place where café terraces look out onto traffic; where designer shops and luxury hotels create an exclusive, snobby atmosphere; where museums are so popular you have to queue for hours. But this is also one of the city's most spectacular areas, where architecture and urban planning never fail to impress, and children's imaginations are fired by some of the world's most famous cultural attractions.

ORIENTATION

The Musée du Louvre, Tuileries gardens, Madeleine church, and Avenue des Champs-Elysées are so huge they've all given their names to entire neighbourhoods which fall into two large arrondissements (1st and 8th) sprawling from the centre westwards. Most attractions can be reached by Métro line 1, which cuts right through central Paris from the Château de Vincennes (east) to La Défense (west) and links the Louvre to the Champs-Elysées. With children you can Métro-hop when your feet get tired, or follow it in a straight line on foot, station by station, without getting lost (approx. five-minute walk between Métro stations, 10 minutes with small children).

GETTING AROUND

The main bus routes are line **72,** which parallels Métro line 1 along Rue de Rivoli, the quayside, past the Louvre up the Champs-Elysées; and line **24**, which links Gare St-Lazare to the Madeleine, Concorde and then the Left Bank. Useful **Batobus** riverbus stops are **Louvre**, **Champs-Elysées**, and **Musée d'Orsay**.

VISITOR INFORMATION

The closest Office de Tourisme is at 25 rue des Pyramides (1st arr., 10am–7pm Mon–Sat, 11am–7pm Sun and public holidays) towards the Opéra district. A smaller office is also open daily (10am–6pm) in the Carrousel du Louvre underneath the inverted pyramid (*08 92 68 30 00*; ***www.parisinfo.com***).

WHAT TO SEE & DO

Children's Top 5 Attractions

❶ **Marvelling** at real-life mummies in the Louvre (see below).

❷ **Learning** to cook like a professional chef at L'Ecole Lenôtre (see p. 61).

❸ **Experiencing** lightning striking overhead at the Palais de la Découverte (see p. 57).

❹ **Testing** the toys and gadgets in Nature et Découvertes (see p. 66).

❺ **Watching** the world go by from the top of the Arc de Triomphe (see p. 60).

Culture & Museums

Musée du Louvre ★★ ALL AGES

*Pyramide du Louvre, 1st arr. and Carrousel du Louvre, 99 rue de Rivoli, 1st arr., ☎ 01 40 20 50 50; **www.louvre.fr**. M° Louvre Rivoli and Palais Royal Musée du Louvre.*

Whatever your children's ages, the biggest museum in the world is as beautiful as it is intriguing. The bad news is that it's so humungous you could spend a day in each wing and still not see everything. Families, especially those with youngsters, should avoid overdosing by deciding what you want to see in advance. If you can't squeeze it all in, you can always come back another day (the Paris Museum Pass allows unlimited access to the Louvre and around 70 other museums see p. 39).

Four floors and three wings (Sully, Denon, and Richelieu) house the Oriental, Egyptian, Greek, Etruscan, and Roman antiquities, European Paintings and Sculptures, the Decorative and Graphic Arts, and Islamic arts departments.

Four sections that will appeal particularly to young eyes are:

Département des Antiquités Egyptiennes ★ In the Sully and Denon wings, I went along with a mummy-obsessed eight-year-old studying ancient Egypt. Once we had inspected the human mummy, contemplated how cats, fish, and crocodiles became animal mummies (**room 19**), and whether her cocker spaniel could be mummified when he dies, we back-tracked to the beginning and the spectacular **crypte du sphinx**, reigned over by a 5m-long granite sphinx. **Room 3**, dedicated to the **River Nile**, is a favourite for children

Egyptian display at the Louvre

who learn how boats were buried in the pharaohs' tombs. **Room 6,** devoted to **Egyptian writing**, intrigues with hieroglyphics, on papyrus, decoded by Egyptologist Jean-François Champollion in 1824. With pen and paper, smaller children can have a go at writing them themselves. **Room 8** shows a typical Egyptian household; **Room 12** has the reconstruction of a temple, watched over by the goddess Sekhmet, whose lion's head is a sign of her destructive power; and in **Room 25** are statues of two ancient superstars, pharaoh Akhenaton and his queen Nefertiti.

Antiquités Grécques & Romaines Edited highlights here in the Denon wing are the **Venus de Milo** in **Room 7,** *Winged Victory* at the top of the stairs (off **Room 4**), and fragments of a Tunisian mosaic in **Room 30** that shows what Romans ate at banquets – lots of bread, wine, fruits, and roasted meat. A wall mural from Pompeii also shows how Romans dressed, with long tunics, cloaks, and sandals. Battle-loving little boys will appreciate **Room 22** with Domitius Ahenobarbus's marble altar (200 B.C.), depicting

Venus de Milo

Roman military costume and the altars used by soldiers for sacrificing bulls, rams, and pigs in a bid to secure a victory. On one 3rd-century sarcophagus you can see an episode of the War of Troy – Achilles giving Hector's body back to his father Priam.

Medieval Louvre ★ Originally situated outside the city boundaries, the Louvre once upon a time had 10 towers, two main entrances, a dungeon, and a moat. The base of the twin

FUN FACT

Flatulent Spook

A mysterious spirit named Belphégor is said to haunt the Egyptology departments. Although a fictional character brought to life by the author Arthur Bernède in 1927, Bernède didn't invent the ghost. According to Christian demonologists, he is a demon who seduces his victims by granting them the genius to create inventions that will make them rich. Even more interesting for children, he can be linked to the little-known Roman god Crepitus – god of farting and obscenity.

HISTORY Give Us a Smile Mona!

François I first acquired Leonardo's **La Giaconda (Mona Lisa)**, the 'smiling one' to hang above his bathtub. It was stolen in 1911 and found in Florence in 1913. At first, both the poet Guillaume Apollinaire and Picasso were suspected, but it was soon discovered in the possession of a former Louvre employee, who had apparently carried it out under his overcoat. Theories about why La Giaconda is smiling range from her being pregnant to the picture being a feminised, self-portrait of Leonardo Da Vinci himself. Get your children to think up their own stories.

round towers of Philippe Auguste's castle and the drawbridge support can still be seen in an excavated area 7m below street level under the Sully wing. Models on the walls are of the original 12th-century fortress and 14th-century modifications. The **Taillerie** tower features heart-shaped engravings – the signature of a stonemason, designed to indicate the work he needed to be paid for. Don't forget to look out for the latrines, which usually amuse.

Leonardo da Vinci in the Denon wing. Even if they've never heard of Leonardo, most children know something about the **Mona Lisa**. Offer them the chance to see her wily smile and use the opportunity to point out some of da Vinci's other masterpieces like **La Belle Ferronnière** (1495–1500) – a lady whose gaze is as haunting as Mona Lisa's; and **La Vierge à l'Enfant avec Sainte Anne** (Mary on her mother's knees, trying to stop Jesus from embracing a lamb – the Passion of Christ), religiously inspired but treated more as a scene of motherly love. If visiting with teens, you could opt for the Da Vinci Code guided tour (book in English on *01 40 20 51 77*), which goes into more detail about Leonardo's paintings (see box above) and reveals the truth behind some elements that inspired Dan Brown.

***Open** Wed–Mon 9am–6pm (until 10pm Wed and Fri). **Admission** 9€ adult, 6€ after 6pm (Wed and Fri). Under-18s free (under-26s free Fri after 6pm).*

INSIDER TIP

Cut the queues and buy an online ticket at ***www.louvre.fr***, or use the automatic ticket machines inside the Carrousel du Louvre (99 rue de Rivoli). In general, queues are shorter there. Tickets also include access to the Musée Eugène Delacroix (see p. 156).

Louvre History Highlights

You can chart Paris's history in the building of the Louvre.

In the 12th century King Philippe Auguste constructed a fortress to protect his city from invaders. It was the centrepiece of a 5km-long defensive wall, still partly visible in the Marais

Tours

The Louvre's website features several downloadable thematic trails for families such as 'Rituals and Symbolism of the meal', as seen in paintings and sculpture from antiquity to the 18th century or 'A canter through the Louvre', which looks at man's relationship with horses in paintings, sculptures, and objects.

today (see p. 133), equipped with a dungeon and treasure room.

In the 1360s Charles V transformed the austere fortress into a residence fit for a king, kitted out with gardens, a zoo, and a tennis court.

The Renaissance king François I tore down the remaining medieval towers and added his own flamboyant Renaissance-style wing.

Henri III and Henri IV In the late 16th and early 17th century both kings Henri added their Grande Galerie (the vast decorative expanse visible today along the south side of the Seine) to Charles IX's Petite Galerie.

The Sun King, Louis XIV, lavished most of his money on Versailles but did complete the Cour Carrée and introduce the name 'Carrousel' to the Louvre after a horse event that took place on today's Place du Carrousel (the roundabout in between the Pyramid and Napoléon's Arc de Triomphe).

Napoléon Bonaparte's memoirs, perhaps typically, claimed the credit for building the Louvre. He did, however, build the wing along Rue de Rivoli, now home to the Musée des Arts Décoratifs (p. 53) and filled it with trophies from his invasions. He also ordered the Arc de Triomphe at the Carrousel to be copied from the Septimus Severus Arch in Rome. The Percier and Fontaine rooms in the Denon wing were where he married Marie-Louise in 1810.

Napoléon III (1852–70) Almost all the Cour Napoléon was built for Napoléon III, under the watchful eye of Baron Haussmann, recognisable by its highly ornate stonework.

François Mitterrand added I M Pei's controversial glass pyramid, today's main entrance, finished in 1989 as part of Mitterrand's 'Grands Travaux' cultural campaign. Like the Eiffel Tower, it was considered so ugly that locals protested. Nowadays, nobody could imagine the Louvre without its light-catching centrepiece.

Musée des Arts Décoratifs ★

AGES 13 AND ABOVE

Palais du Louvre, 107 rue de Rivoli, 1st arr., ☎ *01 44 55 57 50;* ***www.lesartsdecoratifs.fr****. M° Palais-Royal or Tuileries.*

Take a Break

For a quick drink and a snack near the Louvre try the self-service restaurants in the underground Carrousel du Louvre. The Café Marly (93 rue de Rivoli, 1st arr.) under the Louvre's arcades has pleasant views on to the Tuileries gardens and an inside window overlooking the Louvre museum for children to enjoy. Le Fumoir (6 rue Amiral de Coligny, 1st arr.) next to the St-Germain l'Auxerrois church serves delicious snacks and meals in a cosy dining area.

In the northwestern end of the Louvre (Pavillon de Marsan), but separate from the Louvre museum, is one of the world's primary collections of design and decorative art. Set over nine floors, a chronological trail demonstrates how fashion and lifestyle have evolved, featuring medieval liturgical items, Art Nouveau and Art Deco furniture, Gothic panelling and Renaissance porcelain, 1970s psychedelic carpets, chairs by Philippe Starck, and soft furnishings from France's high-speed TGV trains.

For youngsters, star attractions are 10 period rooms ★ showing how the furniture and objects would have looked in a real house. Best are couturier Jeanne Lanvin's early Art Deco purple boudoir and an ostentatious Louis-Philippe bed chamber, both reproduced in the minutest detail.

Between the floors, galleries display miscellaneous collections (glass, wallpaper, chairs, etc.), including an assortment of toys retracing 150 years of play.

Budding fashion designers should combine their visit with the **Musée de la Mode** – a fashion museum open for temporary exhibitions, offering excellent ever-changing retrospectives of the world's biggest designers. Alongside the historical pieces, expect to see sit creations by great 20th-century designers like Christian Dior and Sonia Rykiel.

While the bright posters and funny characters of the exhibits at the **Musée de la Publicité** may capture the attention of youngsters for a while, it's the older ones who will get the most out of the collections (open for temporary exhibitions only) and the way the museum explores the historical, creative, and socio-cultural dimensions of advertising.

There are posters from the 17th century, and film, TV, and radio commercials from the 1930s onwards – all set in architect Jean Nouvel's (famous for the Musée du Quai Branly) cutting-edge interior.

Open *11am–6pm Tues–Fri (until 9pm Thurs); 10am–6pm Sat–Sun.* ***Admission*** *8€ adults, 6.50€ 19–25s, free under-18s, temporary exhibitions extra.*

Musée des Arts Décoratifs

INSIDER TIP

The Musée des Arts Décoratifs is linked to the Musée Nissim de Camondo (p. 58) so grab joint tickets and do both.

Musée de l'Orangerie ★
AGES 8 AND ABOVE

Jardin de Tuileries, 1st arr., ☎ 01 44 77 80 07; ***www.musee-orangerie.fr****. M° Tuileries or Concorde.*

The freshly renovated Orangerie (a winter garden during the Second Empire) is where Monet created his eight gigantic Water Lilies. It's frequently overlooked in favour of bigger, more famous Monet-related museums (Musée d'Orsay p. 154, and the Musée Marmottan p. 84) but here you won't be fighting to see the paintings, and because it's small it suits children better.

The French government lent the Orangerie to Monet after the First World War in exchange for his works. Monet wanted his *Nymphéas* (Water Lilies) to hang as low as possible to recreate the effect of seeing them from above the water. The new layout respects his wishes and the oval rooms make you feel enveloped in colour. You can also introduce your family to other great Impressionists like Renoir (including his self-portrait as a clown), Cézanne, Utrillo, and Picasso. Audio-guides are available in English (5€).

Game Plan: If your children are keen on art, add some spice by asking them to note down what they notice about Monet and Renoir's paintings. Then combine your visit with the Musée d'Orsay (p. 154) and see if they can pick out paintings by the same artists (without reading the labels).

Open *12.30pm–7pm Wed–Mon (until 9pm Fri) Closed some public holidays.* ***Admission*** *6.50€ adult, 4.50€ 19–25s, free under-18s.*

Comédie Française

Five minutes from Place de la Concorde and opposite the Louvre, the Comédie Française is the home of Molière – France's Shakespeare. Children studying GCSE or A-level French can take in the sparkling productions at this national theatre established by the Sun King in the 17th century to keep the dramatic arts alive. The company has been in the present building since 1799. The main box office is open daily 11am–6pm, ☎ 08 25 10 16 80. Prices 11–45€. Closed mid-July to early Sept.

Jeu de Paume ★

AGES 8 AND ABOVE

1 place de la Concorde, 8th arr., ☎ 01 47 03 12 50; ***www.jeudepaume.org****. M° Concorde*

Set in Napoléon III's personal tennis courts, this photography and image museum is a must for families whose adolescents are into photography, film, and anything avant-garde. It explores the world of images, their uses and the issues they have raised from the 19th century to the present. Most exhibits will be lost on under-eights, but if you're coming with children of mixed ages, opt for a 'Family Tour' (call in advance to request English) on Wednesdays at 3pm and Sundays at 4.30pm, aimed at 8–12-year-olds and their parents.

The sister Hôtel de Sully (Place des Vosges or 62 rue St Antoine, 4th arr., ☎ *01 42 74 47 75*, M° Bastille or St-Paul) is a breathtaking Renaissance mansion (1651) and garden, with an ever-changing parade of temporary photo exhibitions.

Open *12pm–7pm Tues–Fri (until 9pm Tues), 10am–7pm Sat–Sun.* ***Admission*** *6€ adults, 3€ under-25s and families with three or more children, free under-10s.*

Grand Palais **AGES 8 AND ABOVE**

3 avenue du Général Eisenhower, 8th arr., ☎ 01 44 13 17 17; ***www.rmn.fr****. M° Champs-Elysées Clémenceau or Franklin Roosevelt. RER C Invalides*

Halfway up the Champs-Elysées, the Grand Palais is a masterpiece of Belle Époque architecture, initially built in 1900 for the World Fair. It has an imposing classical stone façade with a festival of Art Nouveau ironwork, and a huge glass roof (wonderful at night when the light shines through) adorned with bronze flying horses and chariots.

A national art exhibition centre, **Les Galeries Nationales du Grand Palais** is one of France's most important exhibition centres, showing famous and rare art by historically important artists, resulting in queues of up to two hours. You could cheat the system by taking it in turns to have a coffee in the palace's trendy new café, **Minipalais** (they also serve meals and snacks including a children's menu at 15€. ☎ *01 42 56 42 42*, open Mon–Fri 8.30am–1am, Sat–Sun 10.30am–1am).

Open *for exhibitions 10am–8pm Wed–Mon (to 10pm Wed).* ***Admission*** *10€ adult, 8€ 13–25s, free under 13s (with ID).*

Palais de la Découverte ★★
ALL AGES

Avenue Franklin Roosevelt, 8th arr., ☎ 01 56 43 20 20/21 ***www.palais-decouverte.fr****. M° Champs-Elysées Clémenceau or Franklin Roosevelt; RER C Invalides*

Why not take the young ones round the back of the Grand Palais to the **Palais de la Découverte**. It's no match for the massive Cité des Sciences (p. 247) and some parts look outdated, but it covers all the basics of chemistry, physics, maths, biology, earth sciences, and astronomy in a fun and informative manner including interactive demos by presenters often dressed as mad scientists.

One of the best sections for non-French-speakers covers electricity. Your children can watch in wonder as a metal disk hovers as if by magic (thanks to alternative currents), tremble with excitement as real fork lightning strikes just above their heads ★, and watch mum or dad showing how difficult it is to hold a steel bar vertical when standing between the bobbins of a two-tonne electromagnet (one of the biggest in the world).

Star-gazing youngsters should visit the planetarium, which, although in French, is visually stimulating and atmospheric, recreating the night skies as seen through the ages and predicting the next total eclipse of the sun.

Open *9.30am–6pm Tues–Sat, 10am–7pm Sun (and some public holidays).* ***Admission*** *7€ adult, 4.50€ under-18s, free under-5s. Planetarium* ***Open*** *11am, 2pm, 3.15pm, and 4.30pm Tues–Sun (weekends 5.45pm).* ***Admission*** *3.50€ adult and children.*

Musée Jacquemart-André
★★ **AGES 7 AND ABOVE**

158 boulevard Haussmann, 8th arr., ☎ 01 45 62 11 59; ***www.musee-jacquemart-andre.com****. M° Miromesnil or St-Philippe-du-Roule.*

This is the finest museum of its type in Paris, and one of the most family-friendly places around. More a stately home than a museum, it was created

The Grand Palais

by Edouard André, the last of a family that made a fortune in banking and industry in the 19th century. He spent most of his life as an army officer stationed abroad but eventually returned to marry a well-known portraitist, Nélie Jacquemart, and together they gathered a collection fit for a king.

The salons drip with gilt and *fin-de-siècle* style. Works by Bellini, Carpaccio, Uccello, Van Dyck, Rembrandt, Tiepolo, Rubens, Watteau, Boucher, Fragonard, and Mantegna are complemented by Houdon busts, Gobelin tapestries, della Robbia terracottas, and an awesome collection of antiques. This may all sound heavy for the children, but there are audio-guides in English and a museum-themed activity book, packed with puzzles and titbits on the exhibits for 7- to 12-year-olds.

At the end, treat the family to tea and cakes in Madame Jacquemart's high-ceilinged dining room, adorned with 18th-century tapestries. Salads, tarts, *tourtes* (pastries filled with meat or fruit), and Viennese pastries are all delicious and served from 11.45am to 5.30pm.

***Open** daily 10am–6pm. **Admission** 9.50€ adults, 7€ 7–17s, free under-7s.*

Musée Nissim de Camondo ★

AGES 7 AND ABOVE

63 rue de Monceau, 8th arr., ☎ 01 53 89 06 40. M° Villiers.

This pre-World War I townhouse is rich with needlepoint chairs, tapestries (many from Beauvais or Aubusson), antiques, paintings, bas-reliefs, silver, Chinese vases, crystal chandeliers, Sèvres porcelain, Savonnerie carpets, and even an Houdon bust. But most impressive for the children are the downstairs kitchens. Capable of serving hundreds of dinner guests at once, they were insulated with concrete to ensure the cooking smells didn't disturb the visitors. All dishes were washed in the *laverie* (wash-room) inside big, copper plunging pots and there's a *monte-plat*, the contraption used for sending the dishes up to the master's dining-room.

***Open** 10am–5.30pm Wed–Sun. Closed 1 Jan, 1 May, Bastille Day (14 July) and 25 Dec. **Admission** 6€ adults, 4.50€ 18–25s, free under-17s.*

Free Museum – Le Petit Palais

*Avenue Winston Churchill, 8th arr., ☎ 01 53 43 40 00 **www.petitpalais.paris.fr**. M° Champs-Elysées Clémenceau*

If you're counting the pennies, take your family to the Grand Palais' little sister over the road. Also built in 1900 for the World Fair, and lit entirely by natural light, the Petit Palais houses a free fine arts museum with collections by artists such as Ingrès, Delacroix, Courbet and the Impressionists, as well as other paintings and sculptures from the Renaissance to 1900.

***Open** 10am–6pm Tue–Sun. **Admission** free.*

Pause Pipi in Cool Loos

On the right side of the Madeleine you'll find Paris's oldest public loos – a testimony to the good taste French people had during the Belle Époque. Everything looks as it did in the 19th century (white tiles, wooden panelling) – even Madame Pipi (slang for toilet attendant) looks like she's been there for years. The smiley lady seems to have made herself quite at home, with postcards pinned to the walls and family photos.

INSIDER TIP

Joint tickets can be purchased for the Musée des Arts Décoratifs (p. 53).

Places of Worship

Eglise de la Madeleine ★

ALL AGES

Place de la Madeleine, 8th arr., ☎ 01 44 51 69 00 ***www.eglise-lamadeleine.com****. M° Madeleine.*

A colonnade of 20m-high Corinthian columns encircles the Madeleine church – a huge building that gives its name to the surrounding Place de la Madeleine, famous for its gourmet food shops (see shopping p. 64). Your children can make out the church from Place de la Concorde as, thanks to its columns, it's a mirror image of the Palais de Bourbon or *Assemblée National* (home of the French parliament) on the opposite side of the Seine. Though construction began in 1764, it wasn't consecrated until 1845, and almost didn't become a church at all, with alternative uses put forward, ranging from a

Eglise de la Madeleine

government building to a stock exchange and public library. Two famous parts to point out to the children are Rude's **Le Baptême du Christ,** to the left as you enter and the *bas-reliefs* of the **Ten Commandments** on the bronze doors. If your children enjoy classical music, there are free Sunday afternoon concerts (4pm two Sundays a month).

***Open** daily 9am–7pm. **Admission** free.*

St-Germain l'Auxerrois ★★

ALL AGES

2 place du Louvre, 1st arr., 01 42 60 13 96. M° Louvre-Rivoli.

This church, one of the prettiest in Paris, is a jewel of gothic architecture and deserves a visit for its 78m of stained glass, including rose windows, intricately carved church-wardens' pews, based on 17th-century designs by Le Brun, and an austere 15th-century triptych.

***Open** daily 8am–7pm. **Admission** free.*

Streets & Monuments

Arc de Triomphe ★★ ALL AGES

*Place Charles-de-Gaulle-Etoile, 8th arr., 01 55 37 73 77; **www.monuments-nationaux.fr**. M° Charles-de-Gaulle–Etoile.*

At the western end of the Champs-Elysées, the Arc de Triomphe is the starting point of many national festivals, including Bastille Day on 14th July. It's like an ancient Roman arch, only larger. In fact it's the biggest triumphal arch in the world, about 49m high and 44m wide. To reach it, *don't* try to cross the island: with a dozen streets radiating from the 'Star,' the roundabout has been called a 'vehicular roulette'. Take the underground passage, and live to see your family grow up.

Although commissioned by Napoléon in 1806 to commemorate the victories of his Grande Armée, it wasn't completed until 1836, under the reign of Louis-Philippe. Four years later, Napoléon's remains, brought from St. Helena, passed under the arch on their journey to his tomb at the Hôtel des Invalides. Since that time it has become the focal point for state funerals. It's also the site of the Tomb of the Unknown Soldier, in whose honour an eternal flame burns.

If you have a buggy, or children too young to climb the stairs, you can take a lift to the top where there's an exhibition hall with lithographs and photos depicting the arch throughout its history, as well as an observation deck with one of the best views of the city ★.

Guided tours in English can be arranged by calling *01 44 54 19 30*.

***Open** daily 10am–11pm Apr–Sept, daily 10am–10.30pm Oct–Mar. **Admission** 8€ adults, 5€ 18–25s, free under-18s.*

Les Champs-Elysées ★★

ALL AGES

Called 'the highway of French grandeur,' this boulevard, ordered by Louis XIV in 1667, was designed for promenading. It's witnessed some of the greatest moments in French history – and

Cooking for the Children ★★

Want France's culinary *je ne sais quoi* to rub off on your youngsters? Leave them in the famous Lenôtre cooking school on the Champs-Elysées and they'll be proper little chefs in no time. Most Wednesdays (Sept–Jun), children's cooking classes for 8 to 11s and 12 to 17s teach whippersnappers how to cook scrumptious dishes such as salmon guacamole, pear and raisin crumble, and chocolate brownies. Older children can also try their hand at more challenging options like sea bass in a herb crust with vegetable confit, and tiramisu. Prices begin at 40€ – nothing compared to the priceless meals they'll be preparing for you when you get home. *To reserve call* 📞 *01 42 65 97 60 or E:* ***lepavillonelysee-ecole@lenotre.fr****. Pavillon Elysée, 10 avenue des Champs-Elysées, 8th arr. M° Champs-Elysées Clémenceau. Duration 2–3½ hours.*

some of the worst. Bismarck was so impressed with it when he invaded with his victorious Prussian army in 1871, that he had a replica, the Ku'damm, built in Berlin. If you've never seen it before, the 'prettiest avenue in the world' can be a let-down, having swapped much of its late 19th-century elegance for chain stores and expensive street-side cafés. But aesthetics aside, you and your children won't get bored. You'll stroll past gardens, theatres, puppet shows, flashy car showrooms, cinemas, designer and high street clothes shops, and fast-food joints. But make sure you get to the end and climb to the top of the Arc de Triomphe (p. 60) – a truly memorable experience for the whole family once you get your breath back.

Place de la Concorde ★

ALL AGES

Built in 1757 and dominated by two fountains and eight statues representing French cities, this octagonal traffic hub also features an Egyptian obelisk from Luxor, the oldest man made object in Paris, dating to circa 1200 B.C. In the Reign of Terror at the time of the French Revolution, the dreaded guillotine was erected on this spot. For a spectacular view, look down the Champs-Elysées.

The grandest walk in Paris begins here, leading all the way to the Arc de Triomphe (see below). It's a distance of 3.2km and is the most popular walk for visiting families.

In winter (end Oct–Jan) a huge Ferris wheel, **La Grande Roue de Paris** ★★, sits just outside the Concorde entrance to the Tuileries gardens, offering fabulous panoramas all the way up the Champs-Elysées and on to the futuristic business district of La Défense (the high rises beyond the Arc de Triomphe). On the wheel, looking northwards, you can draw your children's attention

FUN FACT Champselyséesaurus

When dinosaurs ruled the earth, the Champs-Elysées lay below sea level. Fossils of prehistoric marine creatures and plants have been found underground.

to Montmartre's **Sacré Coeur** church that sits proudly on the Butte de Montmartre like a giant wedding cake; and southwards, the gold dome of **Les Invalides** and Paris's only inner-city skyscraper, the **Tour Montparnasse** (p. 159). The best time to ride is at night when all the monuments are lit up.

Place Vendôme ALL AGES

In between the Louvre and the Opéra, bring your children to see Paris's gleaming treasure, **Place Vendôme** – the most exclusive and expensive square in the world and home to numerous jewellers including Chopard, Dior, and Bulgari. Designed by the architect Jules Hardouin-Mansart, the Duc de Vendôme gave his name to the 18th-century square by buying a private mansion, Chopin died at no. 12 in 1848, Princess Diana spent her last few hours at the Ritz in 1997, and Napoléon erected a colossal column to his glory, modelled on Trajan's column in Rome and decorated with a spiral comic strip showing off his victories.

Parks & the Outdoors

Jardin des Tuileries ★★ ALL AGES

Jardin des Tuileries, 1st arr. M° Tuileries or Concorde

Children of all ages love the spectacular statue-studded **Jardin des Tuileries** where 18 enormous bronzes by Maillol are installed in the formal Jardin that Le Nôtre, Louis XIV's gardener and planner of the Versailles grounds, designed in the 17th century.

Ferris Wheel in Place de la Concorde

Arc de Triomphe

It's especially popular in summer when toy boats float on the fountains, donkeys and ponies take children up and down the shaded alleys, and a funfair, equipped with a giant Ferris wheel just like the one on Place de la Concorde in winter, offers games and panoramas over the city.

Its central location makes it a draw for both Parisian families and tourists – even if it is forbidden to walk on the grass. Two cafés provide refreshments in a laid-back environment, with shaded terraces – a godsend on a sunny day.

Open *7.30am–7pm daily.*

Parc Monceau ★★ **ALL AGES**

Access via Boulevard de Courcelles, Avenue Vélasquez, ave Van Dyck, Avenue Ruysdael. M° Monceau or Courcelles.

Ringed with 18th- and 19th-century mansions, the Parc Monceau is a favourite with well-dressed Parisian children, their nannies, and mothers with prams. The park was designed in 1778 as a private hideaway for the Duke of Orléans, a man noted for his debauchery and pursuit of pleasure. It was laid out with an Egyptian-style obelisk, a medieval dungeon, a thatched farmhouse, a Chinese pagoda, a Roman temple, an enchanted

Off with their Heads!

The horrible head-chopping guillotine – perfected by Dr Joseph-Ignace Guillotin as a 'more humane execution method' (the first victim was reportedly a sheep) – claimed the lives of almost 1200 people at Place de la Concorde in just two and a half years. Among the victims were Queen Marie-Antoinette, who died in view of her secret apartment at 2 rue Royale, and the revolutionary leaders Robespierre and Danton.

Style

Smack-bang in the middle of the Champs-Elysées gardens, the Théâtre des Guignols (Punch and Judy puppet show) has been entertaining little ones since 1818. Watch the master (Jodé-Luis Gonzalez) at work on Wednesdays, Saturdays, Sundays, and school and public holidays at 3, 4, and 5pm. 3€ per child. The theatre is at the Rond-Point des Champs-Elysées on the corner of Avenues Matignon and Gabriel. 8th arr. M° Champs-Elysées Clémenceau. ***www.theatreguignol.fr***.

grotto, various chinoiseries, and a waterfall. These fairytale touches have largely disappeared, but when picnicking in spring with family friends and their children, we found the park, although small, had something for everyone, with its play area, mini skate park, statuary, and flowers.

Open *daily 7am–8pm winter, 7am–10pm summer.*

Shopping

The area around the Champs-Elysées isn't known as the Golden Triangle (*Triangle d'Or*) for nothing. Dripping in wealth, it's home to top-end jewellers and designer clothes shops as well as gourmet food stores and luxury car showrooms. For a special treat or to initiate your family in the art of window shopping, stroll past the designer offerings along **Place Vendôme**, **Rue de la Paix**, **Rue Faubourg St Honoré**, **Rue St Honoré**, and **Avenue Montaigne** where big names (Hermès, Chanel, Dior etc.) are a shopaholic's A-list.

If you're looking for reasonable prices, the **Champs-Elysées** (see shops box p. 67), the **Carrousel du Louvre** underground shopping centre (see below), and **Place de la Madeleine** have plenty of well-priced boutiques for the family to spend their hard-earned cash and pocket money in. For more choice, however, see the shopping sections of Chapters 5 and 6 (p. 114 and p. 141).

Carrousel du Louvre ★

Underneath the Louvre Museum, the Carrousel du Louvre is a shopping mall with high-street brands, independent boutiques, and a food court. The shop at the top of every child's list is **Nature et Découvertes** (shop no. 1, see box p. 66), but you could check out the crystal jewellery in **Swarovski** (no. 3), familiarise your youngsters with French music at the **Virgin Megastore** (no. 9), look at the fossils and minerals in **Les Minéraux** (no. 23), go bag-hunting in **Le Tanneur**, compare the chocolates in **La Maison du Chocolat** with those in **Trésors du Palais**, and find some unusual foodstuffs and presents to take home at **Résonance** (no. 33). Most shops are open 10am–8pm daily.

Jardin du Palais Royal

The Palais Royal, once the home of Cardinal Richelieu, is now government offices and the shaded, sandy alleys of the palace gardens feel like one of Paris's hidden treasures. It's a fabulous enclosure, bordered by trees, the palace's arcades, shops, cafés, and with a surprising courtyard covered in oddly striped columns by the sculptor Buren (1986). Youngsters love to climb on them and older children appreciate their surreal look. It's a great place to enjoy a lunchtime picnic and watch a game of *boules* (bowls, otherwise known as *pétanque*). Treat the children to some sticky French pastries while you sip the traditional drink of all boules players, pastis.

2 place Colette, 1st arr. M° Palais Royal. ***Open*** *daily 7.30am–8pm.*

Books

If your children want something to read or you're hankering after an English newspaper, **WH Smith** ★ (248 rue de Rivoli, 1st arr. M° Concorde) is a carbon copy of its UK stores. Just further down the road, **Galignani** (224 rue de Rivoli, 1st arr., M° Tuileries) is Paris's oldest English bookstore (since 1802), stocking fine and decorative art books, magazines, and literature.

Just for Children

If you fancy dressing your little ones like a Parisian, **Jacadi** (17 rue Tronchet, 8th arr.) behind the Madeleine sells its own range of cute clothes. **Une Etoile est Née** (74 Champs-Elysées, 8th arr.) sells designer shoes and outfits for newborns to 16s. Also on the

Carrousel du Louvre

Having Fun with Nature

Nature et Découvertes ★★ is a wonderful French chain dedicated to nature and science. Children are so welcome here, they're actually encouraged to pick up the games, books, and objects that cover everything from birds and outer space, to wild animals, minerals, telescopes, plants, relaxation, and the environment. Parents are also catered for with excellent gift items such as jewellery, camping and walking gear, and aromatherapy massage kits. ☎ *01 47 03 47 43*; ***www.nature-et-decouvertes.com***. ***Open*** *daily 10am–8pm.*

Champs-Elysées, **Petit Bateau** (no. 116) and **Catimini** (no. 114) next door, sell a range of baby and children's clothes and accessories. For everything from furry animals to electronic games, **Au Nain Bleu** ★ (5 boulevard Malesherbes, 8th arr.) is France's oldest (1836) and most prestigious toyshop. Finally, for low-priced sportswear and materials try **Décathlon** (26 avenue Wagram, 8th arr.).

Markets ★★

If you or your children are avid stamp collectors, don't miss Paris's stamp market, the **Marché aux Timbres**, where all sorts of rarities change hands (Avenue Gabriel and Avenue Marigny 8th arr., M° Champs-Elysées Clémenceau. Thur, Sat-Sun 10am–6pm or until 4.30pm in winter). For freshly cut flowers try the **Marché aux Fleurs,** which brightens up the right-hand side of the Madeleine.

Nightlife

Lido de Paris ★

AGES 4 AND ABOVE

116 avenue des Champs-Elysées, 8th arr., ☎ *01 40 76 56 10;* ***www.lido.fr.*** *M° Georges V*

Bonheur (happiness) is the name of the Lido's current production – a dramatic reworking of the classic Parisian cabaret show, with eye-popping special effects and new themes, both nostalgic and contemporary, including aerial and aquatic ballets, an ice rink that magically appears and disappears, and enough sequins to cover the Eiffel Tower. The legendary topless Bluebell Girls are still here; but don't worry about bringing your children along – there's nothing sleazy about any of the acts. Youngsters will be enchanted by the fast-moving dancers and extravagant costumes. It's recommended that families come for the first sitting (7pm), when a 30€ children's menu (4 to 12s) can be ordered. The show starts at 9.30pm and costs 20€ per child without dinner. The next show starts at 11.30pm and is free for under-12s. Lunchtime shows also take place some Sundays and Tuesdays (call to check).

Open *for dinner 7pm daily; champagne-revue 9.30pm and 11.30pm daily; lunch-revue and morning champagne revue (call). Dinner 140€–250€ (children 30€ 4–12s). Champagne-revue 90€–100€ (children 20€ 4–12s).* ***Credit*** *AmEx, MC, V.*

High-street Shopping on the Champs-Elysées

On the most famous avenue in the world find girls' and women's clothes at **Naf-Naf** (no. 52), **Zara** (no. 44, plus a men's and children's range), and **Morgan** (no. 92). Perfume superstores include a huge **Séphora** (no. 70) and **Guerlin** (no. 68). For music and films, check out the **Virgin Megastore** (nos. 52–60) and its French equivalent **FNAC** (no. 74).

FAST FACTS

Internet Café Cour-Jardin (inside Hôtel du Lion d'Or), 5 rue de la Sourdière, 1st arr., *01 42 60 79 04*; ***www.cour-jardin.com***. M° Tuileries or Pyramides. Open 7am–midnight daily.

Pharmacy Pharmacie Anglaise, 62 avenue des Champs-Elysées, 8th arr., *01 43 59 22 52*, M° Georges V or Franklin Roosevelt. Open 8.30am–midnight daily.

Post Office La Poste du Louvre 52 rue du Louvre, 1st arr., *01 40 28 76 00*. M° Louvre Rivoli. Open 24/7.

Supermarket Monoprix, 52 avenue des Champs-Elysées, 8th arr., *01 53 77 65 65*. Open daily 9am–midnight.

FAMILY-FRIENDLY ACCOMMODATION

VERY EXPENSIVE

Le Crillon ★

*Place de la Concorde, 8th arr., 01 44 71 15 01; **www.crillon.com**. M° Concorde.*

Never has luxury been finer or more welcoming for families. All equipment is supplied for babies, and there are trained nursery nurses who offer services from babysitting to keeping your children entertained with toys and games. This all comes at a price, but that's to be expected when staying in one of Paris's most historic and beautiful hotels. For your money you get unfaultable service, unrivalled views over Place de la Concorde, chef Jean-François Piège's fabulous gastronomique creations in Les Ambassadeurs (p. 70) and in l'Obélisque his lower-key brasserie, and rooms fit for a king and his family.

***Rooms** 147. **Rates** for the best rates check the website. 695€–890€ doubles; 1160€–8200€ suites and family rooms. **Credit** AmEx, MC, V. **Amenities** A/C, Tea-room, 2 gourmet restaurants, bar, private valet parking, Internet, lift, gym. **In room** safety box, TV/DVD, hi-fi.*

EXPENSIVE

Hôtel Keppler ★

*10 rue Kepler, 16th arr., 01 47 20 65 05; **www.hotelkeppler.com**. M° Georges V or Charles-de-Gaulle Etoile. RER Charles-de-Gaulle Etoile*

This newly renovated boutique hotel welcomes families with open arms and is in a perfect spot for exploring the Champs-Elysées

Le Crillon

quarters. The ostentatious, but chic, décor amuses children with its textured cushions (the animal prints cry out to be cuddled), large mirrors, bold striped walls and intriguing knick-knacks. Extra beds and cots can be added to rooms if necessary. The suites already have a bed-settee that can sleep one child. Breakfast is served in the basement with an open kitchen, where children can see the food being prepared. Babysitting can be organised on request too. On a direct RER line to Disneyland.

Rooms *39 (including 2 rooms for disabled).* ***Rates*** *300€–490€ doubles, 550€–1000€ suites; extra bed 60€–100€, cot free.* ***Credit*** *AmEx, MC, V.* ***Amenities*** *bar, gym, sauna, chauffeured car hire (on request).* ***In room*** *A/C, safe, TV, mini-bar, Internet plug.*

MODERATE

Hôtel Astrid

27 avenue Carnot, 17th arr., 01 44 09 26 00; ***www.hotel-astrid.com****. M° Argentine or Charles-de-Gaulle Etoile; RER Charles-de-Gaulle Etoile.*

This family-run hotel, named after Queen Astrid of Belgium, is good value for money (considering the high prices of the neighbourhood), and although often used by businessmen, it can easily adapt to families. Cots, highchairs, and extra children's beds are available free of charge, and superior rooms are big enough for you all to share comfortably. Just 100m from the Arc de Triomphe (you can see it from some rooms), you are handily placed for catching Métro line 1 to the Louvre, line 2 to Parc Monceau, and the RER A to Disneyland. Décor is plain but tasteful, with light warm tones and simple furniture. Should you decide to eat nearby, the L'Arc Café, literally next door (open 8am to 2am), has a large terrace and serves delicious steaks, salads, and pasta as well as French specialities like sausage cassoulet (a white bean hotpot with tomatoes, sausages, and duck) and Boeuf Bourguignon.

***Rooms** 40. **Rates** 148€–165€ doubles, 180€ triple, extra bed free, cot free. **Credit** AmEx, MC, V. **Amenities** Internet sockets, WiFi, small animals permitted 6€. **In room** A/C, TV, safety box.*

Relais du Louvre ★

*19 rue des Prêtres Saint-Germain-L'Auxerrois, 1st arr., 01 40 41 96 42; **www.relaisdulouvre.com**. M° Louvre Rivoli.*

This hotel next to the Louvre is infused with history. Revolutionaries printed their anti-royalist literature in the cellar and the hotel inspired Puccini's Café Momus in La Bohême. As for families, the star of the show is the huge top-floor, self-contained apartment that sleeps four very comfortably. It has a large sitting room, a dining area, a decorative fireplace, and a kitchen, giving the option of self-catering. In other parts of the hotel, two adjoining rooms per floor can make a family suite. The décor throughout is full of character, with antiques and oriental rugs. If your children like gargoyles, ask for a front room which looks out on to the St Germain l'Auxerrois (see p. 60) church's gothic monsters.

***Rooms** 16. **Rates** 160€–200€ doubles, 205€ triple, 230€–270€ suites, 420€ apartment, extra bed 5€, cot free. **Credit** AmEx, MC, V. **Amenities** Internet sockets, private parking 22€. **In room** TV, safety box.*

INEXPENSIVE

Hôtel Lion d'Or ★★ VALUE

*5 rue de la Sourdière, 1st arr., 01 42 60 79 04; **www.hotel-louvre-paris.com**. M° Tuileries*

Whether you're looking to save money by self-catering, or have two or three children and would all like to sleep in one room, L'Hôtel Lion d'Or is the mother of family-suited hotels, offering a choice between rooms with an extra bed or cot (free of charge), and furnished studios (with a kitchenette) that can sleep up to five, in a location so central you could easily visit Paris on foot. If

Relais du Louvre

Sunday Brunch at the Showcase FIND

Paris's hippest new address, set under the Alexandre III bridge in old, vaulted boat hangars, opens its doors to families with action-packed Sunday brunches. While parents tuck into a delicious brunch buffet, 6 to 14s can go to the 'Kid's Party' where monitors run games, painting and music workshops (including piano and trumpet lessons) and a children's buffet is served away from the boring old folks. Call in advance to request an English speaker. Noon–4pm Sun. 29€–39€ adult, 20€ child. Pont Alexandre III, Port des Champs-Elysées (Right Bank), 8th arr., ☎ 06 28 28 82 88; ***www.showcase.fr***.

you or your children need to surf the net, there's an Internet café next door (Côté Jardin, ***www.cour-jardin.com***). Décor is simple and bright (yellows, green, and mauves), the bathrooms are small but practical, and the buffet breakfast is perfect for filling up before a day's sightseeing. Children also like the clocks in the lobby, set to times in NYC, Tokyo, and Paris.

Rooms *20.* ***Rates*** *95€–115€ doubles, 145€–165€ triple, 135€–165€ studio apartment, extra bed free, 1 cot only (free).* ***Credit*** *MC, V.* ***Amenities*** *safety box at reception, WiFi.* ***In room*** *TV in some rooms.*

FAMILY-FRIENDLY DINING

For a snack during the day, try the food court in the **Carrousel du Louvre** (see p. 64). The previously mentioned **Le Fumoir** (see p. 54), and **Café Marly** (p. 54) are in great spots near the Louvre. The **Minipalais** (p. 56) restaurant in the Grand Palais offers a good children's menu and has excellent, inventive cuisine for grown-ups. Several other museums (**Louvre**, **Arts Décoratifs**, and **Musée Jacquemart-André**) also have handy cafés.

EXPENSIVE

Les Ambassadeurs ★★

Hôtel Crillon, 10 place de la Concorde, 8th arr., ☎ 01 44 71 16 17; ***www.crillon.com****. M° Concorde.*

If you'd like to give your children their first taste of Michelin-starred cuisine, this is the place to do it. For children, the Crillon Hotel's restaurant is like eating in a fairytale castle. The walls are marble, the chandeliers sparkle like diamonds, and gilded cherubs keep watch over the doorways. A special children's menu can be concocted (price on request), while you sit back and sample rare and outstanding classics (foie gras, lobster, duck, caviar and white truffles) reworked with modern flair. The wine list is, of course, exemplary. To save money but experience the same cuisine, come for the more reasonably priced lunch menu.

Open Noon–2pm, 7.30pm–10pm Tues–Sat. 3-course average 185€. Lunch 80€. ***Credit*** AmEx, MC, V.

MODERATE

Atelier Renault

52 avenue des Champs-Elysées, 8th arr., 08 11 88 28 11. M° Franklin D Roosevelt.

If the boys, tomboys, and dads in your family love cars, this futuristic-looking café, all clad in glass, aluminium, and swish contemporary furniture, awaits you above the Renault showroom. Try to grab a table on one of the five walkways from where you have views onto the Champs-Elysées or over the showroom. If you're only mildly hungry opt for an ice cream or the club sandwiches (15€) and pasta dishes (13 to 15€). A child's menu gets you a small plate of ham pasta, a burger, or chicken nuggets with fries, an ice cream or a waffle and a soda for 9€. Adult menus start at 20€ and offer a French take on world food (think scallops served in a tagine with lemon zest). If dad can't afford a flashy new car, you could buy one for your three- to six-year-olds at the boutique, where pedal cars start at 120€.

Open *10.30am–12.30am Sun–Thur; 10.30am–2.30am Fri–Sat. Average 35€, fixed-price 20€, 24€, 29€. Children's menu 9€.* ***Credit*** *AmEx, MC, V.*

Fermette Marbeuf 1900

5 rue Marbeuf, 8th arr.. 01 53 23 08 00; ***www.fermettemarbeuf.com****. M° Franklin D Roosevelt.*

There is something truly magical about bringing your children to a turn-of-the-century dining room with no windows to the outside world, but lots of glass; no plants but plenty of greenery. La Fermette's splendid conservatory is an Art Nouveau masterpiece uncovered during renovations in 1978 and full of the curvaceous floral ironwork and coloured glass that made this era so architecturally unique. I often come here for a special family dinner and delight in dishes such as mussel soup perfumed with saffron, perfectly roasted lamb served with crunchy green beans, and an unsinkable Grand Marnier soufflé. Special children's meals can be ordered on request.

Here's a Scoop

Scoop is an avant-garde ice-cream parlour that dishes out home-made ice cream in a setting that could well be a New York diner. The recipes, all with exotic names like '*tortue*' (tortoise), put ordinary sundaes to shame with lashings of sauces and real fruits. Healthy salads banish any guilt, and the juicy-looking burgers go down a treat with the little ones.

154 rue St-Honoré, 1st arr, M° Palais-Royal. 11am–7pm Sun–Wed, 11am–10pm Thur–Fri.

Macaroon Heaven

If every sweet-toothed family died and went to heaven, then heaven would be **La Durée**. Famous for their fabulous macaroons and other naughties, including the best pistachio-filled *pains au chocolat* I've ever tasted, their two tearooms are in handy spots on the Champs-Elysées (no. 75) and Rue Royale (no. 16) near Concorde. If you sit inside the period 19th-century tearooms (as opposed to the takeaway counters), over-indulging in thick, melted hot chocolate is something best embraced by the whole family. Salads and sandwiches are also available.

***Open** noon–3pm, 7pm–11.30pm daily. Fixed-price menus 32€, 3-course average 50€. **Credit** MC, V.*

PDG

20 rue de Ponthieu, 8th arr., 01 42 56 19 10. M° Franklin D Roosevelt.

Tell your youngsters to tuck their napkins into their collars: the giant burgers at this place are so enormous that eating them without spillage is impossible. You can choose between 10 different varieties including an extravagant Jumbo Bacon Cheese (double burger with double bacon and gooey cheese), the Mexican, which comes with guacamole on the side, and chicken or vegetarian burgers. The bread is baked by a '*meilleur ouvrier de France*' baker (best baker award), and the meat is high-grade and juicy. For your health-conscious teenagers, fries can be replaced with lightly sautéed potatoes or spinach.

***Open** 7.45am–2.30pm, 7pm–11pm daily. Average 30€, fixed-price 30€. **Credit** MC, V.*

INEXPENSIVE

Le Châlet du 8ème

8 rue du Commandant Rivière, 8th arr., 01 45 61 18 10. M° St-Philippe du Roule.

Cheap choices are limited around the Champs-Elysées, but this is an excellent spot, off the beaten track and little-known to tourists. Done up like a Swiss chalet, it serves lip-smacking galettes and crêpes for around 6€ to 12€ a piece. Crêpes are made with the freshest ingredients and are so well-filled small children won't need more than one. Even adults might struggle to gobble down a dessert. My favourite savoury was a goat's cheese, apple and honey galette. Chocolate-mad youngsters won't be disappointed with several chocolaty delights on the dessert menu. Cider is served in traditional bowls and there's an excellent fixed-price lunch menu at just 10.70€.

***Open** noon–2pm, 7.30pm–10.30pm Mon–Fri, 7.30pm–10.30pm Sat. Closed 3 weeks in Aug. 3-course average 20€. **Credit** MC, V.*

4 Invalides to the Eiffel Tower & Chaillot Quarters

INVALIDES TO THE EIFFEL TOWER

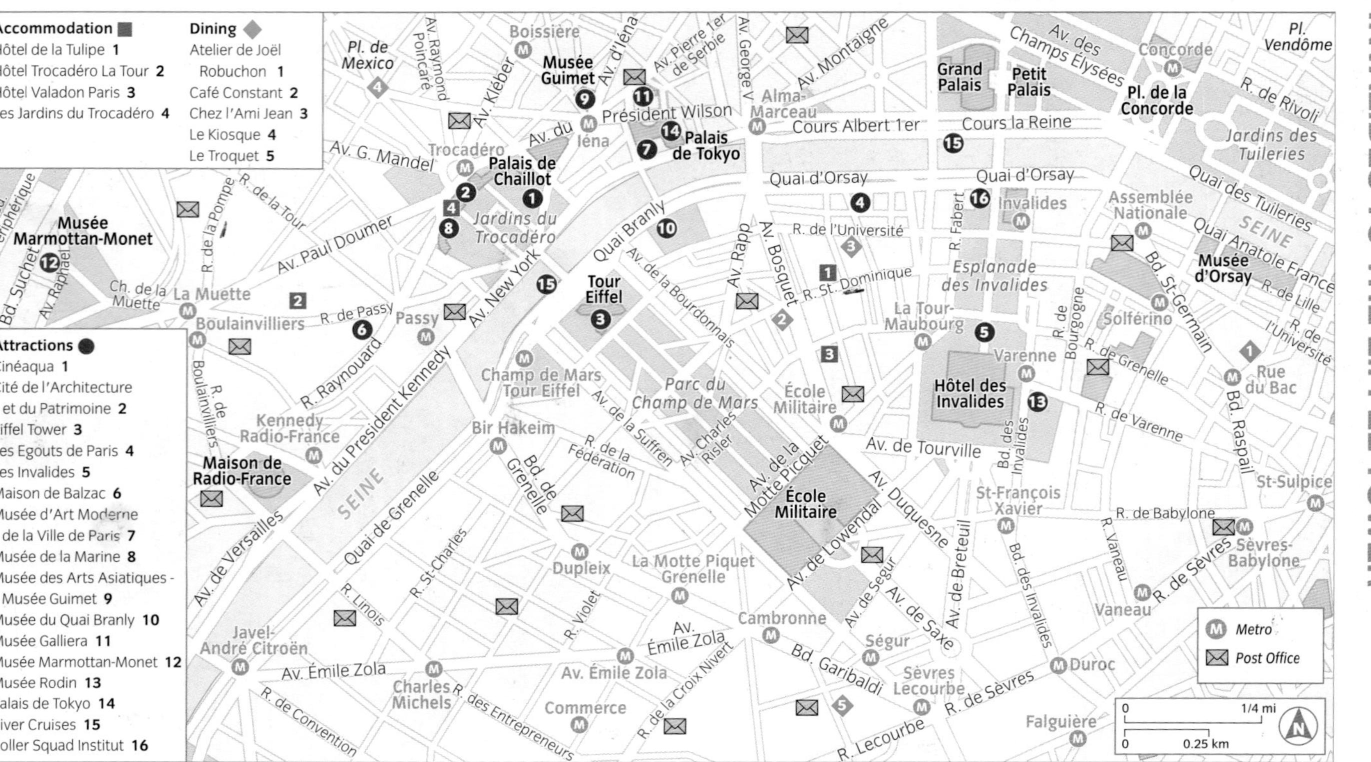

This is one of the grandest areas in Paris, where everything seems to have been built on a monumental scale. The wide, Second Empire avenues are lined with stately, luxurious buildings, embassies, company headquarters, and some of the chicest residences in town – those to the east hiding 18th-century buildings behind later façades. This is the lair of the *haute bourgeoisie*, who parade in designer suits and flashy cars, and live in highly secure, if not sober, Belle Époque apartments.

The Place du Trocadéro (Right Bank) is the convergence point of six arteries, including Avenue du Président Wilson, which has a greater concentration of museums than anywhere else in Paris – but don't try to visit them all at once. It is also home to the stunning Palais de Chaillot. The Palais du Trocadéro, built for the 1878 World Fair, was torn down in the 1930s to make way for the current imposing, two-winged, Neoclassical Palais de Chaillot, revealed at the 1937 World Fair. Between the wings is a viewing terrace that affords the best views of the Eiffel Tower. In summer, the area is sometimes used as an open-air cinema – a magical location, particularly at night when the Tower shimmers for 10 minutes, on the hour.

Crossing the Seine to the Left Bank, Gustave Eiffel's iron lady imposes her colossal grace over everything around it. In the surrounding houses that border the 18th-century Ecole Militaire, Champ de Mars, and Les Invalides military museum, grandeur oozes from every stone, doorway, and window-box. This is where you'll find some of the city's most beautiful Art Nouveau façades.

ESSENTIALS

This area covers three large *quartiers* and as many arrondissements (7th, 15th, 16th), so while buggy-pushers might only break out in a light sweat (except when navigating the stairs in the Métro), those with young walkers could struggle with the distances. My advice is to split the area into chunks, deciding what you really want to see and heading there first. Also, take a bottle of water: there are cafés (most of the museums have one), but around the Seine between Trocadéro and the Eiffel Tower, they are few and far between. The good news is that the area is well served by the Métro, RER, and buses.

GETTING AROUND

The principal bus routes are no. **80**, which crosses the Champs-Elysées to Ecole Militaire; no. **42**, which links the Champ de Mars with the Gare du Nord; no. **82** crosses the river near Trocadéro; no. **30** links Trocadéro with the Champs-Elysées and Montmartre: no. **69** travels along Rue St-Dominique (east) and Rue de Grenelle (west); no. **87** passes along Avenue de Suffren; and no. **28** links Porte d'Orléans in the south to Gare St-Lazare in the north via Ecole Militaire (see p. 37 for advice on using public transport with children and buggies). Also don't forget the **Batobus** river bus (see p. 39) with stops at the **Eiffel Tower** and **Champs-Elysées.**

VISITOR INFORMATION

There are no tourist offices in this area so stock up on maps and any brochures you need beforehand, or bring this guidebook.

WHAT TO SEE & DO

Culture

Cineaqua ★ ALL AGES

2 avenue des Nations-Unies, 16th arr. ☎ 01 40 69 23 23, ***www.cineaqua.com****. M° Trocadéro and Iéna.*

Originally built in 1878 for the Universal Exhibition, this state-of-the-art aquarium plunges you deep into the heart of ocean life, thanks to the biggest tanks in France, full of shimmering fish, eels, sea horses, lobsters, and a whole host of other creatures, including 30 rather fearsome-looking sharks. Surefire hits with the children are the '*bassins caresses*' (touching pools) where they can stroke and feed the koi carp and sturgeon. Children also enjoy the *cinés* (cinemas) dotted around the aquarium, showing a constant stream of lively cartoons, short films and documentaries (some in English or with English subtitles) about nature, sea-life, sustainable development, and why it is important we humans get on swimmingly with our fishy friends.

When tummies rumble, the café offers snacks and sandwiches, and, for something more substantial, the restaurant OZU is an ode to Japanese cuisine (*Ozu* in Japanese means little fisherman's port), with a Japanese-themed dining room, open kitchen and a glass wall, behind which schools of silvery fish swim in what looks like a non-stop underwater ballet. With older children, you could have dinner here before heading downstairs to the lounge-bar for some live music (usually jazz or Brazilian electro) on Thursdays, Fridays, and Saturdays.

Cineaqua open daily 10am–8pm. Ozu ☎ 01 40 69 23 90. ***Open*** *daily 12pm–3pm, 7.30pm–11pm (Thurs–Sat until 4am)* ***Admission*** *19.50€ adult, 12€ 3–12s, free under-3s.*

Cité de l'Architecture et du Patrimoine AGES 5 AND ABOVE

Palais de Chaillot, 1 place du Trocadéro, 16th arr. ☎ 01 58 51 52 00, ***www.citechaillot.org****. M° Trocadéro.*

Paris's newest cultural attraction, the 'City of Architecture and Heritage', covers 8 sq km in the east wing of the Palais de Chaillot, with more than 850 copies of portions of churches, châteaux and cathedrals, plus reconstructions of modern architecture, including an apartment created by Le Corbusier. The

A 19th-century Philanthropist

At Villa Mulhouse, near the edge of the 16th arrondissement (access via 86 rue Boilveau), you can see rows of workers' houses built in 1835 by the cotton giant Dollfus for his employees. He believed that cleanliness and morality went hand in hand, so good housing would improve their behaviour.

wall-painting gallery downstairs in the Pavillon de Tête, offers a stunning collection of frescos copied from medieval murals.

The museum has been designed with children in mind, each floor containing interactive games such as stained-glass making and domed roof building, and in the Galerie des Moulages scaled-down moveable models of structures show how ancient architects overcame engineering problems. While explanations are in French, the games are still absorbing for non-French-speaking children.

A family audio-guide in English is planned for 2008, so ask when you buy your tickets. And don't set off without a map: the museum is huge and difficult to navigate.

For a snack, head to the Café Carlu (*01 53 70 96 65*) on the ground floor and enjoy the panoramic view of the Eiffel Tower. The shop opposite sells beautiful architecture-orientated books, plus children's building games.

***Open** 12pm–8pm Mon, Wed, Fri; until 10pm Thurs; 11am–7pm Sat–Sun. **Admission** 7€ adults, Free under-18s.*

Eiffel Tower ★★ ALL AGES

*Champ de Mars, 7th arr. 01 44 11 23 23; **www.tour-eiffel.fr**. M° Trocadéro, Bir-Hakeim. RER C Champs-de-Mars-Tour-Eiffel.*

No single structure is the source of as much excitement and revelry as Gustave Eiffel's 7,000 tonne, 324m iron masterpiece. Built in 1889 for the World Fair, it was meant to be a temporary exhibit that would 'unlock the unlimited possibilities of metal construction'. However, despite the delicate criss-crossing of the pig-iron girders and the tower's impeccable symmetry, it was considered by some to be so ugly (the author Guy de Maupassant

The illuminated Eiffel Tower

used to dine there just so that he didn't have to look at it) that it's a wonder it's still here.

What saved it from demolition was the advent of radio. As the tallest structure in Europe (it was the tallest building in the world until 1931, when New York's Empire State Building was completed), it made a perfect spot to place a radio antenna (now a TV antenna).

Today, it's practically a village unto itself with shops, restaurants (Altitude 95 *08 25 56 66 62* and the Michelin-starred Jules Verne *08 25 56 66 62*), a post office (send a postcard home from here), and a tiny cinema (Cineiffel) showing short movies about the tower. From the panoramic viewing galleries, on a clear day, you can see for more than 65km – including to Chartres Cathedral, some 89km away (you'll need binoculars).

If you're feeling brave you can climb the stairs to the second floor and avoid the queues for the lifts. You'll have to get the lift if you want to go to the top, however, if you dine at Altitude 95 (first floor, 30–40€ per person), you can cut to the head of the line. If not, take a bottle of water – the wait could be long.

While the tower is awe-inspiring up close, it's best appreciated at night from a distance, when thousands of bulbs make the edifice sparkle for 10 minutes on the hour, until 2am (1am in winter).

The Champ de Mars next to the tower is an ideal spot for a lazy family picnic, with a children's play area.

Open *daily: by lift 9.30am–11.45pm Jan–mid-Jun, 2 Sept–Dec; 9am–12.45am mid-Jun–1 Sept. By stairs 9.30am–6.30pm Jan–mid-Jun, 2 Sept–Dec; 9am–12.45am mid-Jun–1 Sept.* ***Admission*** *lift to 1st floor – 4.50€ adult, 2.30€ 3–11s. Lift to 2nd floor – 7.80€ adult, 4.30€ 3–11s. Top floor – 11.50€ adult, 6.30€ 3–11s. Stairs to 1st and 2nd floors – 4€ adult, 3.10€ under 25s, free under-3s.*

Les Invalides ★★

AGES 6 AND ABOVE

129 rue de Grenelle, 7th arr., 01 44 42 38 77; ***www.invalides.org*** *and* ***www.ordredelaliberation.fr****. M° Invalides, La Tour-Maubourg, Varenne and Saint-François Xavier. RER C Invalides.*

Napoleon's tomb occupies centre-stage of the gilded **Dôme**

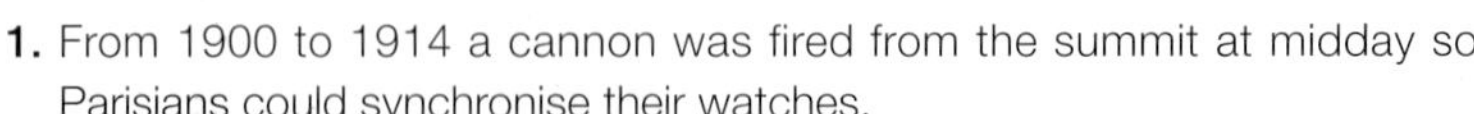

Three Eiffel Tower Facts

1. From 1900 to 1914 a cannon was fired from the summit at midday so Parisians could synchronise their watches.
2. In 1948 an 85-year-old elephant from the Bouglione circus (see p. 135) was hauled up to the first floor for a walk.
3. In 1989, the circus artist Philippe Petit crossed the Seine from the Trocadéro to the 2nd floor of the tower on a 700m tightrope.

Visit Napoleon's tomb at Invalides

church (commissioned by the Sun King, Louis XIV in 1676), the sparkling centrepiece of the Invalides military complex – once an enormous residential centre for disabled French soldiers, injured in battle. Nowadays, the wards have been replaced with four attractions.

The largest is the **Musée de l'Armée** – one of the most comprehensive military museums in the world with Viking swords, Burgundian battleaxes, 14th-century blunderbusses, and American Browning machine guns. Children will love the armoury collections. Look out for the suit Henri II engraved with the monogram of both his mistress, Diane de Poitiers, and his wife, Catherine de' Médici.

The **Musée des Plans-Reliefs**' collection shows scale models of French towns and monuments as well as military fortifications since the days of Vauban (Louis XIV's military engineer). The model of Marseilles' Château d'If, shows the off-shore prison that inspired Alexandre Dumas to write the Count of Monte-Cristo.

The third museum is the **Musée de l'Ordre de la Libération**, dedicated to those who offered 'outstanding service in the effort to procure the liberation of France and the French empire' in World War II; and the fourth attraction is the Historical Charles de Gaulle – a state-of-the-art audiovisual monument sunk 12m below the Invalides' Cour de Valeur wing, that deals with the whole of de Gaulle's life.

One ticket gains access to all museums. Audio-guides in English are available.

For running-around space try the lawns leading up to *Les Invalides,* one of the few parks in Paris where sitting on the grass isn't prohibited.

Open *10am–6pm daily Apr–Sept (until 5pm Oct–Mar). Closed 1st Mon/month.* ***Admission*** *8€ adult, 6€ 18–26s, free under-18s.*

INSIDER TIP

The best way to approach the Invalides is by crossing the Seine via the **Pont Alexandre-III**. A display of massive cannons makes a formidable welcome.

Maison de Balzac

AGES 10 AND ABOVE

47 rue Raynouard, 16th arr. 01 55 74 41 80; ***www.balzac.paris.fr****. M° Passy or La Muette. RER C Boulainvilliers or Radio France.*

It was here, from 1840 to 1847, that the French novelist Honoré de Balzac lived under the false name of Mr de Brugnol to dodge the debt collectors sent by his numerous creditors. The house still has the back entrance he used to flee during emergencies and, aside from a reference library, is little changed since Balzac's day.

The streets around have retained much of their old, country-like appeal, and recent excavations have even uncovered medieval troglodyte dwellings below the house.

Open *10am–6pm Tues–Sun.* ***Admission*** *4€ adult, 2€ 14–26s, free under-13s.*

Musée d'Art Moderne de la Ville de Paris ★

AGES 6 AND ABOVE

11 avenue du Président Wilson, 16th arr. 01 53 67 40 00. ***www.mam.paris.fr****. M° Alma-Marceau or Iéna. RER C Pont d'Alma.*

This fantastic modern art museum is in the east wing of the Palais de Tokyo (constructed in 1937 for the Universal Exhibition) and takes the whole family on a journey through 20th-century 'isms': Fauvism, Cubism, Surrealism, Realism, Expressionism, and Neo-realism, with works by artists like Braque, Dufy, Picasso, Leger, and Matisse, all presented in chronological order. If your children are studying art it's a must, and even if they're not – or perhaps they're too young – the bright colours and often simple forms of many 20th-century art movements generally appeal. I was surprised by how enthusiastically my friend's six-year-old reacted to our challenging him to find the dove and the green peas in Picasso's rather abstract *Pigeon aux petits pois* (Dove with Green Peas). He was equally enchanted by the gargantuan exhibits at the end of the visit including Dufy's 1937 *La Fée Électricité,* which, at 60m by 10m, is one of the largest paintings in the world.

Open *10am–6pm Tues–Sun (until 8pm Fri and Sat for temporary exhibitions).* ***Admission*** *free for permanent collections. 4.50€–9€ temporary collections. Under-13s free.*

Musée de la Marine ALL AGES

Palais de Chaillot, 17 place du Trocadéro, 16th arr. 01 53 65 69 69; ***www.musee-marine.fr****. M° Trocadéro.*

Paris might be miles from the nearest coast, but in the west wing of the Palais de Chaillot this museum (along with St. Petersburg's marine museum) houses the oldest nautical-themed collection in the world,

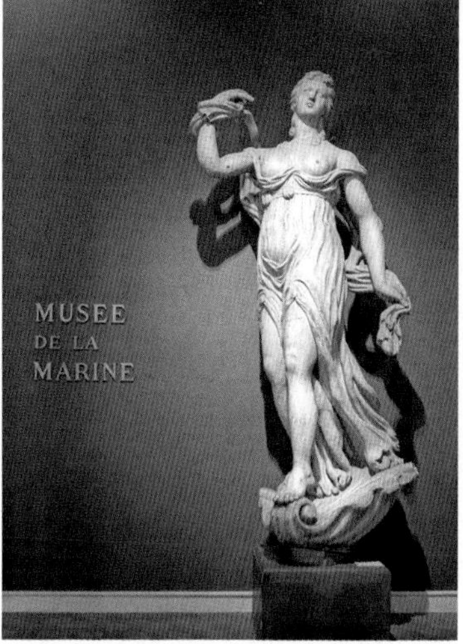

Musée de la Marine

most of the items being donated to Louis XV (1710–1774) by one of his generals, on the condition they be used to instruct marine engineers.

The visit begins with an ensemble of boats, including an ornate barque that belonged to Napoléon Bonaparte, and the prow of the gondola Marie Antoinette used to sail up and down the canal in Versailles. There are striking sculptures used to decorate galleons; models of the old royal fleet; a quarter-sized model of *Le Velox*, France's largest schooner (1903–1907); and, in the final room, a scaled-down replica of the *Charles de Gaulle*, France's nuclear aircraft carrier, able to house 2,000 crew members. Also look out for a model of the world's first steam boat, from 1783.

There are games sheets to fill in during the visit.

Open *10am–6pm Wed–Mon.* ***Admission*** *9€ adults, 7€ students under 25, 5€ 6–18s, free under-6s.*

Musée des Arts Asiatiques – Musée Guimet ★

AGES 5 AND ABOVE

6 place d'Iéna, 16th arr. ☎ 01 56 52 53 00. ***www.museeguimet.fr****. M° Iéna.*

This temple to Asian and Oriental arts is a magical museum, where the treasures (mostly collected and donated by the 19th-century industrialist Emile Guimet) are displayed chronologically over four floors that spill out from around a monumental staircase. You will find more than 45,000 artworks, representing traditions from China, Japan, Korea, Vietnam, India, and Afghanistan, plus the most splendid collection of Cambodian (Khmer) art in the West.

The museum is jam-packed with mythical imagery that children can either draw (perhaps pick out their favourite monsters) or invent stories about. On the way in on the left, the seven-headed Cambodian cobra, Naga, is believed to protect the riches of the earth and, once you've counted each head, your children will be able to find other Nagas in the following rooms. The Naga's arch-enemy is Paravani 'the snake-killer', found further along on the left next to the Hindu war god, Skanda.

For children due to take exams, you could point out the meditating elephant in the Vietnamese room. He is the god of schoolchildren, ensuring success to all those who offer him sweets.

Both the Calligraphy and Chinese-painting workshops for

Musée du Quai Branly

children (7s and over) are easy to follow whatever their mother tongue (*01 56 52 53 45*).

Adjacent to the museum is the **Panthéon Bouddhique** (free entry) containing Japanese religious art from 1876. In spring and autumn the main attraction here is the Japanese tea pavilion in the garden, where 12- to 15-year-olds can participate in traditional tea ceremonies.

***Open** 10am–6pm Wed–Mon.*
***Admission** 6.50€ adult, 4.50€ 18–25s, free under-18s.*

Musée du Quai Branly ★

AGES 6 AND ABOVE

*37 quai Branly, 7th arr. 01 56 61 70 00; **www.quaibranly.fr**. M° Iena, Alma Marceau, RER C Pont de l'Alma.*

Open since 2006, this Jean Nouvel-designed temple to the primitive arts showcases more than 3,500 anthropological and ethnological artefacts from Africa, Oceania, Asia, and the Americas, with Vietnamese costumes, Aztec statues, rare Ethiopian frescos, sculptures from the Cameroon, and the **cabinets des curiosités** – cabinets grouping objects such as divinatory tools from Africa.

Music is a key feature of the museum with a spectacular *tour aux instruments*, a circular glass tower that cuts through the centre of the building showing instruments from all over the world.

For snacks head to the **Café Branly** (open museum hours), but for something special, take the lift to the rooftop restaurant, **Les Ombres** (*01 47 53 68 00; **www.lesombres-restaurant.com***). It's not suitable for very young children, but if your older children enjoy fine dining and you can afford the treat (80–100€ per head), the delicious French food is served in a chic dining room where the views are sensational.

Mum, Dad, What's Impressionism?

When the killer question crops up, here's what to say: Impressionism was an art movement that lasted from around 1870 to the 1920s. The term was coined during an exhibition in 1874, in which Claude Monet showed his painting *Impression, Sunrise* (1874), now in the **Musée Marmottan** (see p. 84). One critic hated the exhibition, calling everything 'Impressionist'. Far from being insulted, the show's artists adopted the word for their movement.

Impressionism is a style of painting that concentrates on the effects (or *impression)* of light on atmosphere, colours, and shapes. The artists often painted with visible, broken brushstrokes (not smooth and unnoticeable like their predecessors), and used lots of different colours that blurred into each other. To make the most of the changing light, they usually painted outside, which is why many Impressionist paintings depict landscapes and scenes of daily life.

Impressionist artists and where you can see their most famous works in Paris:

Claude Monet (1840–1926). *Impression, Sunrise* (1874) in the **Musée Marmottan** (see p. 84). *Water Lilies* hangs in Paris's **Musée de l'Orangerie** (see p. 55), and you can visit Monet's studio and gardens at **Giverny**, north of Paris.

Edouard Manet (1832–83). The groundbreaking *Picnic on the Grass* (1863) and *Olympia* (1863) are both in the **Musée d'Orsay** (see p. 154)

Pierre-Auguste Renoir (1841–1919). A porcelain painter, which helps explain his figures' ivory skin and chubby pink cheeks, many of his works including *Boy with a Cat* and *Barges on the Seine* (1869) are at the **Musée d'Orsay** (see p. 154)

Open *11am–7pm Tues–Sun (until 9pm Thurs–Sat).* ***Admission*** *museum only: 8.50€ adult, 6€ under-18s. Museum and temporary exhibition: 13€ adult, 9.50€ under-18s.*

INSIDER TIP

Arrive for 9.50am and wait for the doors to open – it's when the museum is at its most empty. By 2pm queues are reasonable, after 2pm, bring games or books so that the children can occupy themselves.

Musée Galliera AGES 4 AND ABOVE

10 avenue Pierre 1er de Serbie, 16th arr. 01 56 52 86 00; ***www.galliera.paris.fr****. M° Iéna or Alma-Marceau. RER C Pont d'Alma.*

This fashion museum is only open twice a year but holds more than 50,000 clothes items and 40,000 accessories (jewellery, hats, canes, gloves, and umbrellas) spanning the 18th century to the present day. English audioguides are planned for 2008.

Open *during temporary exhibitions only 10am–6pm Tues–Sun.* ***Admission*** *8€ adults, 3.50€ 14–26s, free under-13s.*

Musée Marmottan-Monet

AGES 8 AND ABOVE

2 rue Louis-Boilly, 16th arr. 01 44 96 50 33; ***www.marmottan.com****. M° La Muette. RER C Bouilainvilliers.*

This former hunting pavilion, on the edge of the Bois de Boulogne is where historian Paul Marmottan kept his collection of Renaissance, Consular and First Empire paintings, furniture, and artefacts. On his death it all passed to the Académie des Beaux-Arts and remained largely ignored until 1966, when Claude Monet's second son Michel died in a car crash, leaving the little museum a multi-million bequest of his father's art.

The Académie suddenly found itself with 130-plus paintings, watercolours, pastels, and drawings, allowing Monet lovers to trace the evolution of Impressionism and the great man's work in a single museum. To Monet's works and the original collections private donors have added treasures by Boudin, Corot, Gauguin, and Renoir plus countless miniatures.

There are no specific activities organised for children but you can point out highlights like Monet's water lilies, plus the *Houses of Parliament* (1905), a Renoir portrait of the 32-year-old Monet, and Monet's *Impression, Sunrise* (1872), from which the Impressionist movement got its name (see p. 83).

Open *10am–5.30pm Tues–Sun.* ***Admission*** *8€ adults, 4.50€ ages 8–25, free under-7s.*

Musée Rodin ★ ALL AGES

79 rue de Varenne, 7th arr. 01 44 18 61 10; ***www.musee-rodin.fr****.*

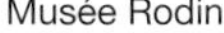

Musée Rodin

M° Varennes, Invalides or St François-Xavier. RER C Invalides

An advantage of being France's greatest 19th-century sculptor was that you were given free board and lodgings in Paris's most elegant mansions, in exchange for your sculptures – left to the state, once you'd chiselled your last. Auguste Rodin made the most of this in the Hôtel Biron (built in 1731) from 1908 to his death in 1917 (alongside Cocteau and Matisse).

Many statues are on display in the museum's stunning rose garden – an exquisite place for families to visit, especially in the summer when the café sells giant ice creams of *'une'* or *'deux' boules* (scoops) that children can drip down their clothes as they explore the shaded alleyways among works like *The Thinker*, *The Gates of Hell*, and *Balzac*.

Indoors, the exhibits are arranged by themes, spanning Rodin's life, including the famous Dante-inspired *The Kiss*. There is also a moving display of works by Camille Claudel, Rodin's long-time lover who tragically spent the last 30 years of her life in an asylum.

Audio-guides are available in English for all the family.

In May don't miss the *Nuits des Musées* (second Saturday of the month), when the museum and gardens can be visited at night by torchlight.

Open *9.30am–5.45pm Tues–Sun (garden until 6.45) Apr–Sept; 9.30am–4.45pm (garden until 5pm) Oct–Mar.* ***Admission*** *1€ gardens only; 6€ adults, 4.50€ 18–25s, Free under-18s (garden and museum). 9€ adults, 7€ 18–25s, Free under-18s (garden, museum and temporary exhibitions). Free entry to garden with a buggy.*

Palais de Tokyo AGES 6 AND ABOVE

13 avenue du Président Wilson, 16th arr. 01 47 23 38 86. ***www.palaisdetokyo.com****. M° Alma-Marceau or Iéna, RER C Pont d'Alma.*

Palais de Tokyo

29 Avenue Rapp

Reveal the delights of Art Nouveau to your family by taking them to see the façade of architect Jules Lavirotte's gorgeous turn-of-the-century building. Its brickwork is intricately decorated with animals, flora, and female figures – perfect for getting the children to count and name what they can see.

Opposite the Modern Art Museum, in the west wing of the Palais de Tokyo, this contemporary arts museum (with the same name as the building), houses an ever-changing succession of avant-garde, temporary exhibitions, that frequently look like a bomb has hit them – chosen to help visitors break away from old school traditions and perceive contemporary creations in a whole new light. In just six years (it opened in 2002), it has become the most-visited contemporary arts museum in the world.

No two visits are ever the same. Just make sure you grab a guide on the latest exhibition and ask as many questions as you feel necessary. The friendly staff are recognisable by their red sashes.

When hunger strikes, the fun continues in the museum's restaurant, Tokyo Eat (*01 47 20 00 29*), where bulbous pink-and-white lights hang over the tables like UFOs. You can combine your entrance fee with the dish of the day and a coffee for 15€.

Open *12pm–12am Tues–Sun.* ***Admission*** *6€ adult, 4.50€ 19–26s, free under-18s.*

Parks & the Outdoors

River Cruises ★★

Kiddie-winkles always get excited by boat trips – which is a good thing, because commentated cruises up and down the Seine are a magnificent way to take in the sweeping vistas and see the intricate underbellies of

River cruise passing under Pont Neuf

Wow that Whippersnapper

Children, speed, and wheels go hand in hand at the Trocadéro, where agile amateurs show off their tricks on rollerblades and skateboards most Saturday and Sunday afternoons. Watch in wonder with the Eiffel Tower as your magical backdrop.

the bridges, often only visible from water-level.

The main companies are **Bateaux Parisiens,** who commentate in English and offer delicious lunch and dinner cruises (plus a special children's cruise in French); and **Bateaux-Mouches** whose open-top boats are a godsend in the summer. In both cases tourist trips last for almost an hour and a half and gourmet cruises last for more than two. For the dinner cruises, smart dress (including jackets for men) is required.

***Bateaux-Parisiens**: 08 25 01 01 01 (0.15 € per min); **www.bateaux-parisiens.com**. M° Trocadéro or Bir-Hakeim, RER C Champs de Mars. Departure Port de la Bourdonnais, 7th arr., on the Left Bank at the foot of the Eiffel Tower. Hours: 10am–10.30pm every 30mins Apr–Sept, 10am–10pm every hour Oct–Mar. **Admission** 10€ adult, 5€ 4–12s, free under-3s.*

***Bateaux-Mouches**: 01 42 25 96 10; **www.bateaux-mouches.fr**. M° Alma-Marceau. RER C Pont de l'Alma. Departure Port de la Conférence, 8th arr., on the Right Bank, next to Pont de l'Alma. Hours: every 45min from 10.15am–3.15pm, then every 20 mins from 4pm–11pm Apr–30 Sept. Oct–Mar private groups only. **Admission** 9€ adult, 4€ 5–12s, free under-4s.*

Roller Squad Institut ★

AGES 6 AND ABOVE

Providing both you and your little monkeys know how to rollerblade, the Roller Squad Institut organises family trips around the urban jungle on Sunday afternoons (weather permitting). This is a unique way to sightsee; and because you'll be gliding along the pavement, babies and toddlers can be pushed in buggies or prams.

Rendezvous at 2.45pm at the Esplanade des Invalides (by Pont Alexandre III, with the Invalides behind you, the Roller Squad is on the left, surrounded by a stone wall, in front of the Air France building). The accent is on safety so padding and helmets are a must for the children. Knee and elbow pads are also obligatory for adults. The circuit is no more than 2km long and takes 2 hours.

*Reserve at least 48 hours before. If it's raining call 06 84 96 99 69 after 1pm. 01 56 61 99 61; www.rsi.asso.fr. M°/RER C Invalides. **Admission** free.*

Underground Paris

Les Egouts de Paris ★

AGES 8 AND ABOVE

Pont de l'Alma (Left Bank, opposite 53 quai d'Orsay, 7th arr. 01 53 68

A Potted History of the Bowels of Paris

In the Middle Ages, drinking water was taken directly from the Seine, while waste water was thrown on to the unpaved streets, transforming the urban landscape into a sea of smelly mud, spreading devastating diseases. In 1370, a vaulted sewer was built in the Rue Montmartre, draining effluents into a tributary of the Seine (where people still drew drinking water). Despite a few improvements during the reign of Louis XIV, waste disposal remained deplorable until the 19th century. By the time Baron Haussmann and the engineer Eugène Belgrand came on the scene (in the 1850s), the Industrial Revolution had improved the manufacture of iron pipes, facilitating a revolutionary system of separate underground channels for drinking water and sewage. Between 1914 and 1977, 966km of sewers were added. Today's network is complete with freshwater mains, compressed-air pipes, telephone cables, and pneumatic tubes, and measures 2,100km.

27 81; ***www.paris.fr****. M° Alma-Marceau. RER C Pont de l'Alma.*

Victor Hugo, in *Les Misérables,* described the Paris sewers as 'all dripping with slime.' He also wrote, 'Paris has beneath it another Paris, a Paris of sewers, which has its own streets, squares, lanes, arteries, and circulation.' The latter description is far more accurate, and the museum, which retraces the history of all 2,100km of Paris's underworld through a series of films, exhibits, and a trip through the tunnels, is fascinating for both children and grown-ups. Visiting times may change in bad weather, when a storm can make the sewers dangerous. Things can also get pretty whiffy in summer – be warned.

Open *11am–5pm Sat–Wed (until 4pm Oct–Apr).* ***Admission*** *4.10€ adult, 3.30€ 5–16s and students with a valid card, Free under-4s.*

Shopping

Paris really is a shopper's paradise – but not in this district. However, museums such as the **Cité de l'Architecture**, the **Musée Rodin,** and the **Musée Guimet** sell interesting gifts and books; **Rue de Passy** has a few neighbourhood offerings. or head south to **Rue de Commerce** (see right), where locals flock to the high-street shops.

Markets ★★

Food *marchés* are fortunately easier to find, and a feast for the senses. **Rue Cler** (7th arr., M° Ecole Militaire or La Tour-Maubourg, Tues–Sat) is a high-class street market, favoured by wealthy families, diplomats, and politicians. Push past the best-dressed shoppers in town to discover the wonderful pâtisseries, fisheries, and cheese shops.

The nearby **Marché Saxe-Breteuil** (Avenue de Saxe, 7th arr.,

M° Ségur, Thurs and Sat 7am–2.30pm) is possibly the most scenic of all Paris's markets thanks to the Eiffel Tower that pokes its head up between the trees and the mouth-watering stalls. If you're into organic food, an excellent **Marché Biologique** (organic market) sells produce every Tuesday and Friday (7am–2.30pm) on Rue St-Charles (15th arr., M° Javel-André-Citroën).

Rue de Commerce

15th arr., M° La Motte-Picquet-Grenelle

This long street, away from the tourist track, offers both French and international brands such as **Gap** (no. 6), **André** (shoes, no. 7), **Comptoirs des Cotonniers** (women's fashion, no. 11), **Zara** (women's fashion, no. 13), **MAC** (makeup, no. 14), **H&M** (no. 15), **Etam Lingerie** (no. 18), **Celio** (men's fashion, no. 23) and **La Compagnie des Petits** (children's clothes, no. 55).

Village Suisse

38-78 avenue de Suffren/54 avenue de la Motte-Picquet Grenelle, 15th arr., M° La Motte-Picquet-Grenelle.

The mock-Alpine village that was built for the 1900 World Fair by the Eiffel Tower, has long gone (it was rebuilt in the '60s), but its tradition for trading in secondhand goods lives on thanks to some 150 antiques dealers who sell a range of collectables from furniture to knick-knacks.

***Open** 10.30am–7pm Thurs–Mon.*
www.levillagesuisseparis.com

FAST FACTS

Internet Café Tetranet Trocadéro, 129 rue de la Pompe,16th arr., *01 47 04 33 00*; ***www.tetranet.fr***. M° Trocadéro or Victor Hugo, open 9.30am–midnight Mon–Fri, 10.30am–midnight Sat, 1pm–9pm Sun and public holidays.

Pharmacy Pharmacie Kleber, 91 avenue Kléber, 16th arr., *01 47 27 95 09*, M° Trocadéro, open 8.30am–9pm Mon–Fri, 9am–8pm Sat–Sun.

Post Office La Poste, 56 rue Cler, 7th arr., *01 53 85 00 09*. M° Ecole Militaire or La Tour-Maubourg, open 9am–6pm Mon–Fri, 9am–12pm Sat.

Supermarket Monoprix, 2 rue de Commerce, 15th arr., *01 45 79 94 86*, open 9am–10pm Mon–Sat. **Franprix**, 56 rue Longchamp, 16th arr., *01 45 05 05 26*. M° Trocadéro, open 8.30am–9pm Mon–Sat.

FAMILY-FRIENDLY ACCOMMODATION

VERY EXPENSIVE

Les Jardins du Trocadéro

Place du Trocadéro/35 rue Benjamin Franklin, 16th arr., 01 53 70 17 70; ***www.jardintroc.com****. M° Trocadéro.*

This 1870s' building is distinctly Empire and lavishly kitted out with period furniture, soft draperies and fabrics you and the children will want to curl up in. Beaux-Arts students are responsible for the dreamy-looking muses and musical monkey frescos over the walls and doorways. The plush downstairs breakfast room doubles as a *salon de thé,* serving snacks and cakes all afternoon. The rooms are not gigantic (this is central Paris), but luxurious touches like jacuzzis please more than just the adults. Children are made to feel very welcome and, staying here, you'll be in walking distance of many main attractions.

Rooms *17.* ***Rates*** *299€–399€ doubles; 399€–599€ suites and family rooms; extra bed 49€–69€; cot 29€.* ***Credit*** *AmEx, MC, V.* ***Amenities*** *A/C, tearoom, bar, private parking (25€ night), babysitting (on request), Internet, lift.* ***In room*** *WiFi, safety box, TV.*

EXPENSIVE

Hôtel Trocadéro La Tour

5 bis rue Massenet, 16th arr. 01 45 24 43 03; ***www.trocadero-la-tour.com****. M° Passy.*

This modernised and charming hotel is listed as a 3-star, but is most definitely 3-star deluxe – something reflected in its prices. Décor is a mishmash of 1920s' Art Deco, Empire, and modern – with plenty of wooden panelling, marble floors, and plush carpet giving a hint of old-style class. The rooms (decorated with bright bedclothes) make up for their moderate size with decent storage space. On warm days the pretty breakfast room opens on to a leafy courtyard so you can all breakfast in the sunshine. As with many Parisian hotels, the lifts are small, so it is best to leave your buggy at reception.

Rooms *41.* ***Rates*** *240€–310€ doubles, 390€ family room, extra-bed 25€, cot (free).* ***Credit*** *AmEx, MC, V.* ***Amenities*** *A/C, bar, terrace, babysitting (on request), WiFi, Internet, lift, small pets allowed.* ***In room*** *Safe, sound-proofing, TV.*

MODERATE

Hôtel de la Tulipe

33 rue Malar, 7th arr. 01 45 51 67 21; ***www.hoteldelatulipe.com****. M° La Tour Maubourg.*

In Paris it's rare to feel like you're in the countryside, but this haven of peace pulls it off, with its rustic Provençal décor, a cobbled, honeysuckle-filled courtyard, and old walls and beams reminiscent of its days as a convent (until 1900). There are only two storeys (no lift), but two rooms in particular (one equipped for disabled guests) are on the ground floor, leading directly to the patio. This is ideal if you have toddlers. Breakfast is a treat, with buttery croissants freshly delivered every morning from a bakery round the corner. If there are more then three of you, enquire about the apartment for up to five.

Rooms *20.* ***Rates*** *140€–150€ doubles, 170€ triple, 270€ apartment, 1 cot only (free).* ***Amenities*** *babysitting on request, Internet, small pets allowed, private parking 26€.* ***In room*** *TV, safety box.*

INEXPENSIVE

Hôtel Valadon Paris

16 rue Valadon, 7th arr. 01 47 53 89 85; ***www.hotelvaladon.com****.*

M° Ecole Militaire. RER C Pont de l'Alma.

The owners made a bold decision when they decorated their budget hotel in huge black-and-white stripes with red trimmings; but it paid off. The whole place feels utterly original – a rarity in the French capital. All ten stripy bedrooms are triples, which makes this popular with families, and there's even a communal fridge where guests can leave lunchtime or evening picnics before eating them on the veranda – a thoughtful extra. Dog lovers can befriend Othello, the owners' gorgeous Harrier Beagle who likes guests and particularly children (and their sticky fingers). Breakfast is copious, with pastries and homemade jams, and can be enjoyed over a free newspaper, magazine, or novel found in the library area. Families can request an entire floor (two rooms per floor) or the Family Cottage (two bedrooms and a terrace), which is entirely non-smoking.

***Rooms** 10. **Rates** 125€–155€ doubles, 150€–170€ triples, extra beds for under-5s free. **In room** TV, fan, heating, safety box.*

FAMILY-FRIENDLY DINING

EXPENSIVE

The Eiffel Tower, Cineaqua aquarium, Bateaux Parisiens, and Quai Branly museum are all excellent family treats; but for an unforgettable gourmet adventure, off the tourist track, try this:

Atelier de Joël Robuchon

*5 rue de Montalembert, 7th arr. 01 42 22 56 56; **www.joel-robuchon.com**. M° Rue du Bac.*

Mr Robuchon is a household name in France, and his Atelier has been causing a stir (not just in the kitchen) ever since it first opened its dark wood and granite dining room in 2003. Well-dressed guests sit amid displays of bright red peppers and overhanging hams while they savour the chef's sophisticated takes on both French and world cuisine. You can expect delicacies like fresh whiting on a bed of potato purée with herb butter; a scallop served in its shell with truffle shavings, or frogs' legs fritters in garlic cream. This is not a place for unruly children, but families are welcome. There are two sittings per meal, but reservations are only taken for 11.30am and 6.30pm sittings.

***Open** 11.30am–3.30pm, 6.30pm–midnight daily. 3-course average 80€. Fixed-price 60€–125€ **Credit** MC, V.*

MODERATE

Chez L'Ami Jean

*27 rue Malar, 7th arr. 01 47 05 86 89; **www.amijean.com**. M° Invalides.*

This place is so popular there are two sittings and booking is essential. The reason for the hype is delicious southwest food like *petit salé* (gammon and lentils) cooked to perfection, and a laidback atmosphere reminiscent of grandma's dining room (providing she lived in southwest France). The 30€

menu is excellent value featuring delectables like pigeon terrine, *petits farcis* (stuffed courgettes) with Pyrenean lamb and parmesan, and traditional *riz au lait* – the French take on rice-pudding and a hit with children.

***Open** Noon–2pm, 7pm–midnight Tues–Sat. 3-course average 50€, fixed-price 30€. **Credit** MC, V.*

Le Troquet

21 rue François-Bonvin, 15th arr. ☎ 01 45 66 89 00. M° Sèvres-Lecourbe.

This foodies' haunt is off the beaten track. You may even find the street dodgy, but don't be fooled: hidden in this distinctly residential area, 15 minutes from the Eiffel Tower, this is chef Christian Etchebest's temple to Basque cuisine – where specialities such as squid (*chipirons*) with ewe's-milk cheese and piquillo peppers are served with cherry jam. If your children aren't adventurous with food, ask the waiters for a child alternative – otherwise, sit back, relax and let the experimentalist in you all take over.

***Open** Noon–2pm, 7.30–11.30pm Tues–Sat. Fixed menus 24€ (lunch), 28€, 30€. 3-course average 45€. **Credit** MC, V.*

INEXPENSIVE

Café Constant

139 rue St-Dominique, 7th arr. ☎ 01 47 53 73 34. M° Ecole Militaire, RER C Pont de l'Alma.

Michelin-starred chef Christian Constant bought this former *tabac* as a low-budget spin-off of his nearby (and very expensive) *Violin d'Ingres* restaurant. Low budget it may be – in fact he's hardly touched the décor – but there's nothing cheap about the quality of the hearty French cuisine that rolls out of the kitchen. We sat upstairs in the tiny dining area, drooling over peppery paté de campagne, steak with dauphinois potatoes, and fresh peach melba. Even the children ate every scrap. For the grown-ups the wine list is a pure gift, with some excellent Cahors and Bordeaux going from 14€.

***Open** Noon–2.30pm, 7pm–10.30pm Tues–Sat. 3-course average 28€. **Main Courses** from 11€. **Credit** MC, V.*

Le Kiosque

1 place de Mexico, 16th arr. ☎ 01 47 27 96 98. M° Trocadéro.

This little restaurant, near Trocadéro, will be a hit with the children thanks to a bicycle hanging from the ceiling, and bright red, green, and purple walls, covered in photographs. The owner used to be a magazine editor and pays homage to his days in journalism with a small kiosk (hence the restaurant name) offering magazines and newspapers. Food and wine draw inspiration from different French regions. When I went we were served delicious prawn-filled samosas with sweet-chilli dip for starters, followed by coriander and olive chicken, and a scrumptious strawberry tiramisu. The lunch menu is a bargain at 26€.

***Open** 12.15pm–3pm, 7.30–11pm daily. 3-course average 35€. Fixed menus: 25€, 26€, 30€. **Credit** AmEx, MC, V.*

5 From Opéra & the Grands Boulevards to Montmartre

OPÉRA TO MONTMARTRE

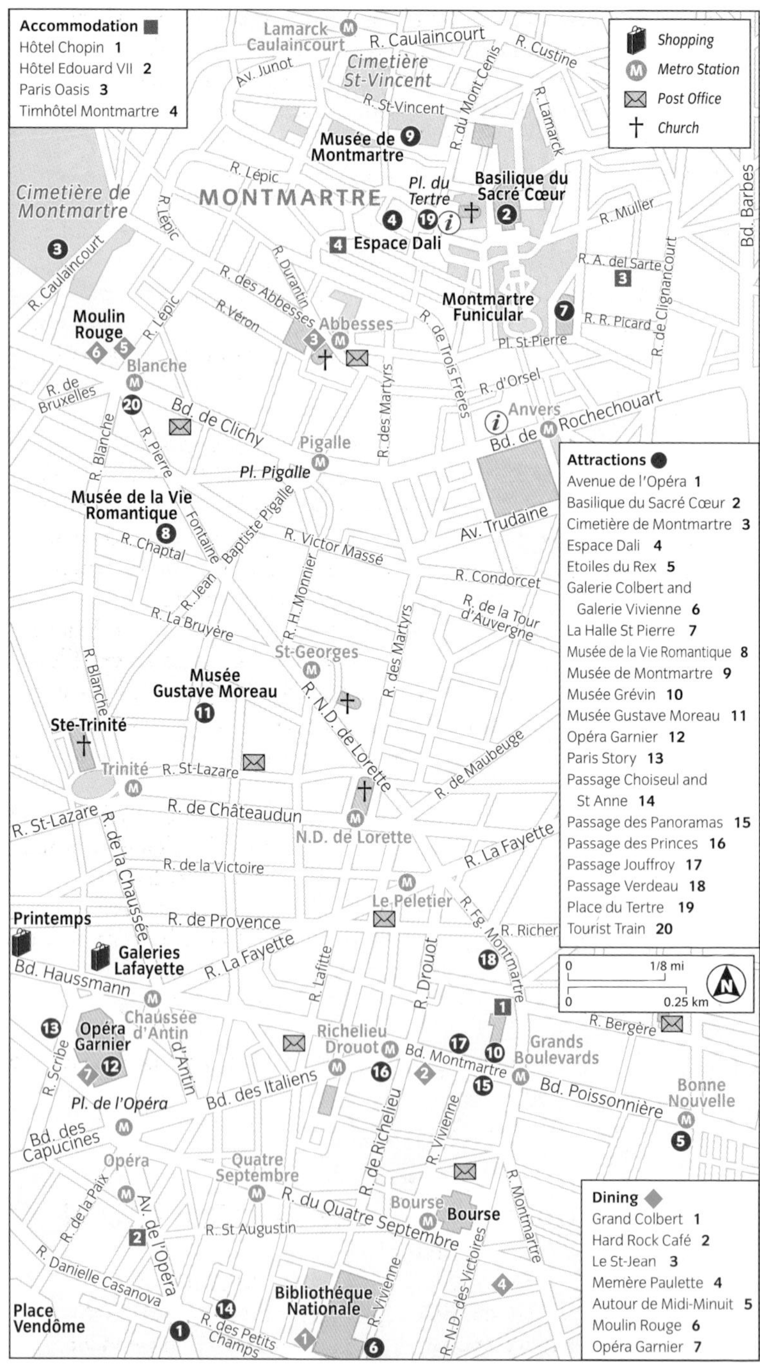

There are remnants of Paris's 19th-century splendour all around the Opéra and Grands Boulevards quarters, where modern-day shoppers, sightseers, bankers, and businessmen scurry in and out of buildings whose façades have changed little in 150 years. This is Napoléon III's Paris, shaped by his favourite city planner, Baron Haussmann, who recreated the city's urban structure, razing medieval quarters. Widening Louis XIV's bourgeois promenades (Grands Boulevards), he turned them into long avenues bustling with theatres, cafés, and department stores. But the jewel in the crown is Charles Garnier's sumptuous opera house (p. 100) – a temple to the arts ordered by Napoléon and so imposing it has given its name to the whole district.

Older Paris is found in delightful, atmospheric shopping arcades (*passages couverts* p. 105), dotted between the Grands Boulevards and Opéra, home to antiques and curiosity shops, tearooms, a waxwork museum for children (Musée Grévin, p. 99), and a giant children's toy store (Joué Club Village p. 114).

With a distinct village feel, the steep *Butte de Montmartre* (Montmartre Hill) is also a fabulous family spot with windmills, old artists' haunts, cabarets, vineyards (the grapes still harvested), and winding, cobbled streets that lead to panoramic views over the whole city. In summer, the steps in front of the Sacré Coeur are smothered with adults and children watching lively street performers.

Between the 9th arrondissement and Montmartre (between Pigalle and Place de Clichy), the main roads are covered with sex shops. The area is safe but visually explicit, so if you'd rather keep young eyes away, take the Métro directly to Abbesses, or walk up from Anvers Métro.

ORIENTATION

The Garnier Opera House, Galeries Lafayette, and Printemps department stores dominate the Opéra area (9th arr.), which is linked to Place de la République in the east by the long, wide Grands Boulevards. It can also be accessed from the Louvre, by the Avenue de l'Opéra, and from the Madeleine by Boulevard des Capucines. If you decide to walk, to help with navigation bear in mind that the Grands Boulevards run parallel to the Seine. Montmartre (18th arr.) borders the 9th arr. and is most easily accessed by Métro on line 12 (via Madeleine) or line 2 from the Champs-Elysées. Walking at a steady pace from the Opéra to the bottom of the Butte takes roughly 20 minutes (add 10 to 15 minutes if you have small children as it's hilly). Only the no. 95 bus (see Getting Around) offers direct access to Montmartre from Opéra.

GETTING AROUND

When in Montmartre the **Funiculaire** takes you to the Sacré Coeur – a godsend with small children and buggies. For steep Montmartre, the special **Montmartrobus** leaves from Pigalle for the village area. Other handy bus routes are no. **95,** which links Montparnasse to Place de Clichy, stopping in St Germain-des-Prés, by the Louvre and along Avenue de l'Opéra. No. **20** follows the Grands Boulevards and no. **30** follows the ring road below Montmartre.

VISITOR INFORMATION

The principal Tourist Office is on Rue des Pyramides, (25 rue des Pyramides, 1st arr., 10am–7pm Mon–Sat, 11am–7pm Sun and public holidays). There's a small booth at the exit of Anvers Métro station (open daily 10am–6pm); and another small office at 21 place du Tertre (open daily 10am–7pm). For all of these addresses call *08 92 68 30 00*; ***www.parisinfo.com***.

WHAT TO SEE & DO

Children's Top 5 Attractions

❶ **Being** photographed next to waxwork celebrities in the Musée Grévin (see p. 99).

❷ **Discovering** Montmartre's hidden secrets with your family (see p. 107).

❸ **Shopping** for toys in Joué Club Village (see p. 114).

❹ **Seeing** Paris at your feet from the top of the Sacré Coeur church (see p. 104).

❺ **Learning** how films are projected at the Grand Rex cinema (see p. 97).

Culture & Museums

Espace Dalí ★ AGES 7 AND ABOVE

*11 rue Poulbot, 18th arr. 01 42 64 40 10; **www.daliparis.com**. M° Anvers or Abbesses and then the Funicular.*

A sofa in the form of giant pink lips, an elephant with spindly legs carrying a pyramid on its back, and melting clocks are just some of the bizarre creations to fire your children's imagination in this small exhibition space devoted to the extravagant and Surrealist works of Salvador Dalí. The weird and wacky forms of his phantasmagorical sculptures (with easily recognisable, recurring themes – see p. 97 and p. 98) will be more accessible to younger children than his etchings. However, teenagers and parents will be able to appreciate the humorous and often philosophical messages in everything, including the wall art (sometimes rude) that completes the museum's collection. Because it's small this is a perfect choice for a quick museum fix (one hour is enough) and it's the only permanent Dalí collection in France.

***Open** 10am–6pm daily. **Admission** 10€ adults, 6€ 8–26s, free under-8s.*

Etoiles du Rex ★★

AGES 5 AND ABOVE

Le Grand Rex, 1 boulevard Poissonnière, 2nd arr. 01 45 08 93 58; ***www.legrandrex.com****. M° Bonne-Nouvelles.*

The Grand Rex Cinema stands proud as one of Europe's last remaining Art Deco picture houses (and the biggest, seating 2,800 people). It witnessed the golden age of cinema from the '20s to the '50s and by the '50s 'going to the Rex' meant not just seeing a film but, before and during the intermissions, a show featuring more than 36 dancers, 60 musicians, and a giant water extravaganza with 2,500 jets of water shooting 20m into the air alongside synchronised swimmers in an on-stage pool. The **Etoiles du Rex ★★** is an audio-guided visit taking you into the heart of cinema projection, backstage into the projection room, behind the giant screen, into the film-director's office, and into a special-effects room where your children can become Hollywood actors and remake scenes from famous movies, such as King Kong. In the sound room, they can learn how sound is added after filming; and the whole visit is finished off

Etoiles du Rex

in the projection room, where you can all laugh at the scenes you've just filmed. Audio-guides in English are provided for all the family. Films in English with French subtitles are also shown in the main cinema year round. Look for the letters VO (*version originale*) after the film title.

Open *10am–7pm Wed–Sun (and public holidays).* ***Admission*** *15.50€ adults, 13.50€ under-16s.*

FUN FACT Dalí in Montmartre

By the 1950s the Catalan genius had become a devoted resident of Montmartre. He loved its artistic heritage and its windmills, which reminded him of Cervantes's Don Quixote – the errant knight he longed to incarnate. In November 1956, he organised a press conference and set about creating the first engraving of his *Don Quixote* series using rhinoceros horns dipped in ink. The whole affair was captured on film so that he could verify the 'moral character' of his audience.

Dad What do Dalí's Sculptures Symbolise?

1. **Watches.** For every human being the notion of time is different from the time shown on a watch.
2. **Walking stick**. From the moment Dalí found a walking stick in the loft of his family home, he was never seen without it. It symbolises death and resurrection.
3. **Snail**. Softness or hardness and time that goes by slowly but surely.

La Halle St Pierre ★

AGES 6 AND ABOVE

2 rue Ronsard, 18th arr. ☎ 01 42 58 72 89; ***www.hallesaintpierre.org****. M° Anvers.*

At the foot of the Sacré Coeur and opposite the Saint Pierre fabric markets, La Halle Saint Pierre is an all-in-one *Art Brut* (Outsider Art – see p. 100) gallery, museum, bookshop, theatre, and café. It's a great place to introduce children to contemporary artistic creations. Don't miss the Halle's organic café, where you can rub shoulders with the artists over a healthy snack.

Open *10am–6pm daily (closed Sat and Sun in August).* ***Admission*** *7.50€ adults, 6€ under-25s.*

Musée de la Vie Romantique

VALUE **AGES 8 AND ABOVE**

16 rue Chaptal, 9th arr. ☎ 01 55 31 95 67; ***www.vie-romantique.paris.fr****. M° St-Georges, Blanche or Pigalle.*

In the early 19th century the sloping orchards and vegetable allotments below the village of Montmartre succumbed to the upper classes' appetite for large mansions with private gardens. Neoclassical *hôtels particuliers* (private townhouses), popped up all over the current 9th arrondissement. The Dutch painter, Ary Scheffer, moved into a pretty house at 16 rue Chaptal in 1830. Considered an exemplary artist of the Romantic movement, he taught the Duc of Orléans' children how to paint and became something of a local figure, welcoming the big names of art and politics into his home. Charles Dickens, Chopin, Rossini, Delacroix, Liszt, and George Sand were just some of his visitors and the whole place still feels like it's lived in.

But the real reason to bring your family (especially smaller children on whom the exhibits will be lost) is for the lovely rose garden and, in the shade of century-old trees and roses, the tearoom (open May to October) serving delicious snacks including scrumptious cakes made at **Les Cakes de Bertrand** tearoom (7 rue Bourdaloue, 9th arr.).

Open *10am–6pm Tues–Sun.* ***Admission*** *free for permanent collections. Prices vary for temporary exhibitions.*

Musée de Montmartre ★

AGES 7 AND ABOVE

*12 rue Cortot, 18th arr. ☎ 01 49 25 89 37; **www.museedumontmartre.fr**. M° Abbesses , Blanche or Anvers (then the Funicular).*

This museum is an oasis of calm and a fabulous way to recapture the atmosphere of old Montmartre, when it was a village separate from Paris. Don't expect to see major works of art – they're in the city's bigger museums: this is more about showing your children how Montmartre used to look, covered in windmills, vineyards, and vegetable patches. The building itself dates from the 17th century when it was the home of Roze de Rosimond, a member of Molière's theatre company. Other famous residents include Renoir, Dufy, and Utrillo. Nowadays, you can see old posters from the famous Chat Noir cabaret (now vanished), photos, etchings, porcelain, and a reconstruction of the Café de l'Abreuvoir that the painter Maurice Utrillo frequented (all too often). On a sunny day, spend time in the quiet garden and you'll feel like you've gone back in time.

INSIDER TIP

Follow your visit with a family walk around *La Butte* and discover the places you've seen in the museum, p. 107.

Open *11am–6pm Wed–Sun.* ***Admission*** *7€ adults, 5.50€ 11–26s, free under-10s.*

Musée Grévin ★★ ALL AGES

*10 boulevard de Montmartre, 9th arr. ☎ 01 47 70 85 05; **www.grevin.com**. M° Grands Boulevards or Richelieu Drouot.*

France's very own kitsch version of Madame Tussauds is a huge hit with families, who can get up close and personal with some 300 wax figures of international stars, artists, sportsmen, and historical figures. The sumptuous Belle-Époque 'Tout Paris' theatre (one of the best preserved in Paris) is where you can meet waxwork stars like Céline Dion, Monica Bellucci, and Elton John. There's also a 'Snap Shots of the 20th Century' section where important historical

FUN FACT **Movie Madness**

In the 1930s Parisians were mad about cinema. On the Grands Boulevards (see p. 106) there were no less than 100 picture houses, all of which popped up after Les Frères Lumière organised the world's first public film projection in the Grand Café, 4 boulevard des Capucines, on 28th December 1885 (nowadays a pleasant brasserie).

Although the Lumière brothers didn't invent moving pictures, they were the first to produce them for the public, the first showing a collection of 10 short films on subjects such as workers leaving the Lumières' factory in Lyon, bathing in the sea, or feeding a baby.

Definition of Art Brut

***Art Brut*, coined in 1945, categorises artistic creations made by** people with no artistic training and who produce art without following trends and without looking for recognition from the mainstream art world.

moments are recreated, such as Armstrong walking on the moon.

One of the most fascinating parts is the *Palais des Mirages* – an eerie hall of mirrors built for the 1900 World Fair and saved in 1906. After extensive renovations it tricks your eyes just like it did 100 years ago. A light and sound show, with music composed by Manu Katche (Sting, Peter Gabriel, and Dire Straits' drummer), makes for a unique experience.

The children I took, however, had a soft spot for the *Children's Corner* where youngsters (and grown-ups) are invited to touch the real hair, the fake eyes, and partially finished faces of the models, and learn about how they are put together.

INSIDER TIP

To avoid the queues, buy tickets online at ***www.grevin.com*** or in Fnac and Virgin stores.

Open *10am–6.30pm Mon–Fri, 10am–7pm Sat–Sun (last entry one hour before closing). From 9am during school holidays.* ***Admission*** *18€ adults, 10.50€ 6–14s, 9€ under 6s.*

Musée Gustave Moreau ★

AGES 13 AND ABOVE

14 rue de la Rochefoucauld, 9th arr. 01 48 74 38 50; ***www.musee-moreau.fr****. M° Trinité.*

The home and works of Symbolist painter Gustave Moreau (1825–98) are a must for teens and parents interested in 19th-century non-Impressionist art. Moreau was a mysterious painter, greatly influenced by Leonardo da Vinci, Michelangelo, Poussin, and Indian art, especially miniatures. He drew inspiration from Greek mythology, biblical stories, and his long-time unrequited love, Alexandrine Dureux. The building still feels like the painter's home where he lived on the first floor, and you'll notice the artist's passion for collecting furniture, knick-knacks, and portraits. Arranged by the artist on the second floor are canvases with mystical beasts, fantasy worlds, and writhing maidens, and on the top floor his masterpiece, *Jupiter and Semele*, featuring Semele struck down by Zeus's lightning, her child Dionysos – god of wine, agriculture, and theatre – clinging to her side.

Open *10am–12.45pm, 2pm–5.15pm Wed–Mon.* ***Admission*** *5€ adults, 3€ 19–26s, free under-18s.*

Opéra Garnier ★

AGES 8 AND ABOVE

Place de l'Opéra, 9th arr. 01 40 01 24 93; ***www.operadeparis.fr*** *M° Opéra, RER A Auber.*

Opéra Garnier

The most beautiful Napoléon III style building ever made is a masterpiece of 19th-century architecture, often referred to as 'the giant wedding cake', thanks to its domed roof and gilt statues. If your girls or boys are studying ballet or love dancing, take a tour of the building, or get tickets for a performance (see Nightlife, p. 116). The interior is a fairytale of marble staircases, imposing statues, and painted ceilings, including one, on the amphitheatre's central vaulted ceiling, by Marc Chagall (1962). Get your children to pick out the famous monuments in the painting (Eiffel Tower, Place de la Concorde, the Arc de Triomphe etc.). Back outside, take a look at the façade, where you can also see Carpeaux's famous *La Danse* sculpture – the original is in the Musée d'Orsay (see p. 154).

The Opéra Garnier was built for Napoléon III after a failed assassination attempt in 1858 at an opera house on Rue Peletier (9th arr.). The new space needed to be open enough to foil any potential attackers and include ramps big enough for Napoléon's carriage to enter. A national competition was won by the hitherto unknown 35-year-old Charles Garnier. Construction was thwarted by money, fire, the Franco-Prussian war and the discovery of a marsh below the foundations (turned into a permanent water source in case of fire and the inspiration behind Leroux's Phantom of the Opera, see p. 106) but eventually the theatre opened in 1875. The Opéra's shop, though small, sells some interesting souvenirs

New Athens

In the early 19th century, the north of the 9th arrondissement was so overrun with 19th-century imitations of ancient Greek and Renaissance architecture that it was nicknamed New Athens. Artists quickly moved in and created ateliers for visiting painters and writers. Among the famous, Eugène Delacroix lived at no. 58 rue Notre-Dame de Lorette (1844–57); Paul Gauguin was born next door at no. 56 (1848); and Pissarro lived at no. 49 (1856).

History of Montmartre

The sacred Roman hill dedicated to the god Mercury became the home of Benedictine monks in the Middle Ages. According to legend, St Denis (the first bishop of Paris, in the 3rd century AD) was beheaded at the top of the hill. Then, a miracle happened: St. Denis picked up his head and washed the blood from his face in a nearby fountain, before walking 6km to die as a martyr.

In the 12th century, the religious importance of the hill led to the building of the powerful Benedictine abbey, funded by Louis VI. The church, St-Pierre-de-Montmartre (next to the Sacré Coeur basilica), is the only remaining part of this Benedictine order.

Like most medieval abbeys, Montmartre's started producing its own wine and before long the hilltop was covered with vineyards. In the 16th century, the first windmills appeared, which were used to press grapes and grind the grain from surrounding villages. At one time there were 30; only two remain – the **Moulin de la Blute-Fin** and the **Moulin Radet** (labelled the Moulin de la Galette, see box right).

By the 18th century, Montmartre was a bustling village and source of Paris's wheat, wine, and gypsum (the famous Plaster of Paris came from here p. 104). The gypsum quarries closed in 1860 (the Métro *Blanche*, meaning white, was named after the colour of the quarries), the same year that Montmartre was annexed as part of Paris; and only one vineyard remains – more for nostalgia than wine.

But Montmartre never lost its village feel and in time, artists and poets moved in and created the legendary Montmartre art scene. Renoir and Utrillo painted street life and the **Bateau Lavoir** (13 place Emile Goudeau, 18th arr.), an old wash house converted into artists' studios, overflowed with talent: Max Jacob, Matisse, Apollinaire, and Braque all worked here, as did Picasso, who created *Les Demoiselles d'Avignon* on the premises in 1907.

Montmartre also became the scene of Paris's wildest nightlife. The **Moulin Rouge** (p. 115) cabaret attracted anyone in search of a good time and Montmartre's windmills were converted into popular 'anything goes' dance halls.

Today, the area is home to an increasingly hip crowd and a new generation of artists, who stick to the less touristy streets around Abbesses.

including Opéra honey (see p. 105).

Open *10am–5pm daily (from 1pm only on matinee performance days).* ***Admission*** *8€ adults, 4€ 11–25s, free under-10s.*

Paris Story AGES 8 AND ABOVE

11b rue Scribe, 9th arr. ☎ 01 42 66 62 06; ***www.paris-story.com****. M° Opéra; RER A Auber.*

On a rainy day, or to get your bearings before you sightsee,

Paris Story gives an overview of the French capital with a 50-minute film (projected on a 12m-wide screen) about Paris's history from its days as the Roman settlement Lutèce through the Middle Ages, the Revolution, Prussian invasions, Liberation from the Nazis in 1944, and other colourful, events. It's all a bit kitsch (Victor Hugo guides you with a serious, literary voice), but it's a good way to pick up historical titbits and familiarise your children with important monuments, museums, and works of art. After the film, an interactive model of Paris shows some 155 famous sites. Your family can have fun finding the street your hotel's on, follow a themed tour through gothic, revolutionary, or Da Vinci Code Paris, and trace the meridian line through town. At the end, five 3D screens (new technology means no need for glasses), show more highlights. Audio guides in English.

Open *10am–6pm (film every hour on the hour).* ***Admission*** *10€ adults, 6€ 6–18s, free under-6s; Family ticket (2 adults and 2 children) 26€.*

Tourist Train ★★ ALL AGES

Place Blanche, 18th arr. 01 42 62 24 00; ***www.promotrain.fr****. M° Blanche*

With children the hilly slopes of Montmartre make the tourist train an attractive option. It goes from Place Blanche near the Moulin Rouge to Place du Tertre, via the vineyards, Le Cimetière de Montmartre (cemetery p. 113) and La Halle and Marché St-Pierre (p. 115). You might lose face with

A Horror Story for the Children – Macabre Windmills

In the 19th century, just two windmills remained on the Butte de Montmartre (both visible on Rue Lepic); the Blute-Fin and the Moulin du Radet. Together they formed the famous *bal populaire* (dancehall), the **Moulin de la Galette**, immortalised by Toulouse-Lautrec, Van Gogh, Utrillo, and Renoir (whose version is in the Musée d'Orsay p. 154). During the 1814 Russian invasion of Paris, three brothers of the Debray milling family were killed defending their hill, while the fourth and his son hid in the Blute-Fin. When discovered, the father killed a Russian officer. In retaliation, the Russians seized the poor man and cut him into four – each piece attached to the sail of his windmill. His widow and son collected his remains and buried them in a tomb topped with a statue of a windmill, painted in red to signify their family's bloodshed. In 1889, that red windmill inspired entrepreneurs Odler and Zidler to create the Moulin Rouge (red windmill) cabaret.

Don't get confused: today's Moulin de la Galette restaurant on Rue Lepic (p. 109) is actually set inside the former Moulin du Radet.

Dinosaurs and Plaster of Paris

Montmartre has been mined for its fine, white gypsum since Gallo- Roman times – it is used to make decorative mouldings and the world-famous Plaster of Paris, so popular at one time that Parisians joked that there was more Montmartre gypsum in central Paris than in Montmartre. In the early 19th century the scientist Georges Cuvier discovered that Montmartre's gypsum contained fossils: the footprint of a small dinosaur and the remains of a prehistoric crocodile led him to discover that, millions of years ago, Paris had a tropical climate. Montmartre today is a hollow hill and ten times more likely to cave in than any other part of the city.

teenagers, but youngsters will love it, and there is an interesting commentary on the history of Montmartre.

Trains leave every 30 min (summer) and 45 min (winter) from 10am–6pm. Return trip: 5.50€ adults, 3.50€ under-10s. Single trip to the top: 3.50€ adults, free under-10s.

Places of Worship

Basilique du Sacré Coeur ★★

ALL AGES

Basilique du Sacré-Coeur de Montmartre, 18th arr. ☎ *01 53 41 89 00;* ***www.sacre-coeur-montmartre.com****. M° Anvers or Abbesses then Funicular.*

Atop the *butte* in Montmartre, the Sacré Coeur's multiple gleaming white domes and bell-tower loom over Paris. After France's 1870 defeat by the Prussians, the basilica was planned as an offering to cure France's misfortunes. Locals contributed the money to build it and construction began in 1876. Although not consecrated until 1919, perpetual prayers of adoration have been made here day and night since 1885. There's a huge mosaic of Christ under the main dome, the face visible wherever you stand in the church. The crypt contains what the devout believe is Christ's sacred heart – hence, the name of the church – but the main attraction for families is the greatest panorama in the capital★★: from the gallery around the church's inner dome, there's a sweep of the city, extending for 48km into the Ile de France.

Basilique du Sacré Coeur

***Open** 9am–6pm daily. **Admission** free to basilica, 6€ joint ticket to Dome and Crypt. Warning: there is no buggy access to the dome or crypt, and the many steps may be difficult for young children to climb.*

Streets & Monuments

Passages Couverts (arcades) ★

Dotted around the 2nd and 9th arrondissements, Paris's 18th- and 19th-century arcades are some of the most original and mysterious places in Paris. Originally built as shortcuts between the main boulevards, they fell into disuse in the early 1900s, but were revamped in the 1970s.

Passage Jouffroy (9th arr., M° Grands Boulevards), built in 1847, looks like it belongs in a Dickens novel with its old bookshops, sweetshop, and a novelty cane shop (advertised by a huge pair of antlers hanging outside). The Musée Grévin (p. 99) and Hôtel Chopin (p. 118) are also tucked away in one corner. Following on from Jouffroy, the **Passage Verdeau** (also built in 1847) displays some lovely façades behind which you'll find antique shops, more bookshops, and a particularly good camera shop (Photo Verdeau, no. 14), selling old and rare models. **Passage des Panoramas** (2nd arr., M° Bourse or Grands

Passage Jouffroy

Boulevards) was built in 1834 and is the hunting ground for passionate stamp and postcard collectors. **Galerie Colbert** and **Galerie Vivienne** (2nd arr., M° Bourse or Quatre-Septembre), built in 1823, feature the most luxurious architecture, a few boutiques, a lovely tearoom, and a good restaurant.

Passage des Princes (2nd arr., M° Richelieu Drouot) was built in 1860 linking Boulevard des Italiens with Rue de Richelieu and houses the outstanding toyshop **Joué Club Village**, And finally, the **Passages Choiseul and Saint**

FUN FACT › Opéra Honey

Ballet dancers and sightseers aren't the only ones to buzz around the Opéra. Bees – thousands of them – inhabit parts of the roof. Their honey is sold in the Opéra's shop and gourmet food stores such as Fauchon.

The Phantom of the Opera

The composer Andrew Lloyd-Webber made the Phantom of the Opera world famous but his musical was based on a 19th-century romantic horror story by the French author Gaston Leroux. The man-made lake beneath the Garnier opera house inspired him to write a macabre tragedy, printed weekly, about Erik, an eccentric, physically deformed genius who terrorises the theatre by pretending to be a ghost (the *fantôme*). He makes the underground lake his home and takes the beautiful soprano Christine under his wing. The consequences are, as everybody knows, disastrous. *Le Fantôme de l'Opéra* was translated into English in 1911 and makes good reading for teenagers.

Anne (2nd arr., M° Bourse or Quatre-Septembre) have hardly changed since their construction in 1829 – although today's cheap shops, galleries, and snack bars give them a 1970s' feel.

Avenue de l'Opéra

2nd arr. M° Palais Royal, Pyramides, Opéra, Quatre-Septembre or RER A Auber.

Shops, law firms, and businesses line the Avenue de l'Opéra – so called thanks to the dramatic view of the Garnier Opera House when looking up from the Louvre. Completed in 1876, it is the only avenue in Paris not to have any trees and a perfect example of how architect Baron Haussmann dramatically modernised Paris by clearing the medieval city to create wide, open boulevards. In doing so he flattened the mound where Joan of Arc started her crusade against the English (to locate it stand with your children outside today's Monoprix supermarket and look to the middle of the road). The unified five-storey buildings along the street are typical of the Haussmann style (see p. 110) and contrast heavily with the narrower surrounding 17th- and 18th-century buildings and covered passages.

Les Grands Boulevards

Although Haussmann is remembered for his long, wide thoroughfares, the parts known as the Grands Boulevards were in fact built in the 17th century under the rule of Louis XIV, to convert Louis XIII's city walls (from Madeleine to Place de la République) into a fashionable promenade. Eight broad avenues – Madeleine, Capucines, Italiens, Montmartre, Poissonnière, Bonne Nouvelle, St-Denis, and St-Martin – became places of entertainment, crowded with street sellers, hawkers, entertainers, and cafés. In the 19th century, Haussmann extended and widened them but they still offer a glimpse of their previous uses. Walking from Opéra to République you'll go past chic shops and cafés, the red light district of Saint Denis, and numerous theatres – remnants of a time when theatre was the only affordable entertainment for ordinary people. The term *théâtre du boulevard*, meaning 'low-brow theatre' comes from these boulevards.

Parks & the Outdoors

A Family Walk around Montmartre

Montmartre is one of the most enchanting places you can bring your family. Its village atmosphere is a long way from the bustle of the big city, the views over Paris are stunning, and your children will be excited to find windmills, vines, cobbled streets and houses, and cafés that look like giant toys rather than real buildings. This walk takes you from **Abbesses Métro** to just beyond **Place du Tertre** and should take less than two hours (see map p. 109), depending on how fast you walk and how many times you stop in cafés, shops, and museums. At the end you can easily carry on into the Sacré Coeur basilica (p. 104), the St-Pierre fabric market (p. 115), the Halle St-Pierre Art Brut museum (p. 96), or walk towards the Musée de la Vie Romantique (p. 98) or Musée Gustave Moreau (p. 100) in the 9th arr.

❶ Abbesses Métro

This is the deepest in the city – 116 ft below street level and, if you're feeling energetic, you could climb the never-ending staircase to show the children the vast fresco of Montmartre scenes created by local artists. You can also take the lift. Designed by Hector Guimard in Art Nouveau style, the Métro entrance is a shell of swirling glass and iron.

The Art Nouveau entrance at Abbesses Metro

FUN FACT Sacré Coeur

To support the weight of the Sacré Coeur and its 17-tonne bell, the hollow Butte had to be reinforced with 83 stone pillars, 38m deep, and joined by stone arches.

❷ Place des Abbesses

This is the centrepiece of the neighbourhood, overlooked by the L'Eglise St-Jean-l'Evangéliste – a redbrick church, completed in 1904, and the first church built of reinforced concrete.

With the church behind you turn left up Rue des Abbesses, a lively street of shops, boutiques, cafes, and restaurants.

INSIDER TIP

As you pass Rue Tholozé on your right, look up to see the adorable windmill Blute-Fin (part of the Moulin de la Galette).

Just past the Rue Tholozé where Rue des Abbesses branches off into Rue Lepic, turn right northwards (go to ❹.) unless your family want to see the famous café (❸) where Amélie worked in the film, in which case you should bear left.

Jazz at Place des Abbesses

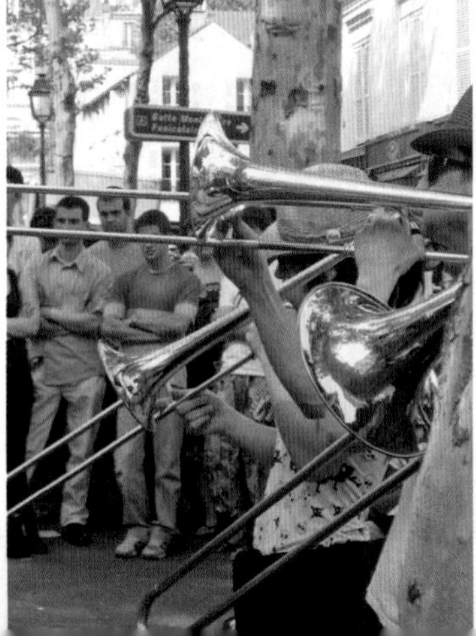

❸ Café des Deux Moulins

Amélie was a quirky French film by Jean-Pierre Jeunet, set in Montmartre, that became an international hit when released in 2001. Amélie Poulain (played by Audrey Tautou) worked as a waitress at the Café des Deux Moulins on Rue Lepic (intersection of Rue Cauchois). Inside, the 1950s' decor, the mustard-coloured ceiling, and the lace curtains are all intact, so if you're in the mood for a quick coffee, this is as good a spot as any.

Retrace your steps north on Rue Lepic, then turn left where it merges with Rue des Abbesses.

❹ Vincent Van Gogh's flat

As Rue Lepic climbs towards the top of the hill, look out for no. 54 on your right. Vincent van Gogh and his brother, Théo, lived here from 1886 to 1888 on the third floor. The gardens and windmills of Montmartre inspired a number of van Gogh paintings and during his time in Montmartre, he became friendly with the painters Toulouse-Lautrec, Gauguin, and Signac.

Continue along Rue Lepic until the windmills are on your left.

❺ Les Moulins (The Windmills)

The Moulin Blute-Fin and Moulin Radet together formed

FAMILY WALK IN MONTMARTRE

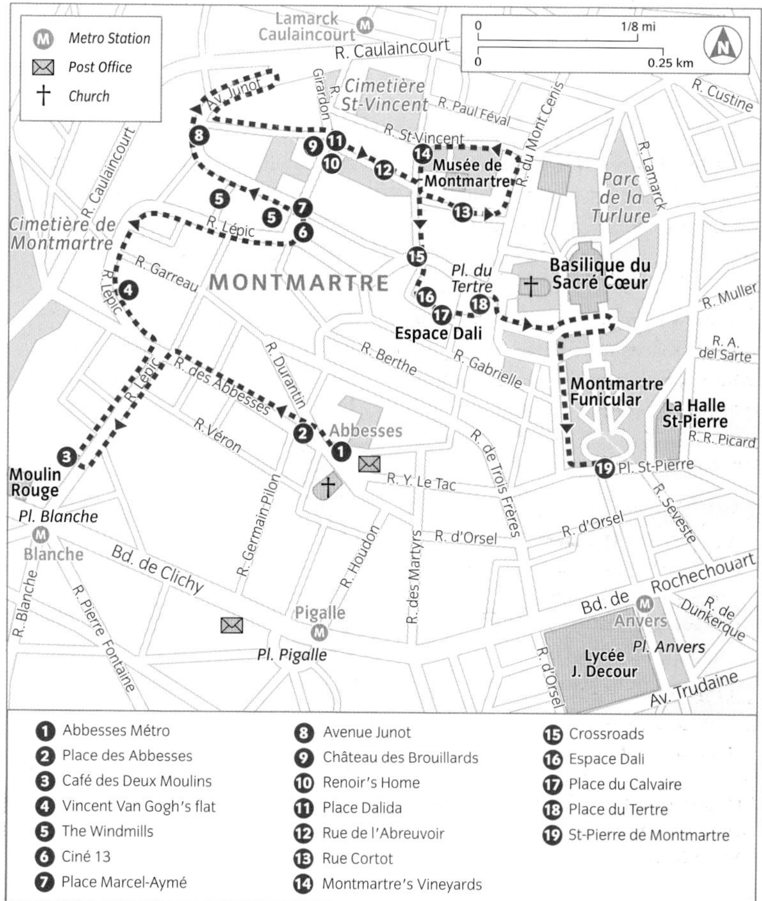

the Moulin de la Galette dance-hall, frequented by Toulouse-Lautrec, van Gogh, Utrillo, and Renoir (also see box p. 103). Nowadays the Blute-Fin mill is private property (protected by radars and guard dogs).

Moulin Radet, at the corner of Rue Lepic and Rue Girardon, is now a pleasant French restaurant called the Moulin de la Galette and, if you're hungry, this a good place for a family lunch.

Take a left on Rue Girardon.

❻ Ciné 13

At the intersection with Avenue Junot, Ciné 13, is a tiny theatre owned by film director Claude Lelouche. Facing the theatre, on the right, is the gated entrance to a private compound. Children find it amusing to read the names

FUN FACT Recognise Haussmann-style

1 They all have 5 storeys plus servants' quarters under the roof (6th floor), and made from cream-coloured stone, usually limestone.
2 A wrought-iron, decorative balcony always covers the 2nd and 5th floors. The 3rd and 4th floors only have decorative window guards.
3 The slate roofs are always punctuated with skylights into the servants' quarters on the top floor.
4 A building never stands alone; it is always part of a block.
5 The roofs are always slanted at 45 degrees.

on the outside intercom: to keep the exclusive residents anonymous, aliases read like a who's who of French art with supposed tenants such as Degas, Matisse, Utrillo, and Toulouse-Lautrec.

With the Ciné 13 behind you walk towards the Place Marcel-Aymé (ahead on the right)

❼ Place Marcel-Aymé

This square was named after the writer Marcel Aymé, who lived in the building here until his death in 1967. The first thing your children will notice is the sculpture of a man emerging from the wall. It was inspired by Aymé's short story the *Passe-Muraille,* 'The Man Who Could Walk Through Walls', which tells how a petty bureaucrat who used his superhuman powers for mischief, got trapped inside a wall forever. Tip: if your children are young enough to believe, get them to put their ears to the wall to see if they can hear the man shouting to get out.

Facing the Ciné 13, turn right down Avenue Junot, a curving street planted with linden trees.

❽ Avenue Junot

No. 11, on the left, is an artists' hamlet where Maurice Utrillo lived from 1926 to 1937. Utrillo was born in Montmartre in 1883, and painted many neighbourhood street scenes. **No. 13** was the studio of Francis Poulbot, a designer known for his drawings of street urchins. His distinctive illustrations gave rise to the term *petits poulbots* to describe street urchins. Several of his designs decorate the top of the building.

No. 15 was the home of Romanian-born French poet Tristan Tzara, best known as the founder of the Dadaist movement. Tzara's house gives no ground to frivolous decoration – all-white cement on a beige stone block. At **no. 23** is the unusual leafy passage, M18 where, should you venture up it, you'll find a mysterious rock on the left known as *le rocher de la sorcière,* or 'The Witch's Rock'. Get your children to put their hand on the rock and make a wish.

Back on the avenue, **no. 25** is the Villa Léandre (built in 1926) – a short cul-de-sac of houses that look so English that one, on the right, bears the sign 10 Downing Street.

Back on Avenue Junot, walk down the hill, then turn right at Rue Simon-Dereure.

9 Château des Brouillards

Down the street on your right is an entrance to the pretty square Suzanne-Buisson, the former grounds of an 18th-century white country manor known as the Château des Brouillards (Fog Castle) named after the mist that crept up from a nearby spring when the water contacted the cold morning air. The mansion became a shelter for homeless and impoverished artists around 1890. A family of musicians has been living here since 1928.

Take the stairs on the left that lead to the Allée des Brouillards.

10 Renoir's Home

This tranquil path leads past a number of massive houses, including the studio and family home of Pierre-Auguste Renoir from 1890 to 1897 at no. 6.

Walk to the end of the Allée des Brouillards to Place Dalida.

11 Place Dalida

Yolanda Gigliotti, aka Dalida, was one of Montmartre's most beloved residents and one of France's biggest stars, recording hundreds of hits and winning 70 gold records. Dalida's personal life was less successful however: three of her ex-lovers killed themselves and after at least one attempt of her own, Dalida committed suicide in 1987. Her statue looks out on one of the most prototypical views of Montmartre: a cobbled lane leading up a hill with the Sacré Coeur in the background.

Take the road opposite, the Rue de l'Abreuvoir.

12 Rue de l'Abreuvoir

This leafy street was a country lane used by horses and cattle on their way to the *abreuvoir* (watering trough). The Café de l'Abreuvoir, a former artists' hangout, was at **no. 14**. Impressionist painter Camille Pissarro rented **no. 12** as a *pied-à-terre* between 1888 and 1892. The ivy-covered cottage at **no. 4** belonged to Henry Lachouque, the noted historian of Napoléon, whose symbol was an eagle. Test your children's French by getting them to translate the legend on the sundial next to the rooster: QUAND IV SONNERA, JE CHANTERAI – 'when four rings, I'll sing.' The charming little café at **no. 2**, La Maison Rose, was made famous by Utrillo in one of his first successful paintings.

Cross Rue des Saules and walk down Rue Cortot.

FUN FACT **What's in a Name?**

The word boulevard derives from the Middle Dutch word *Bulwerc*, meaning ramparts – in this case Louis XIII's ramparts.

⓭ Rue Cortot

You might be so absorbed in looking around this pretty street that you walk right past the 17th-century building that houses the **Musée de Montmartre** (**no 12**, see p. 99). At **no. 6**, composer Erik Satie lived in a tiny room he called his 'closet.' He earned his living banging out tunes in Montmartre cabarets, and in his spare time composed the haunting piano cycles *Les Sarabandes, Les Gymnopédies,* and *Les Gnossiennes.*

Walk to the end of Rue Cortot. Turn left on Rue du Mont-Cenis and go down the stairs. Turn left on Rue St-Vincent.

⓮ Montmartre's Vineyards

Down the street you'll find the **Vignes de Montmartre**, the last remaining vineyard in Paris. On your right is **Au Lapin Agile**, a working cabaret so named in 1880 after artist André Gill who painted a picture of a rabbit (*lapin*) in a bow tie on the front. People began saying that it was the *Lapin à Gill* (Gill's Rabbit), which gradually changed into *Lapin Agile* (agile rabbit). Picasso, Renoir, and Utrillo were just some of the young upstarts that came for wine, women, and song.

Montmartre's Vineyard

Turn left up Rue des Saules and walk to the corner of Rue Norvins and Rue St-Rustique.

⓯ Crossroads

This crossroads was frequently painted by Utrillo, only his version didn't have the shops selling postcards and T-shirts.

Walk up Rue Norvins a few feet and turn right on Rue Poulbot.

⓰ Espace Dalí

Follow the curve to **no. 11** to see a permanent display of Dalí's works (see p. 96).

If you're coming out of the museum, turn left.

⓱ Place du Calvaire

Here you have a wonderful panoramic view of the back of Paris. If your children are football or rugby mad, they can try to spot the *Stade de France* in the distance.

Turn left and walk straight on.

⓲ Place du Tertre ★★

ALL AGES

Place du Tertre, 18th arr. M° Abbesses or Anvers then the funicular.

This is one of the most frequented tourist spots in Paris – if not the world. More than 6 million people visit this small, cobbled square *tertre* (hillock or a mound in old French) every year. It's the highest point in Paris at some 130m, and drips with touristy restaurants and cafés selling crêpes and ice cream. During the 19th century, Montmartre's artists traditionally exhibited their paintings here – and it's a legacy that continues today with dozens of so-called 'artistes' who paint the local streets and do caricatures. You won't be looking at the next Picasso; nevertheless, a few euros for a portrait or a caricature of your children is money well spent and a fun experience for the youngsters who can be the centre of everyone's attention.

Walk across the square to Rue Norvins, then take a right.

⑲ St-Pierre de Montmartre

Behind the Sacré Coeur basilica you can show your family one of the oldest churches in Paris – the last remnant of a Benedictine abbey that held sway in Montmartre until the Revolution. The chancel and the nave date from 1147 when the church was consecrated. The west façade through which you enter was reconstructed in the 18th century.

Tip: *If you're fed up of walking, the funicular takes you down the steep flights of steps effortlessly.*

Spooky Paris

Cimetière de Montmartre

ALL AGES

20 avenue Rachel, 18th arr. M° Place de Clichy or Blanche.

This final resting place is second in fame only to Père-Lachaise cemetery (see p. 248). Established in 1795 you'll find some of Paris's most famous defunct inhabitants. The graveyard, with its house-like tombs, maze-like streets, weird and wonderful statues, hidden staircases, and sometimes over-grown flora, is quite exciting for children, who feel like they're in a forbidden land where ghosts could jump out at any moment. In reality, it's a peaceful spot and a place to see the final haunts of people like Emile Zola, the French novelist who made his living as a journalist (as a novelist, he was once so poor he had to sell his raincoat and trousers and stay at home working in only his shirt); the French painter Jean-Honoré Fragonard; Impressionist painter Hilaire Germain Edgar Degas; New-Wave film director François Truffaut; and Vaslav Nijinsky,

Cimetière de Montmartre

the Russian-born ballet dancer. Don't forget to grab a map on your way in or you'll easily get lost.

***Open** 8am–5.30pm 6 Nov–15 Mar; 8am–6pm 16 Mar–5 Nov (9am–5.30pm Sun and public holidays).*

Shopping

Along Boulevard Haussmann, you'll find the flagship department stores **Galeries Lafayette ★★** (no. 40) and **Printemps ★★** (no. 64) and a host of high-street offerings such as **H&M** (no. 54), **Zara** (no. 39), and **C&A** (no. 49, which here still provides a range of cheap adults' and children's wear). Galeries Lafayette is famous for its stunning Art Nouveau cupola, underneath which clothes by more than 90 established designers, high-street brands and Parisian creators sit alongside lingerie, make-up, jewellery, perfume, and toys. On the first floor **Galeries Lafayette Gourmet ★★** is a foodie's paradise with nosh galore and wonderful high-end take-away sections; and just over the road, **Galeries Lafayette Maison** is five floors dedicated to home design. **Printemps** houses the largest shoe department in Paris, with more than 200 different labels. The household section, **Printemps de la Maison**, has excellent kitchenware, home decoration and furniture, and for a quick pitstop, the Paul Smith decorated **World Bar ★** restaurant on the 5th floor of the men's department is great for lunch, with décor that'll amuse the children (think chairs that would look at home in a crèche) and decent French cuisine. The 9th floor in the main building also sports a brand new restaurant-cum-tearoom underneath a Belle Époque glass dome. Other areas with an interesting mix of shops suitable for families are **Rue des Abbesses** in Montmartre (18th arr., M° Abbesses) and **Rue des Martyrs** just below (9th arr., M° Notre-Dame de Lorette).

Books

For literature, newspapers, magazines, and children's books in English, the American bookstore **Brentano's** (37 avenue de l'Opéra, *01 42 61 52 50;* 2nd arr., M° Opéra.) has an excellent choice, plus a few gifts and cards. The children's section in the basement has a wide range of storybooks, plus French-language books aimed at French learners.

Just for children

With over 2,000 sq m of space devoted to toys, dolls, teddies, and games, **Joué Club Village ★★** (3–5 boulevard des Italiens, *01 53 45 41 41*; ***www.villagejoueclub.com***. 2nd arr. M° Richelieu Drouot. Open 10am–8pm Mon–Sat) is a children's dream and the biggest toy shop in Paris. Set in the beautifully conserved **Passage des Princes** more than 12 different sections sell everything from Lego to board games, dolls and jigsaw puzzles. **Section 4** has hundreds of models to choose from. For educational games and activities, head to **section 3**; modelling kits for aeroplanes, ships, and houses can be bought in **section 7**; a special department for under 4s is in **section 5**; and you'll find masks and party costumes for all ages in **section 11**.

INSIDER TIP
For uninterested teens there's an Internet café and video games centre just next door with enough high-action machines to keep them occupied for hours.

Markets ★★

There is a small food market around the classy **Place du Marché St-Honoré** (12.30pm–8pm Wed and Sat, M° Pyramides) and at the **Bourse** (12.30pm–8.30pm Tues and Fri, M° Bourse), but the main draw in these districts is the **Marché St-Pierre** fabric market at the base of the Sacré Coeur (10am–6.30pm Mon–Sat, M° Anvers) where the whole of Paris rolls up for bargain fabrics. **Dreyfus** is one of the best established, with little model dolls dressed up in outfits made from the fabrics on sale – inspiration for little girls and boys interested in fashion. Warning: the crowds round here know how to use their elbows!

Nightlife

Autour de Midi-Minuit ★★

AGES 12 AND UP

*11 rue Lepic, 18th arr. ☎ 01 55 79 16 48; **www.autourdemidi.fr**. M° Blanche.*

Paris and jazz go hand in hand, so if you're coming with older children or teenagers and want to see where Parisians go for some syncopated rhythm and a good old be-bop, this jazz club and restaurant is in a great spot just above the Moulin Rouge, and a fine way to combine dinner with an evening concert. The traditional French cuisine, served in the main café, is never disappointing, and the music, performed in the vaulted cellar, is always by well-established local and international musicians.

***Open** 12pm–2.30pm, 7pm–11pm Tues–Sun. Shows usually start at 9.30pm Tues–Sat. **Admission** varies. **Credit** MC, V.*

Moulin Rouge ★

AGES 6 AND ABOVE

*82 boulevard de Clichy, 18th arr. ☎ 01 53 09 82 82; **www.moulinrouge.fr**. M° Blanche*

The most famous cabaret in the world is the only place in Paris

The windmill of the Moulin Rouge

still to perform the traditional Cancan: in fact it created the dance, originally called *Quadrille Réaliste*, back in 1889, to please crowds of raucous men looking for a good time. Nowadays, the affair (a show called *Féerie*) is far more wholesome, and a great place to bring your over-6s, who will be mesmerised by the sparkly costumes, feather head-dresses, ever-changing shimmering sets, a giant aquarium with boa constrictors, and funny ventriloquists and magicians that intersperse the dance numbers. Sixty bare-breasted Doriss Girls do still strut their stuff, but as far as children are concerned, that will be secondary to the perfectly synchronised dancing and cheesy songs. For dinner (7pm) you have a choice of three menus plus vegetarian. Unlike at the Lido, there is no special children's meal, but dishes can be ordered à la carte and children between 6 and 12 get half-price show tickets. Show-only tickets include a half-bottle of champagne. Elegant attire is mandatory (no shorts, trainers or sportswear – even the children).

Dinner 7pm daily; champagne-revue 9pm and 11pm daily. Dinner 145€–175€, champagne-revue 99€ at 9pm and 89€ at 10pm. ***Credit*** *AmEx, MC, V.*

Opéra Garnier ★★

AGES 6 AND ABOVE

Place de l'Opéra, 9th arr. 📞 08 92 89 90 90 (in France) and 📞 +33 172 29 35 35 (from abroad); ***www.operadeparis.fr****. M° Opéra or Chaussée d'Antin Lafayette; RER A Auber.*

A performance in Paris's Opéra Garnier is a truly memorable experience and since the Opéra de Bastille opened in 1989 almost exclusively for opera (including special family-orientated performances), the Garnier's programme has focused on a mix of traditional ballet and contemporary dance performed by the resident **Ballet de l'Opéra de Paris** or visiting international companies. Book well ahead. You can try your luck on the night (reduced tickets are sometimes available), but will probably get the worst seats. Tickets can be bought at branches of Fnac, Virgin Megastore, on the Garnier's website, or by phone.

Show times vary. Prices from 80€–100€. ***Credit*** *AmEx, MC, V.*

FAST FACTS

Internet Café Cybernity, 74 rue de Clichy, 9th arr., 📞 *01 45 26 02 67*; M° Place de Clichy. Open 9am–midnight daily.

Pharmacy Pharmacie Haussmann, 19 boulevard Haussmann, 9th arr., 📞 *01 47 70 83 88*, M° Chausée d'Antin Lafayette. Open 8am–7.30pm Mon–Fri, 11am–7.30pm Sat.

Post Office La Poste, 19 rue Chauchat, 9th arr., 📞 *01 44 83 87 47*. M° Le Peletier or Richelieu Drouot. Open 8.30pm–7pm Mon–Fri or 8 rue des Abbesses, 18th arr., 📞 *01 53 09 93 20*. M° Abbesses. Open 8am–7pm Mon–Fri, 8am–noon Sat.

Supermarket Monoprix, 21 avenue de l'Opéra, 1st arr. M° Pyramides. *01 42 61 78 08*. 9am–10pm Mon–Fri (until 9pm Sat).

FAMILY-FRIENDLY ACCOMMODATION

MODERATE

Paris Oasis ★★ VALUE

Rue André del Sarte, 18th arr. 01 42 55 95 16; ***www.paris-oasis.com****. M° Anvers.*

Just imagine having your own family apartment with heated swimming pool in the middle of Montmartre: stay in this charming guest house, where devoted owner Hélène spoils her guests rotten, and that's just what you'll get. Almost all of the one- and two-bedroom flats have their own kitchenette, which gives the option of self-catering (although there are plenty of restaurants and cafés nearby); there's a charming little garden, bursting with greenery (great for the little ones as it's away from the road). If you are coming with babies, only the Lucie loft and the Liette studio have cots. For families with older children you could rent two separate apartments. Note: cash only. Minimum stay is three nights. A deposit in traveller's cheques or a bank transfer is required to secure bookings.

Rooms *6.* ***Rates*** *Jack's room (1 person) 60€, Iris's room, Amélie's studio and Nino studio 100€, Lucie loft 130€–180€, Liette studio 150€–200€, cot (free).* ***Credit*** *Cash only.* ***Amenities*** *TV, DVD, free Internet, heated swimming pool, linen, kitchenette.*

Hotel Ambassador ★

16 boulevard Haussmann, 9th arr. 01 44 83 40 40; ***www.hotelambassador-paris.com****. M° Chausee d'Antin Lafayette.*

This chic Haussmann-era hotel, just 2 minutes from the Galeries Lafayette and Printemps department stores, is a great choice for large families in need of two bedrooms, with 50% off the price of the second room (availability permitting). This can save you quite a bit of money. Connecting rooms and triples are also available. Décor is thoroughly modern with an Art Deco twist; there's a good on-site restaurant if you don't fancy going out. The Butte de Montmartre is also just a pleasant 15-to-20-minute walk away, as is the Louvre.

Rates *Doubles 230€–400€, Suites 500–900€. Cot (free). Units: 294. Amenities: A/C, bar, Wifi (in lobby), babysitting (on request), ADSL, gym. In-room: Safe, sound-proofing, minibar, TV.* ***Credit*** *MC, V, AmEx.*

Timhôtel Montmartre ★

11 rue Ravignan, 18th arr. 01 42 55 74 79; ***www.my-paris-hotel.com****. M° Abbesses or Blanche*

Perched high on Place Emile-Goudeau, right next to the former Bateau-Lavoir artists' workshop, this chocolate-box hotel looks so picture-perfect you'd be forgiven for taking snap shots to send home as postcards. That and reasonable prices make it popular with families looking to be in the heart of Montmartre.

Vegetarian Grain de Folie

For a warming vegetarian meal in a cosy restaurant (maximum 14), this homely address, hidden on a cobbled backstreet in Montmartre, serves delicious soup (a mini-meal in itself) and fresh vegetable dishes such as avocado with Roquefort, vegetable pâté, and a scrumptious apple and hazelnut tart – delicious treats for all the family, vegetarian or not.
24 rue de la Vieuville, 18th arr., M° Abbesses.

The renovated rooms are tasteful and comfortable, and children are well catered for with the option of extra beds and cots. Specially designed family rooms can take up to five and rooms on the 4th or 5th floors have breathtaking views over Paris.

***Rooms** 60. **Rates** 85€–95€ doubles, 180€ triples and suites. Cot free. Check the website for deals with under-12s. A Sunday-night stay is usually 25% cheaper than on other days. **Credit** AmEx, MC, V. **Amenities** lift (useful for buggies), WiFi. **In room** TV, safety box. Small animals permitted.*

INEXPENSIVE

Hôtel Chopin ★★

*46 passage Jouffroy/10 boulevard de Montmartre, 9th arr. 01 47 70 58 10; **www.hotelbretonnerie.com/chopin** M° Richelieu Drout.*

Smack-bang in the middle of Paris's most atmospheric covered arcade (Jouffroy see p. 105), and right next to the Musée Grévin, this budget hotel (built at the same time as the arcade in 1846) is a bargain, considering its central location, and it's great for families of three or four with extra beds and cots free in Category 2 priced rooms. The whole place feels attractively old-fashioned, almost like you're in the middle of a 19th-century novel. The only downside is views that mostly look out on to surrounding buildings. However, top floor rooms have typical Paris rooftop panoramas.

***Rooms** 36. **Rates** 68€–76€ singles, 81€–92€ doubles, 109€ triple. Extra bed and cots free. **Credit** MC, V. **Amenities** lift. **In room** TV, safety box.*

FAMILY-FRIENDLY DINING

When it comes to food, the Opéra, Grands Boulevards, and Montmartre districts are one big paradox: while some streets are full of restaurants and cafés, others have hardly any at all – and when tummies rumble, the last place you want to be is in one of the latter. So, for an off-the-cuff family meal, fail-safe streets to try are **Rue St-Anne** (2nd arr., M° Pyramides or Quatre-Septembre) with its dozens of authentic Japanese restaurants; **Place du Marché St-Honoré** (2nd arr., M° Tuileries or Opéra), which has a spattering of high-end eateries mixed in with an affordable

Two Heavenly Lunch Spots

For a quick pitstop near Montmartre, head to Rue des Martyrs (9th arr., M° Notre-Dame de Lorette, Pigalle or Anvers) where your children can choose between two lip-smacking addresses: for the familiar taste of home, **Rose Bakery** (no. 46 – closed Mondays) has a gorgeous organic takeaway counter laden with Anglo-Saxon carrot cakes and flapjacks, plus quiches, salads, and soups. There's also a coveted sit-down area at the back if you're lucky enough to get a table. Just opposite, **Delmontel** (no. 39 – closed Mondays) is a prizewinning bakery with wonderful cake creations. Children devour their *Petits Pains* – little bread rolls baked with delights like bacon and cheese or olives.

Italian (*Fuxia*, no. 42), an excellent brasserie (*Le Zinc d'Honoré*, no. 36) and an organic bakery that serves excellent salads and cakes (*Pain Quotidien*, no. 18); **Rue des Abbesses and Rue Lepic** (18th arr., M° Abbesses) in Montmartre, are covered with trendy and touristy restaurants and cafés (the best salads are in *Un Zebre à Montmartre*, 38 rue Lepic); and **Boulevard des Italiens** (9th arr., M° Opera) has several big bistros, including *Le Grand Café* (see p. 99), two decent pizzerias, and some sandwich bars. For a planned meal try one of the below.

MODERATE

Grand Colbert ★

*2 rue Vivienne, 2nd arr. 01 42 86 87 88; **www.legrandcolbert.fr**. M° Bourse or Pyramides.*

Set in a former 19th-century perfumerie, this typical Belle Époque restaurant, favoured by actors, politicians, and models, is a wonderful place to introduce your family to the bustling atmosphere and hearty cuisine of a traditional Parisian Brasserie. The menu is extensive, with plenty of familiar choices (steaks, roasted chicken, salmon, and pasta), daring dishes (frogs' legs and snails), and gourmet options (seafood platters that look like veritable works of art, foie gras with sauternes jelly, and chocolate profiteroles) to satisfy even the pickiest of eaters. Décor is sumptuous without being showy and the waiters are friendly and accommodating with children. For a spot of afternoon tea, pop in between 3 and 6pm – the hot chocolate is dreamy.

Open *Noon–1am daily. 3-course average 45€.* ***Credit*** *MC, V.*

Hard Rock Cafe ★

*14 boulevard de Montmartre, 9th arr. 01 53 24 60 00; **www.hardrockcafe.com**. M° Grands Boulevards.*

The food's not French and you could argue that the HRC is old hat; however, there sometimes comes a time when a meal of junk food is the only thing that will do. For those moments the

Especially for your Wee Ones

If travelling with a baby, the Poussette Café (meaning buggy café) is a welcome rarity, with space to park your buggy, a games area for under 3s, a place to heat a bottle, a baby-orientated shop, and decent salads and sandwiches. It was initially conceived as a meeting point for desperate new mothers, but it has quickly turned into a prized local café for anyone with a baby. *6 rue Pierre-Sémard, 9th arr., M° Poissonnière or Cadet. 10.30am–6.30pm Tues–Sat.*

burgers, fries, nachos, and free refills of the Hard Rock Cafe, handily situated on the Grands Boulevards, won't disappoint – especially families with young children, who will enjoy seeing all the music paraphernalia of international pop stars: look out for Eminem's pristine trainers.

Open *8.30am–1am (until 2am Fri–Sat) daily. Average 30€.* ***Credit*** *MC, V.*

INEXPENSIVE

Le St Jean ★

23 rue des Abbesses, 18th arr. ☏ 01 46 06 13 78. M° Abbesses.

Chicken and chips, salads, steaks, and croque-monsieurs make up the menu of this buzzing locals' café frequented by Montmartre's artists, trendy residents, and tourists alike. Set just opposite the Place des Abbesses, it's handy for a snack with the children, day or night. The toilets are conveniently situated on the ground floor. In the summer, grab a table outside.

Open *8am–midnight daily. 3-course average 20€. Salads: 10€.* ***Credit*** *MC, V.*

Memère Paulette ★★

3 rue Paul Lelong, 2nd arr. ☏ 01 40 26 12 36. M° Bourse.

You'd never find this place unless you knew about it first: on a backstreet behind the Bourse, it's practically invisible, with a dining-room full of faithful followers dead-set on keeping their favourite address a secret (whoops!). Wooden tables and funny pictures and objects laid out in a higgledy-piggledy fashion all over the walls and ceilings make it cosy. Food is simple (think egg mayonnaise, sausage and mash, and chocolate mousse), copious, and consistently delicious. If mums and dads are into wine, the owner is passionate about his cellar and will treat you to his favourites if you give him a free rein (his Château La Liquière is some of the best Faugères you can find). With young children beware the spiral staircase to the toilets: it is very steep and difficult to navigate – the only downer in this wonderful, homely restaurant.

Open *Noon–2.30pm, 8pm–10pm Mon–Fri. Closed 3 weeks Aug. 3-course average 20€.* ***Credit*** *MC, V.*

6 From Châtelet & Les Halles to the Marais & Bastille

CHÂTELET TO BASTILLE

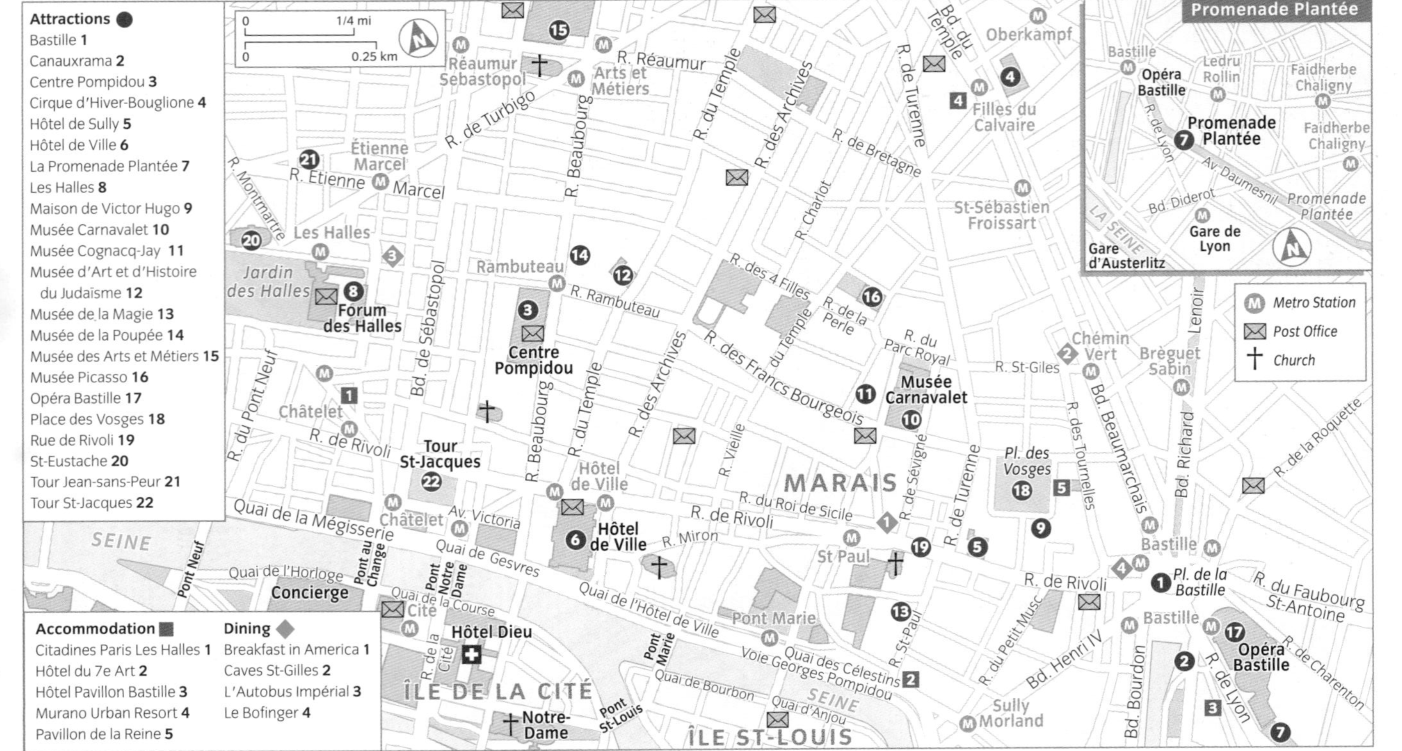

Châtelet, the Marais, and Bastille include some of the oldest parts of Paris, with winding narrow streets leading to medieval and Renaissance mansions (often converted into museums), hidden historical buildings (like **La Tour Jean-sans-Peur** p. 135 and 15th-century alchemist **Nicolas Flamel's house** p. 134), remnants of old **city walls** (p. 133) and **fortresses** (see Bastille p. 136). In sharp contrast, however, your family will also see modern Paris – the parts that, despite residents' protests, have dared to deviate from tradition and fly the flag of avant-garde architecture – **Les Halles** underground shopping centre (p. 137), the **Pompidou Centre** (p. 127), and **Bastille Opera House** p. 136.

Châtelet and Les Halles are the epicentre of high-street fashion and fight their reputation as seedy areas (particularly Les Halles) with constant refurbishments and a spattering of specialised food shops. The Marais, a former marshland (*marais* means swamp) then a place of royal residence in the 17th century, is now the main gay and Jewish quarter, and a hotspot for designer shopping, museums, and family attractions such as the **Musée des Arts et Métiers** technology museum (p. 131).

Bastille, forever linked to the 1789 French Revolution, is a fashionable area dominated by architect Carlos Ott's modern, grey opera house, and filled with restaurants, bars, and cafés. It's also the gateway to outer Paris thanks to the **Canal St Martin** that heads north-eastwards (see **Canauxrama** p. 139) through the old working-class quarters towards the über-modern **Parc de la Villette** (p. 246), Boulevard Beaumarchais, with its 150-year-old **Cirque d'Hiver** (winter circus) near the République district, and a converted railway line, **La Promenade Plantée** (flowery walkway, p. 140), that takes your family along the top of a viaduct towards the **Bois de Vincennes** with its **zoo** and **château**.

ORIENTATION

The Châtelet, Les Halles, Marais, and Bastille quarters cover central Paris and part of the east, touching on the 1st, 2nd, 3rd, 4th, 11th, and 12th arrondissements. Rue St Antoine, which becomes Rue de Rivoli near the St-Paul Métro, is the central axis, running parallel to the river and linking Bastille to Concorde (and the Champs-Elysées) in the west. Métro line 1 is the most useful, touching on all these districts. If you're planning a trip to Disneyland Paris, RER A runs directly from Châtelet-Les-Halles and Gare de Lyon (near Bastille) to Marne-la-Vallée. The Louvre, Notre-Dame, and the Latin Quarter can all be reached on foot from here too.

GETTING AROUND

The most useful bus routes are no. **76,** which links Bastille and Châtelet to the Louvre; no. **29**, which runs from Bastille, past the Marais and Etienne Marcel to the Opéra district (the open platform at the back is a hit with children); no. **85** links the Louvre and Les Halles to Montmartre; no. **47** travels between Hôtel-de-Ville and the Latin Quarter, near Cardinal Lemoine; and no. **75** cuts through the Marais to République and the Canal St Martin. A handy **Batobus** stop is **Hôtel de Ville**. Also remember that Canauxrama runs canal trips between Bastille and La Villette (p. 139).

INSIDER TIP

RER B from Châtelet-Les-Halles is direct to the Gare du Nord and the Charles-de-Gaulle (north) and Orly (south) airports.

VISITOR INFORMATION

The nearest Tourist Offices are in the Carrousel du Louvre (99 rue de Rivoli, 1st arr., M° Palais-Royal-Musée du Louvre), or in the Gare de Lyon (20 boulevard Diderot, 12th arr., M° and RER Gare de Lyon) *08 92 68 30 00*; ***www.parisinfo.com***.

WHAT TO SEE & DO

Children's Top 5 Attractions

❶ **Learning** a magic trick at the Musée de la Magie (see p. 130).

❷ **Being** wowed by the horses, clowns and acrobats at the Cirque d'Hiver p. 135).

❸ **Following** the trail of Nicolas Flamel, the maker of the Philosopher's Stone (see p. 134).

❹ **Taking** a canal boat (Canauxrama, see p. 139) from Bastille to the Parc de la Villette (p. 246).

❺ **Discovering** your favourite planes, trains, and automobiles in the Musée des Arts et Métiers (see p. 131).

Culture & Museums

Centre Pompidou ★★

ALL AGES

Place Georges-Pompidou, 4th arr. 01 44 78 12 33. ***www.centre-pompidou.fr****. M° Rambuteau, Hôtel de Ville or RER A and B Châtelet–Les Halles.*

When it opened in 1977, this was hailed as 'the most avant-garde building in the world'. Even by today's standards it looks eccentric, with its bold, 'exoskeletal' architecture of brightly painted pipes and ducts (green for water, red for heat, blue for air, and yellow for electricity) plus transparent escalator tubes criss-crossing on the outside. Designed by Richard Rogers and Renzo Piano, it was

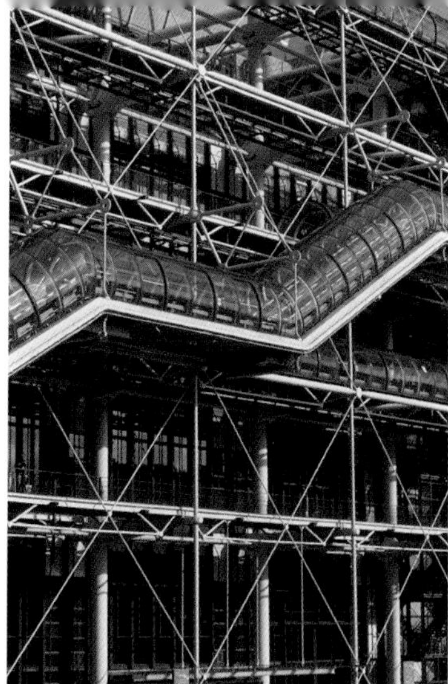

Centre Pompidou

the dream of former president Georges Pompidou, who wanted a centre to house 20th- and 21st-century art. The result is one of the world's finest modern and contemporary art collections.

INSIDER TIP

The Centre Pompidou sells its own guide in English for 12€, online and in the ground-floor shop. It's money well spent for both teens and parents wishing to guide their children using the concise explanations.

Get your bearings The Centre Pompidou is almost a city unto itself, with six levels to explore: On floors 4 and 5 you'll find the permanent collections of the **Musée National d'Art Moderne** (National Museum of Modern Art); Floor 6 contains a **temporary exhibition space**, a bookshop, a panoramic viewing point, and the minimalist (and expensive) restaurant **Georges**; Floors 2 and 3 offer a **library** (and café) with free access to masses of French and foreign books, periodicals, films, records, slides, and microfilms; Level 1 houses the **Printemps** (as in the department store p. 114) modern furniture boutique, a **café**, and a **cinema**; and on the ground floor you'll find the **ticket offices**, a **cloakroom** (where you can leave anything bulky including buggies), an **education centre**, the **Galerie des Enfants** (children's gallery p. 126), a **post office**, and a **bookshop** with lots of fun postcards to send home.

To avoid artistic indigestion, particularly if you have small children, restrict yourself to the sections below, which are child-friendly and stimulating for all the family. As the museum rotates its permanent collection, some of the works listed might not be visible, however there's plenty more to see, and you could opt for the **guided visit** ★★, in English on Saturdays at 3pm (call *01 44 78 12 33* to book a place).

❶ The **Musée National d'Art Moderne (National Museum of Modern Art)** ★★ ALL AGES The permanent collections cover 20th- and 21st-century art, with some 40,000 rotating works. The 5th floor covers 1905–1960 (Fauvism, Cubism, inter-war art, Surrealism, Abstraction, and Neo-realism) and floor 4 covers 1960 to the present day. On the 5th floor seek out Fernand Léger's **Composition à la Main et au Chapeau (1927)**, (hand and hat composition in room 9) and ask younger children to say what they can see (hats, a face, cards, etc.). In the Terrace Nord, youngsters will appreciate Takis's **Signals** (weird spirals that seem to grow out of the floor. Room 10 houses Mondrian's geometrically abstract **New York (1942)** with yellow, blue, and red lines which can be copied if you bring along colouring pencils and paper. Room 15 is entirely devoted to Picasso. Both of his **Femme Couchée** (1932, Woman Lying Down) paintings amuse younger children who notice that the lady's breasts look like eyes, which in turn make her look rather like a cartoon elephant or octopus. Picabia's **Dresseur d'Animaux** (Animal Trainer, room 20) is also fun, showing the silhouette of a man with a strange, curly nose, an owl, and multi-coloured dogs. If your children can only draw stick men, take them to room 12 where they can copy Calder's **Josephine Baker** (1928). Every time I visit with my friend's children, I am dragged to floor 4 to see the piano that can't play, German artist Joseph Beuy's **Infiltration Homogen für Konzertflügel** (1966, room 16) and the next door **Plight** (room 15), a felted space, filled with one solitary piano: both children take piano lessons and find the two exhibits fascinating.

At the other end of floor 4, the brand new **Espace Nouveaux Médias** is a great place for adolescent computer fans, who can surf through a CD of the museum's collections and check out the sound and graphic installations of France's most innovative video makers.

❷ La Galerie des Enfants ★

AGES 11 AND UNDER This section of the museum, on the ground floor, has been wonderfully thought out to make art, design, and architecture as accessible as possible to 2 to 5-year-olds and 6 to 12s, with interactive toys, games, and installations

❸ L'Ecran des Enfants

AGES 5 TO 13 A children's cinema showing the best of French and international cinema with the occasional English-language option.

❹ Atelier Brancusi ★★

AGES 8 AND ABOVE This re-creation of the Jazz Age studio of Romanian sculptor Brancusi is a minimuseum separated from the rest of the action. It was painstakingly moved from Brancusi's home in Montparnasse to this spot opposite the Centre Pompidou in 1997. Your children can meander round bronzes, plasterworks, drawings, photos, and the sculptor's tool, poised as if Brancusi might come home any second – a humanscale museum in which to wind down after your day's visit.

Open *11am–10pm Wed–Mon (11pm some Thurs for temporary exhibitions).* ***Admission*** *10€ adults, 8€ students and 18–25s, free under-18s.*

INSIDER TIP

The museum is free the first Sunday of the month, but be prepared to queue; or jump the queues and buy your ticket online.

Entertainment While You Queue

The Pompidou Centre is a popular place and queuing is inevitable. However, the museum's forecourt, overshadowed by a giant, golden flowerpot, is a free 'entertainment centre' featuring mime, fire-eaters, circus performers, and, sometimes, musicians. Children hardly notice the wait when the street performers are there. Also, don't miss the nearby **Fontaine Stravinsky**, (Place Igor-Stravinsky, 4th arr.), an automated fountain in which wacky mobile sculptures by Jean Tinguely and Niki de Saint-Phalle spit water at each other.

Maison de Victor Hugo ★

AGES 8 AND ABOVE

6 place des Vosges, 4th arr., ☏ *01 42 72 10 16.* ***www.musee-hugo.paris.fr.*** *M° St-Paul, Bastille, or Chemin-Vert.*

If you've ever taken the children to see the *Les Misérables* musical, or they've read one of Victor Hugo's books, consider visiting this little museum – his former house – tucked away on the Place des Vosges (p. 138), which includes more than 450 of his drawings, illustrating scenes from his own works, along with mementos. To get the most out of the visit, hire an audio guide in English, aimed at families, with anecdotes about the items on display. The museum is free to enter, so 5€ per audio guide is money well spent.

Open *10am–6pm Tues–Sun.*
Admission *free.*

Musée Carnavalet ★

AGES 5 AND ABOVE

23 rue de Sévigné, 3rd arr. ☏ *01 44 59 58 58.* ***www.carnavalet.paris.fr.*** *M° St-Paul or Chemin-Vert.*

Here Paris's past comes alive in details like the chessmen Louis XVI used to distract himself while waiting to go to the guillotine. The building, a Renaissance palace, was built in 1544 but is best known because one of history's most famous letter writers, Madame de Sévigné, moved here in 1677. Fanatically devoted to her daughter (she moved in with her because she couldn't bear to be apart), she poured out nearly every detail of her life in her letters, virtually ignoring her son.

Musée Carnavalet

Several rooms cover the Revolution, with a bust of Marat, a portrait of Danton, and a model of the Bastille (one painting shows its demolition). Another room tells the story of the captivity of the royal family at the Conciergerie (p. 177), including the bed in which Madame Elisabeth (the sister of Louis XVI) slept, and the Dauphin's exercise book.

Exhibits continue at the **Hôtel le Pelletier de St-Fargeau,** across the courtyard, with furniture from the Louis XIV period to the early 20th century, including a replica of Marcel Proust's cork-lined bedroom with his actual furniture, plus artefacts from the museum's archaeological collection, including Neolithic pirogues – shallow oak boats used from about 4400 to 2200 B.C.

Guided visits for families in English (1hr 30min) need to be reserved 6 to 8 weeks beforehand. Themes can cover the Renaissance to the 20th century and prehistory or archaeology departments (4.50€ adults, 3.80€ under-18s). Also look out for the concerts some Saturdays and Sundays in intimate venues ideal for introducing your children to classical music.

Open *10am–6pm Tues–Sun.*
Admission *free.*

Musée Cognacq-Jay

AGES 5 AND ABOVE

In the Hôtel Donon, 8 rue Elzévir, 3rd arr. 01 40 27 07 21. ***www.cognacq-jay.paris.fr****. M° Chemin Vert or St-Paul.*

The founders of La Samaritaine department store (now closed), Ernest Cognacq and his wife, Louise Jay, were fabled for their exquisite taste, and their collection is now on show in the 16th-century Hôtel Denon, which, with its Louis XV and Louis XVI panelled rooms, looks rather like a giant dolls' house. The works include some of the 18th century's most valuable works including ceramics and porcelain, delicate cabinets, and paintings by Canaletto, Fragonard, Greuze, Chardin, Boucher, Watteau, and Tiepolo. While none of this is set out for children, they will enjoy the feeling of being in someone's home rather than a 'real' museum. **Tip:** If you find your children losing interest, mum or dad can

Quick Snack in Rue des Rosiers

All along Rue des Rosiers (4th arr., M° St-Paul), Jewish bakeries and restaurants tempt passers-by with sweet 'n' sticky gateaux, tasty falafels, and sizzling chawarmas. **L'As du Fallafel** (no. 34) is the local hotspot for exceptionally well-prepared, savoury sarnies, and for Yiddish cakes filled with poppy seeds, apple, and cream-cheese, bring the family to **Finkelsztajn** (no. 27).

take them for a breath of fresh air in the nearby **Square Georges Cain** or the **Square Léopold Achille** (both just off Rue Payenne, 4th arr.) while the rest of you finish the visit. A good spot to meet up afterwards is the **Café du Centre Culturel Suédois** (Swedish cultural centre, 11 rue Payenne, 3rd arr.) – a lovely shaded courtyard in an old mansion, the Hôtel de Marles. They sell delicious homemade cakes and sandwiches and have a free contemporary Swedish art exhibition section opposite.

Open *10am–6pm Tues–Sun.* ***Admission*** *free.*

Musée d'Art et d'Histoire du Judaïsme

Musée d'Art et d'Histoire du Judaïsme ★ AGES 7 AND ABOVE

Hôtel de St-Aignan, 71 rue du Temple, 3rd arr. ☎ 01 53 01 86 60. ***www.mahj.org****. M° Rambuteau or Hôtel de Ville.*

Security is tight, but it's worth the effort. In the Hôtel De St-Aignan, dating from the 1600s, this museum of Jewish history has been handsomely and impressively installed. The development of Jewish culture is traced not only in Paris, but across France and Europe. Many of the exhibitions are devoted to religious objects, including menorahs, Torah ornaments, and ark curtains, in both the Ashkenazi and Sephardic traditions. Some of the most interesting documents for teenagers studying French or history relate to the notorious Dreyfus case (the affair that saw Captain Alfred Dreyfus, a Jew and fervent French Nationalist, wrongly accused of espionage against France after the Germans seized Alsace. His case – pure anti-Semitism – rocked the nation and led to many years of political unrest). Also on parade is a collection of illuminated manuscripts, Renaissance Torah arks, and paintings from the 18th and 19th centuries, along with Jewish gravestones from the Middle Ages. The best display is of the artwork by leading Jewish painters and artists ranging from Soutine to Zadkine, Chagall to Modigliani.

Tip: A visit to the museum can be combined with the moving WW2, Jewish deportation memorial (**Mémorial de la Déportation**) behind Notre-Dame cathedral p. 186.

Open *11am–6pm Mon–Fri, 10am–6pm Sun.* ***Admission*** *6.80€ adults, 4.50€ 18–26s, free under-18s.*

Musée de la Magie ★★ FIND

AGES 5 AND ABOVE

*11 rue St-Paul, 4th arr. 01 42 72 13 26, **www.museedelamagie.com**. M° St-Paul.*

Magic wands, vanishing chairs, magic mirrors, and live shows all unite to make this place a thoroughly captivating family experience. The main museum is set in atmospheric vaults, with walls covered in old posters advertising magic, around which are scattered all sorts of strange curiosities (many from the 19th century, a time when Paris was a world centre for illusionists) including an early box used to saw a woman in half and magically put her together again. Although your children can't touch the Secret Objects Cabinets, they can see magic wands, old toys, trompe-l'oeil boxes used to hide secret stashes of tobacco, jewellery, or money, and 'spirit objects' used in the 19th century to simulate ghost writing and the paranormal moving of objects. In the magic mirror room, you'll find optical illusions including cubby holes into which youngsters can put their heads and see things in a strange new way. At certain times of day, live magic shows for children take place in the little theatre. The tricks are simple to understand even if your French is non-existent (most magicians speak broken English anyway). Children are usually asked to step up on stage and pick a card or hold the end of a rope.

To finish off your visit, there is the **Musée des Automates**, where more than 100 automated toys charm adults and children alike. In the museum shop are all sorts of tricks and spell-books (many in English) so your children can wow their friends when they get home.

***Open** 2pm–7pm Wed, Sat, Sun (daily during school holidays). **Admission** 9€ adults, 7€ under-18s.*

Musée de la Poupée

AGES 2 TO 12

*Impasse Berthaud, 3rd arr. 01 42 72 73 11, **www.museedelapoupeeparis.com**. M° Rambuteau.*

This all-in-one doll hospital, museum, and shop is heaven for little girls who love dolls (and boys who appreciate teddy bears and quacking toy ducks). From the moment you step away from the noisy Rue Rambuteau into this old-fashioned, flower-filled alley, you're in another world – where porcelain faces, miniature ball dresses, and golden locks have been preened and curled as if they belonged to real children. Started in 1994 by two avid doll collectors, Guido Odin and his son Samy, the collection shows more than 500 dolls chronologically from 1800 to today. There are no flashy installations and some grown-ups may find the whole affair quite kitsch, but children will see past the cheesiness and simply enjoy looking and learning how dolls are put together. If you have a sick doll at home (from any era), bring it along for an assessment and estimate in the doll hospital. Also, on your way out, don't miss the little shop where your children

Musée de la Poupée

can spend their pocket-money (and yours) on books, dolls, and teddy bears.

Open *10am–6pm Tues–Sun.* ***Admission*** *7€ adults, 5€ 12–25s, 3€ 3–11s, free under-3s.*

Musée des Arts et Métiers ★★

FIND **AGES 5 AND ABOVE**

60 rue Réaumur, 3rd arr. ☎ 01 53 01 82 00. ***www.arts-et-metiers.net****. M° Arts et Métier or Réaumur-Sébastopol.*

This museum, founded in the 18th century by the Abbot Grégoire as 'a store for useful, new inventions' is, along with the Parc de la Villette (p. 246), one of Paris's best children's attractions. Split into seven departments, whether your youngsters are budding scientists, mechanics, astronomers, pilots, or simply curious about the world around them, it's a mesmerising place. Audio guides are available in English for adults and teens, and 7 to 12-year-olds. The adult audio guides suggest three possible trails. The one-hour trail (red ticket) covers 30 of the museum's must-see exhibits. The two-and-a-half hour trail (red and yellow tickets) highlights 65 objects linked to the history of science and technology. And the 'Liberté' trail (red, yellow, and blue tickets) allows you to wander at will. For the Junior audio guide (one-and-a-half hour-long trail), a little robot takes children to 34 different objects to find a hidden key and solve the enigma of what it was made for.

If you go it alone, four themes make for appealing family visits:

❶ An all-round overview

Start on the 2nd floor with the scientific instruments. Here, even non-mathematical children will admire **Pascal's 17th-century calculator**, which can be tested in the wooden vaulted room next door (left). Downstairs, on the 1st floor, the construction section displays interesting **model bridges**. In the Energy department children will be impressed by the **motor,** which roars if they press a button. The mechanical department shows how movement is produced with machinery. But the best part, especially for under-fives, is the **Théâtre des Automates** (automated theatre), where, several times a day, automated children's toys and models are set in action.

❷ Astronomy

In the Prieuré de Saint-Martin-des-Champs Chapel (a stunning building in itself), hangs Foucault's Pendulum. In 1851, French physician Léon Foucault decided to make the rotation of the Earth visible to the human eye. He developed a weighted sphere, with a pointed tip, suspended from a steel thread. Marks are left in sand placed beneath the pointed sphere. As the sphere is still, the marks come from the movement of the Earth around the sphere. This visual demonstration is truly fascinating for children and there are more centuries-old scientific instruments like celestial spheres, astrolabes, and sundials upstairs.

❸ Planes and Rockets

Clément Ader's **Avion III**, the world's first working aeroplane (1897), is suspended from the roof in the Prieuré de Saint-Martin-des-Champs Chapel right by the entrance to the Transport department. He called it an *Avion* (aeroplane) from the Latin word *Avis*, meaning 'bird'. Three wheels, two steam motors, and two rotors were required to get the rickety old thing into the air. Although Ader abandoned attempts to fly when his machine hit the ground after just a few seconds, magnificent men in their flying machines were crossing the Channel just 11 years later. You can see the **Blériot 11**, the first plane to cross the Channel, at the end of the section. Look out also for the world's first **helicopter**, a 1907 **gyroplane**, a model of the **Ariane 5 space shuttle**, and the **Breguet 14 biplane**, kitted with a ski so that it could land in the desert.

❹ Cars

You have to get to the 19th-century part of the Transport department before you can see a glimmer of a motorcar. Its predecessor, a 25km/h **steam-powered tricycle** (1888) is interesting for children, however,

FUN FACT **Belly of a Giant Machine!** 

The Arts et Métiers Métro stop on line 11 is the most interesting station in the city. Entirely covered in copper panels, it was designed to make passengers feel like they're in the belly of a giant machine.

Mum, Dad, What's Philippe Auguste's City Wall?

The reign of Philippe Auguste (1180–1223) was a defining moment in Paris's history (until he was defeated by Richard the Lion Heart in 1194). Philippe Auguste centralised many of the city's feudal powers and encouraged the guilds (butchers, drapers, furriers, etc.) to grow, thus spurring the rise of the bourgeoisie. He built the first permanent market in Les Halles (p. 137) and a castle – now the Louvre. With such a prosperous city, he needed to defend it from Normandy (whose duke was also the King of England) and so he built a defensive wall all round it. You can see the remains in the Tour Jean-sans-Peur (see p. 135), the **Jardins-St-Paul** in the Marais (4th arr., M° St Paul) and the **Louvre Medieval**, (p. 51, 1st arr., M° Louvre-Rivoli or Palais Royal Musée du Louvre) beneath the Sully wing, and **Cour du Commerce St-André** (6th arr., M° Odéon).

who can see that petrol and electricity aren't the only ways of making vehicles move. Star exhibits are **Peugeot's 1889 quadricycle**; Henry Ford's **'T' model**; a sliced-in-half 1931 **Citroën C6**, the first **motor engine** (1892), and a strange car with rotor blades, the **Helica**, created by Marcel Leyat in 1921. To finish off, little boys will love Alain Prost's 1983 yellow **Formula 1** racing car.

INSIDER TIP

Tuesday to Saturday the museum café offers a healthy 'steamed' menu (7–9€), salads, and terrines. On Sundays a family brunch (17€ over-16s, 10€ under-16s) is also available from 11.30am–2pm.

Open *10am–6pm Tues–Sun, until 9.30pm Thurs.* ***Admission*** *6.50€ adults, 4€ 6–25s, free under-5s. Audio guides 5€.*

Musée Picasso ★★

AGES 7 AND ABOVE

Hôtel Salé, 5 rue de Thorigny, 3rd arr. ☎ 01 42 71 25 21. ***www.musee-picasso.fr****. M° St-Paul, Filles du Calvaire, or Chemin Vert.*

When it opened in the Marais at the beautifully restored Hôtel Salé (*Salt Mansion*, built by a man who made his fortune controlling salt distribution in 17th-century France), the press hailed this as a 'museum for Picasso's Picassos.' Acquired by the state, in lieu of millions of euros of inheritance taxes, are more than 200 paintings, 160-odd sculptures, 16 collages, 29 bas-reliefs, 107 ceramics, and more than 1,500 sketches and 1,600 engravings, along with 58 notebooks, plus works by Corot, Braque, Matisse, and Miró (Picasso's private collection). Picasso's works span some 75 years and collections are regularly changed or moved around but the bright colours and weird

Story-Time: On the Trail of the Maker of the Philosopher's Stone

In the first of J.K. Rowling's Harry Potter books, a 700-year-old alchemist called Nicolas Flamel owns the Philosopher's Stone, a magical rock linked to the elixir of life. Rowling didn't invent the character or his association with eternal life. Flamel was a 15th-century Parisian. His house is still standing and his epitaph can be seen in a museum (see below).

The Story: One night a poor man came to Nicolas Flamel's door to sell him a mystical book entitled *Abraham the Jew*. It contained symbols which, if deciphered, would tell him how to turn base metal into gold and create the Philosopher's stone – the secret of making the elixir of eternal life. After 21 years, Flamel finally cracked the enigma, turning lead into gold and became very rich indeed. He and his wife Pernelle used their wealth selflessly – building shelters (including **La Maison de Nicolas Flamel**, see below), donating to hospitals (such as the **Quinze-Vingts** hospital still running today), and cleaning up cemeteries (notably la Cimétière des Innocents whose macabre treasures are on display in the **Paris Catacombes** p. 162). After Flamel's official death, the book *Abraham the Jew* supposedly made its way into the court of Louis XIII, via Flamel's descendent, a man called Dubois. To impress the king, Dubois let slip that he possessed the secret of eternal life. Cardinal Richelieu learned of this and decided to find the secret for himself. He condemned Dubois to death, ransacking every building that had ever belonged to Flamel. His tomb (possibly near the current **Tour St Jacques** p. 138 in Châtelet) was also raided, but his body was never found, giving rise to rumours that Flamel never actually died.

Tracing Flamel today: Elements of Flamel's mysterious life have been preserved. Your family can see his house, the **Maison de Nicolas Flamel**, dating from 1407 (51 rue Mortmorency in the 3rd arr.) complete with the original carvings over the entrance. It's now a vibrant restaurant (**L'Auberge Nicolas Flamel**, ☎ *01 42 71 77 78*). In Châtelet, opposite the **Tour St-Jacques** lie the **Rue Nicolas Flamel** and the adjacent **Rue Pernelle** after his wife. And while Flamel's grave and book have been lost, his epitaph is positioned on a wall in the medieval **Musée National du Moyen Age** (p. 182).

forms of his many paintings and sculptures attract children so you can stroll and ask your children to find their favourites. On a sunny day, don't forget the garden, where you can view the building and several of Picasso's biggest sculptures.

Open** 9.30am–6pm Wed–Mon Apr–Sept, 9.30am–5.30pm Wed–Mon Oct–Mar. Closed from Mar 09–2010/11 for refurbishment.* ***Admission

7.70€ adults, 5.70€ 18–25s, free under-18s.

Tour Jean-sans-Peur ★ FIND

AGES 5 AND ABOVE

*20 rue Etienne Marcel, 2nd arr. 01 40 26 20 28. **www.tourjeansanspeur.com**. M° Etienne Marcel, Sentier or RER A Châtelet-les-Halles.*

This solitary, medieval tower is the only remaining part of the Hôtel de Bourgogne, a sumptuous palace built by Jean-sans Peur – Fearless John – in 1409–1411. During the Hundred Years' War with England (1337–1453), Jean-sans-Peur seized power after murdering the king's brother and, along Philippe Auguste's city wall, created a luxurious residence complete with the still-existing vaulted ceiling displaying family symbols of oak, hawthorn, and hop. But he was himself assassinated and the palace confiscated on the death of his grandson.

Split up in the 16th century, one part became the property of a theatre troupe, which in time merged with Molière's troupe to become La Comédie Française (p. 56) in 1680. The building eventually disappeared from view, only rediscovered when Rue Etienne Marcel was built (1866–8), and was eventually restored in the 1990s.

A visit takes about 30 minutes, making it ideal for a cultural quick-fix (no buggies). Children's favourites are the latrines and there are repaired medieval stained-glass windows and a small chunk of Philippe Auguste's ramparts to view.

Information leaflets are available in English.

***Open** 1.30pm–6pm Wed, Sat, Sun mid-Nov–Mar, 1.30pm–6pm Wed–Sun Apr–mid-Nov. **Admission** 5€ adults, 3€ under-18s.*

Children's Entertainment

Cirque d'Hiver-Bouglione ★★

ALL AGES

*110 rue Amelot, 11th arr., 01 47 00 28 81. **www.cirquedhiver.com**. M° Filles du Calvaire or Oberkampf.*

Paris's oldest inner-city circus, set inside the beautiful (if a little crumbly) 19th-century winter circus, has been run by the Bouglione family for decades. International acts from the USA, Hungary, China, Russia, and Italy, as well as France wow the audience with acrobatics, death-defying stunts, a very clever elephant, jugglers, acrobatic cyclists, horses, dogs, clowns, and a 12-strong orchestra playing live, just like in the olden days. The show lasts two hours and 10 minutes with a 20-minute entr'acte so you can rush the children to the loo or give them a chance to wriggle. However, the extravaganza is so captivating even the four-year-olds I took didn't notice the time go by.

***Shows** 2pm, 5.15pm, or 8.30pm (call to check) three times a week. Tickets can be bought online, in Fnac, Virgin Megastore or at the circus between 11am and 7pm Tues–Sun. **Admission** 10€–37€.*

Opéra Bastille ★

AGES 5 AND ABOVE

*Place de la Bastille, 12th arr. 08 92 89 90 90 or +33 1 72 29 35 35 from abroad. **www.operadeparis.fr**. M° Bastille.*

The Bastille Opera (also see Nightlife p. 143) runs children's shows several times a month in the amphitheatre. The 'Petits et Grands' section of the website lists all current performances and tickets can be booked online. Most run for less than an hour and previous shows have included shadow puppets for over-fives, and operatic fairy-stories for over-nines.

*Dates vary. **Admission** 16€ adults, 5€ under-13s.*

Streets & Monuments

Bastille ★

Place de la Bastille, 4th arr., M° Bastille.

The busy, traffic-logged square takes its name from the Bastille prison stormed by the lower classes on the 14th July 1789 – an event that marked the start of the French Revolution and the beginning of France as a republic. Very little remains today (its bricks were used to build the Pont de la Concorde), but you can show your children some foundations on the platform of Métro line 5 (dir. Bobigny) and opposite the entrance to the Métro at Sully Morland. There is also the modern opera house and the giant central **Colonne de Juillet** (column topped by the golden Genius of Liberty) in a trendy part of town with lots of bars, restaurants, and an attractive marina that marks the beginning of Paris's canal system up to Parc de la Villete (p. 246) in the northeast.

Sledging and ice-skating at Hôtel de Ville

Paris Walks ALL AGES

One of the best ways to ways to make Paris come alive for your family is on a guided walk. **Paris Walks** has been taking tourists around the city (in English) since the 1990s and offers wonderful tours of the Marais' narrow streets, medieval courtyards, and Renaissance mansions.

Every Tuesday (10.30am), Saturday (10.30am), Thursday (Apr–Oct 2.30pm) and Sunday 2.30pm. Book by email ***E: paris@paris-walks.com*** *or call Peter and Oriel Caine* ☎ *01 48 09 21 40. Tours last about two hours (in rain and shine). 10€ adults, 8€ students under 21, 5€ under-15s,* ***www.paris-walks.com****.*

Hôtel de Ville

Hôtel de Ville, 4th arr., M° Hôtel-de-Ville.

Paris's original 17th-century town hall burned down in 1871, so the one you see today is a highly ornate 19th-century reconstruction with elaborate masonry, turrets, and rows of statues watching over the pedestrianised square.

The area in front of the hall was once the site of hangings, burnings, and executions. Henri IV's assassin, Ravaillac, was gruesomely quartered alive here by horses that pulled his body in four different directions. Today, from December to March, there's a **mini-ice-rink** ★ just in front of the main building, where children can skate for free (be prepared to queue). Skates can be hired for 5€.

Les Halles

Les Halles, 1st arr., M° Les Halles, Châtelet, Sentier, Etienne Marcel, or Réamur Sébastopol; RER Châtelet-les-Halles.

Les Halles district (pronounced *Laiz Al*) was historically the belly of Paris – a vast marketplace that, for centuries, sold the capital's best meat, fish, fruit, and vegetables. But in the 1960s all that changed and the whole market, including its 19th-century wrought iron and glass pavilions (some of the most beautiful in Europe), were dismantled and sent to Rungis market in the suburbs. In its place a park, underground shopping centre (**Forum des Halles** p. 141), cinemas, swimming pool, and Europe's biggest underground suburban train station were built. On paper all looked good, but in reality Châtelet was, for many years, an unsavoury spot. Nowadays the area has been gentrified and restaurants, gourmet boutiques, and cheap high-street shops have opened. However, it's still best to keep your family away from Châtelet-les-Halles RER stations and the dimly lit park and overground passages after dark. Surrounding streets leading to Beaubourg (around the Pompidou Centre), Rue Montorgueil (p. 141) and Rue de

Window shopping in the arcades around Place des Vosges

Rivoli (p. 138) are fine; just avoid the northern end of Rue St Denis, a well-policed but explicit red-light district.

Place des Vosges ★

Place des Vosges, 4th arr., M° Bastille, Chemin-Vert or St-Paul.

When strolling around the Marais or Bastille, don't miss this beautiful and impressively symmetrical pink-brick square (nine houses line each of the four sides). It's the ultimate, compact, family park with grass where small children can run around, with fountains they can dip their hands into, and benches and spaces for a picnic, while barriers prevent them from running on to the road. Atmospheric covered arcades are filled with art galleries, tearooms, restaurants, and antique shops; and a secret door leads to the Hôtel de Sully photographic gallery (p. 56). The square is more than 400 years old and has been the scene of many an important historic event, including a three-day party celebrating Louis XIII's marriage to Anne of Austria.

Rue de Rivoli

1st and 4th arrs, M° St-Paul, Hôtel-de-Ville, Châtelet, Louvre-Rivoli, Palais-Royal Musée du Louvre, Tuileries, and Concorde.

Running from St-Paul to Concorde, this long and busy thoroughfare, commissioned by Napoleon Bonaparte to celebrate his victory at Rivoli, is mostly about shopping. In the Châtelet district, it's a high-street shopper's dream, with famous international and French brands and a big department store, the BHV.

Tour St Jacques

4th arr., M° Châtelet.

As your family wanders around Châtelet, they will notice this free-standing Gothic tower (partially under cover for restoration works until mid-2009). Dating from 1523, it's all that remains of a church, St-Jacques de la Boucherie, begun in the 13th century and destroyed in 1797 after the Revolution. The tomb of the 15th-century alchemist, Nicolas Flamel, famed for possessing the Philosopher's Stone (p. 134), is rumoured to lie somewhere in the garden round the tower.

Religious Buildings

St-Eustache ★★

Entrance Place René Cassin, 1st arr. *01 42 36 31 05.* ***www.saint-eustache.org****. M° Les Halles or RER Châtelet-les-Halles.*

Louis XIV, Madame de Pompadour (Louis XV's mistress), Molière, and Cardinal Richelieu were all baptised here in one of Paris's most beautiful churches, towering over the Les Halles shopping district. Built between 1532 and 1637 its interior was modelled on Notre-Dame, but the architectural style is mostly Renaissance – noticeable on the columns, arches, and pillars. Its organ, with some 8,000 pipes, is one of the biggest in France and on Sundays at 5.30pm there are free organ recitals, or the mass at 11am on Sundays includes organ and choral performances. Just in front of the church, children often enjoy trying to climb on the huge sculpture of a man's head.

Open *9.30am–7pm Mon–Fri, 10am–7pm Sat, 9.15am–7pm Sun.*

Parks & the Outdoors

Canauxrama ★★ ALL AGES

Embark Port de l'Arsenal (opposite no. 50 boulevard de la Bastille, 12th arr. *01 42 39 15 00.* ***www.canauxrama.com****. M° Bastille.*

If you're visiting Bastille and fancy heading to the fabulous

Rollerblading from Bastille

If your family are bladers, Rollers & Coquillages (***www.rollers-coquillages.org***) run rollerblading excursions around Paris from Bastille (Sunday 2.30pm to 5.30pm) for anyone who can keep up. Parents with toddlers can bring their children in a sturdy buggy and older children can join in as long as they know how to change direction and break. The route covers 17 to 23km in three hours, police and ambulances provide security, and you can hire reasonably priced material from **Nomades** (37 Boulevard Bourdon, 4th arr.; ***www.nomadeshop.com***), a shop near the departure point.

Rules of the game:

1. Bring enough to drink – even in winter – and an energising snack for the break.
2. Bring an extra pair of shoes and a metro ticket in case you get tired, your skates break, or you need to leave early.
3. Make sure you're insured (EHIC's or personal health insurance).
4. The event will be called off if it's raining.

Parc de la Villette in the 19th arr. (p. 246), a two-and-a-half-hour boat trip up the Canal Saint-Martin is a leisurely and pretty way to get there with a commentated ride, interspersed with cheesy accordion music. The canal (p. 246) is part of a wider waterways system linking Paris to the sea.

Historically this was a working class district, made famous in the '20s and '30s by French stars like Edith Piaf. Today it's a 'Bobo' area (Bourgeois-Bohemian) coveted by artists and young professionals. Children love the journey through the locks and you could bring colouring pencils for down time.

Once you get off, follow the canal north (it becomes the Canal de l'Ourcq) on foot or by bike (a self-service Vélib p. 38 bike station is on 14 rue Louis Blanc, 10th arr.) past the MK2 cinema complex (p. 248) to the Parc de la Villette. Children under six ride for free on weekdays.

Departure from Bastille: 9.45am and 2.30pm daily. Departure from Bassin de la Villette: 9.45am and 2.45pm daily. ***Admission*** *15€ adults, 8€ 6–12s, free under-6s. On weekend afternoons and bank holidays just one fee, 15€ is valid for all.*

La Promenade Plantée ★★

FIND **ALL AGES**

Main access: Avenue Daumesnil near Rue Jules-César, 12th arr. Lifts onto the Viaduct walk.

A railway station used to occupy the site of today's Bastille Opera House, part of a suburban line linking Paris to Vincennes and St-Maur in the east. Today all that is visible is a red-brick viaduct behind the opera house – **Le Viaduc des Arts** – so-named for the chic artists' ateliers and shops (1.5km of fashion designers, potters, furniture restorers, and violin and flute makers) nestled under the arches. On top of the viaduct is a promenade, planted with roses, lavender, bamboo, and fragrant shrubs – a popular walk for Parisian families. There are lifts up and the whole route is accessible with a buggy, though you will have to navigate a few steps.

After the viaduct, the walk reverts to ground level near a street called **l'allée Vivaldi** (over a wooden walkway) and carries on into the **Jardin de Reuilly** and then along the old railway line, to the **Bois de Vincennes**.

Access to the 4.5km-long Promenade (which takes 2 to 3 hours) is on **Avenue Daumesnil**

Promenade Plantée

(12th arr.) behind the Opera House (by Rue Jules-César). Mums and dads can enjoy the view into people's apartments. Children love the novelty of walking on top of a railway line, and at the end can run round the Jardin de Reuilly or the Bois de Vincennes (take a ball or outdoor games) where you'll find public toilets, a play area, and drinks stand plus boats, a zoo, Parc Floral, and Château. For a quick snack along the way try the **Viaduc Café** (43 avenue Daumesnil, 12th arr.).

To head back into Paris at the end of the Viaduct take the Métro from Porte Dorée (line 8) back to Bastille.

Open *8am (9am Sat–Sun)– 9.30pm or nightfall.*

INSIDER TIP

For a vitamin-packed fruit drink before you leave, try the fresh juices at **Paradis des Fruits** (12 place de la Bastille, 11th arr., M° Bastille). They also serve healthy salads and milkshakes.

Shopping

Rue de Rivoli, the **Châtelet-les-Halles** (Les Halles) underground shopping centre and its surrounding streets are where most everyday Parisians go shopping, with large crowds and groups of bargain-hunting teens in a veritable rabbit warren of corridors. Just outside, **Rue Rambuteau** is home to several cheap clothes and shoe stores; **Rue Etienne Marcel** and **Rue Ticquetonne** (2nd arr., M° Etienne Marcel) have high-end high-street and designer stores such as **Miss Sixty** (32 rue Etienne Marcel), **Barnara Bui** (23 rue Etienne Marcel), **Naf-Naf** (33 rue Etienne Marcel), and a funky retro clothes shop called **Kiliwatch** ★ selling Diesel jeans alongside vintage clothing and underground clothes brands (64 rue Ticquetonne). For something special, the **Marais** ★ is a treasure trove of designer boutiques around **Rue des Francs-Bourgeois, Rue des Rosiers**, and **Rue Vieille du Temple**.

Books

I Love my Blender ★★ is an odd name for a wonderful bookshop selling books by English-only authors, toys for children, fancy writing paper, candles, incense, tea and coffee (36 rue du Temple, 4th arr., M° Hôtel-de-Ville. *01 42 77 50 32*; ***www.ilovemyblender.fr***). **The Red Wheelbarrow**, is an English-language bookstore specialising in top-notch literature (22 rue St Paul, 4th arr., M° St Paul. *01 48 04 75 08*; ***www.theredwheelbarrow.com***). For bargain coffee-table books **Mona Lisait** (a pun on the painting – *Lisait* means 'was reading') in Les Halles sells hundreds of interesting hardbacks on everything from Parisian history to interior design in New York and 19th-century children's toys, all at permanent sale prices (Place Joachim du Bellay, 1st arr., M° Châtelet or RER A Châtelet-les-Halles. *01 40 26 83 66*; ***www.monalisait.fr***).

Food, Kitchenware, and Gifts

Rue Montorgueil (2nd arr., M° Sentier or Etienne Marcel) is a

Quick Shopper's Snack

Queen Elizabeth II ate cake at Stohrer, on Rue Montorgueil, when she came on an official visit in 2004. Bring your family to try the best rum-babas in Paris.

*51 rue Montorgueil, 2nd arr., 01 42 33 38 20; **www.stohrer.fr**. M° Sentier.*

bustling street with cheese shops, delicatessens, wine cellars, and florists. **Foie Gras Luxe** (26 rue de Montmartre, 2nd arr., M° Les Halles. *01 42 33 28 15*; ***www.foie-gras-luxe.com***) sources the best from across France. For fine copper saucepans and almost every kitchen utensil ever invented, **E Dehillerin** (18 rue Coquillière, 1st arr., M° Les Halles; ***www.e-dehillerin.fr***) has been supplying great chefs since 1820. For quirky gifts for children and adults, try the **Paris-Musées** shop in the Marais (29 bis rue des Francs Bourgeois, 4th arr., M° St-Paul. *01 42 74 13 02*). Finally, **Pep's** (223 rue St-Martin, 3rd arr., M° Arts et Métiers or Etienne Marcel. *01 42 78 11 67*; ***www.peps-paris.com***) is a dying breed of shop, where you or your children can take your broken brollies to be repaired, or treat yourselves to a made-to-measure one.

Just for children

Multicubes (5 rue de Rivoli, 4th arr., M° St-Paul. *01 42 77 10 77*) won me over the moment I happened on it: the owner's children (no older than 8), were helping their mum organise the shop by counting aprons into piles of ten. All around them, wooden music boxes, wall-hangings, lamps, puppets, marbles, and wooden games covered every inch of shelf-space. Not far from here, opposite BHV, *A la Poupée Merveilleuse* (9 rue du Temple, 4th arr., M° Hôtel-de-Ville. *01 42 72 63 46*) is a multi-coloured joke shop filled with dressing-up costumes for children and adults, tricks and enough fake moustaches and wigs to sink a ship. If your boys and girls are into robotics, don't leave without visiting **Robopolis** near the Cirque d'Hiver (p. 135), entirely devoted to dinosaur, animal, and human-like robots (107 boulevard Beaumarchais, 3rd arr., M° Saint-Sébastien Froissart. *01 44 78 01 18*; ***www.robopolis.com***).

Markets ★★

Bastille's food market (along Boulevard Richard Lenoir between Rue Amelot and Rue St-Sabin, 7am–2.30pm Thurs and Sun) offers rows of lip-smacking fare, street performers and, at the bottom nearest the square, a small, year-round funfair. The cheapest market in central Paris is the covered **Marché Aligre** (Place d'Aligre, 12th arr., M° Ledru-Rollin; 9am–1pm, 4pm–7.30pm Mon–Sat, 9am–1.30pm Sun) just east of Bastille;

and the oldest covered market, created in 1615, is the **Marché des Enfants Rouge** (39 rue de Bretagne, 3rd arr., M° Temple or Filles-du-Calvaire; 8.30am–1pm, 4pm–7.30pm Tues–Sat, 8.30am–2pm Sun) on the northern edge of the Marais.

Nightlife

If you want to keep your family out after dinner, Les Halles has two multi-screen cinemas: **UGC Les Halles** (7 place de la Rotunde, 1st arr.) and **UGC Orient Express** (level 4, rue de l'Orient Express inside les Halles, 1st arr.) showing the latest film releases, many in English (look for VO, version originale. *08 92 70 00 00*; ***www.ugc.fr***). For something more high-brow, with older children, you could reserve seats for a production at the **Opéra Bastille** ★ (see p. 136) (Place de la Bastille, 12th arr., M° Bastille. *08 92 89 90 90* or from the UK *+33 172 29 35 35*; ***www.operadeparis.fr***) or at the **Théâtre du Châtelet** ★★ (1 place du Châtelet, 1st arr., M° Châtelet. *01 40 28 28 40*; ***www.chatelet-theatre.com***), which specialises in contemporary dance and musical performances. For older teenagers, **Kong** (1 rue du Pont Neuf, 1st arr., M° Châtelet or Pont-Neuf. *01 40 39 09 00*; ***www.kong.fr***) is a Manga themed, trendy restaurant-bar, designed by Philippe Starck, featured in the US TV series *Sex in the City*.

FAST FACTS

Internet Café Web 46, 46 rue Roi de Sicile, 4th arr., M° Hôtel de Ville. *01 40 27 02 89*. Open 9.30am–10.30pm Mon–Fri, 9.30am–7.30pm Sat, 11am–10.30pm Sun.

Pharmacy **Pharmacie du Forum les Halles**, 1 rue Pierre Lescot, 1st arr., *01 40 41 90 80*, M° Les Halles. Open 8.30am–8pm Mon–Fri, 9.30am–8pm Sat. **Pharmacie du Centre Pompidou**, 4th arr., *01 42 72 96 00,* M° Rambuteau. Open 8.30am–8pm Mon–Fri. 8.30am–1pm, 2.30pm–8pm Sat.

Post Office **La Poste** 52 rue du Louvre, 1st arr., *01 40 28 76 00,* M° Les Halles, Châtelet or Louvre-Rivoli. Open 24/7 or **La Poste** 12 rue Castex, 4th arr., *01 44 54 24 34*. M° Bastille. Open 8.30am–7pm Mon–Fri, 8.30am–noon Sat. There is also a post office in the Pompidou Centre.

Supermarket **Monoprix**, 71 rue St-Antoine, 4th arr., *01 42 74 13 73*. M° St-Paul or Bastille. 9am–9pm Mon–Sat. **Monoprix**, 17 boulevard St-Martin, 3rd arr., *01 44 54 51 52*, 9am–midnight Mon–Sat.

FAMILY-FRIENDLY ACCOMMODATION

VERY EXPENSIVE

Pavillon de la Reine ★★

28 place des Vosges, 4th arr., ☎ *01 40 29 19 19;* ***www.pavillon-de-la-reine.com****. M° Bastille or St-Paul.*

There's a real sense of intimacy from the moment your family steps out of Place des Vosges into this lovely establishment – a haven of peace in an ivy-clad historic building, For children, extra beds and cots can be added to each room, and some rooms are large duplex spaces. Regular packages offer guests seasonal extras: in winter and spring reservations may include a complimentary breakfast for you and the children, tickets to the Louvre, the Bateaux Parisiens, a free parking space, or a bottle of wine. Ask when you reserve or consult the website.

Rooms *56.* ***Rates*** *370€–460€ doubles, 520€–660€, 570€–830€ duplex; extra bed and cot (free).* ***Credit*** *AmEx, MC, V.* ***Amenities*** *private parking, A/C, soundproofing, ADSL, babysitting on request, massage and hairdressing on request.* ***In room*** *safe, TV, Internet.*

EXPENSIVE

Murano Urban Resort ★ FIND

13 boulevard du Temple, 3rd arr., ☎ *01 42 71 20 00;* ***www.muranoresort.com****. M° Filles du Calvaire or République.*

This oddity with furry lifts (loved by children) is a trend-setting, minimalist hotel with a wild and

Pavillon de la Reine

Good, Clean Family Rooms for Around 120€ a Night

www.accorhotels.com **Ibis is a chain (part of the Accor group) but** these two branches, just five minutes from Bastille, are cheap, cheerful, well-situated and good for families on a budget. Rooms can accommodate families of up to four, including babies, for around 120€ a night. All rooms have A/C, WiFi, hotel reception is open 24/7, and there is private parking. Some reduced mobility rooms are available at both addresses: **Ibis Bastille Faubourg St Antoine**, 13 Rue Trousseau, 11th arr., M° Ledru Rollin or Bastille. *01 48 05 55 55*; **Ibis Bastille Opéra**, 15 rue Breguet, 11th arr., M° Bastille or Bréguet-Sabin. *01 49 29 20 20*.

angular interior which is not everyone's cup of tea. However, families into cutting-edge design will find it fun, well thought through, and possibly the most memorable place they've stayed, with details like individual light settings, which include a spectrum of up to six colours to choose from. There are no designated family rooms but extra beds and cots can be added to most doubles and two of the suites have small swimming pools on private terraces – a real family treat in summer. The restaurant on the ground floor serves excellent food, appreciated by locals (children's portions on request).

***Rooms** 52. **Rates** 400€–650€ double; 750€–2500€ suite. **Credit** AmEx, DC, MC, V. **Amenities** bilingual doctor if necessary, babysitting on request; restaurant; bar; 24-hr. room service; car rental; photo service; manicure-pedicure; fitness centre; massage; jacuzzi; spa; some rooms for those with limited mobility. **In room** A/C, TV, safe, Internet.*

MODERATE

Citadines Paris Les Halles ★★ FIND

*4 rue des Innocents, 1st arr., 08 25 33 33 32 (in France); 08-00-376-3898 (in the UK) **www.citadines.com/en/france/paris/les_halles.html**. M° Châtelet or RER A Châtelet-les-Halles.*

If you'd like a self-catering apartment, you won't find one more central than this Citadines apartment block. The chain's no-frill studios and one-bed apartments are adapted for families and can sleep up to four people. Babies are catered for with cots (on request at an extra charge). All come with bedding, a fully equipped kitchen (hobs, microwave, crockery, dishwasher), and cleaning is free once a week. Stay here and you'll be within walking distance of the Marais, Bastille, and the Louvre, plus on a direct RER line to Disney.

***Rooms** 189. **Rates** 1–4 people 207€. **Credit** AmEx, MC, V. **Amenities** lift, A/C, Internet, concierge booking facilities, laundry, dry-cleaning, WiFi, Internet, ADSL.*

In room TV, safety box, fully equipped kitchen. Small animals permitted.

Hôtel Pavillon Bastille ★

65 rue de Lyon, 12th arr., 📞 01 43 43 65 65; ***www.paris-hotel-pavillon bastille.com****. M° Gare de Lyon or Bastille.*

Modern design and comfort are what you get for your money in this converted mansion opposite the Opéra de Bastille. You can book a triple or connecting rooms. The courtyard in front of the main entrance contains a pretty 17th-century fountain and the buffet is almost big enough to keep you going past lunchtime.

Rooms *25.* ***Rates*** *185€–195€ doubles, 390€ family rooms and connecting rooms. Always check for last-minute rates which can be almost 40% cheaper.* ***Credit*** *AmEx, MC, V.* ***Amenities*** *lift, babysitting on request.* ***In room*** *A/C, TV, WiFi, safe.*

INEXPENSIVE

Hôtel du 7e Art ★★

20 rue St-Paul, 4th arr., 📞 01 44 54 85 00; ***www.paris-hotel-7art.com.*** *M° St-Paul or Pont Marie.*

The '7th Art' is a reference to filmmaking and, true to its name, the hotel's décor has been entirely inspired by film. It occupies one of many 17th-century buildings in this part of the Marais, classified as historic monuments, which means that rooms are quite small and there isn't a lift, but extra beds and cots can be inserted, and, if necessary, rooms can be booked side by side. Breakfast is served in the lobby-bar amid film memorabilia. It's

Lobby bar in Hôtel du 7e Art

not the chicest hotel on the block, but fun for all the family, good value for money, and in a top-notch central location.

Rooms *23.* ***Rates*** *65€ single (toilet on the landing); 100€–145€ double; extra-bed 20€* ***Amenities*** *bar; laundry, gym, Internet station.* ***In room*** *TV, dataport, safe.*

FAMILY-FRIENDLY DINING

MODERATE

Caves St Gilles ★

4 rue St Gilles, 3rd arr., 📞 01 48 87 22 62. M° Chemin Vert.

This is a wonderful Spanish tapas restaurant for a lively family meal; it's noisy, bustling, you can see into the kitchen, the waiters run around shouting '*chaud devant*' ('it's hot, move out of the way'), and the food is as copious as it is delicious. If your whippersnappers like seafood, opt for the mixed fish tapas, made up of giant prawns, white fish, squid, and fried octopus. Other dishes include tapas of brochettes (pork, lamb, and chicken), vegetables (stuffed peppers and olives) and tasty paella. One small tapas is big enough for one child, or you could order a selection to share.

Open *8.30am–midnight Mon–Sat (food served noon–3pm, 8pm–11pm),noon–midnight Sun.* ***Tapas*** *5€–14€.* ***A la Carte*** *25€–50€.* ***Credit*** *MC,V.* ***Amenities*** *no disabled access, small terrace, upstairs toilet.*

Le Bofinger ★

5–7 rue de la Bastille, 4th arr., ☎ 01 42 72 87 82; ***www.flobrasseries.com****. M° Bastille.*

Opened in the 1860s, Bofinger is the oldest Alsatian brasserie in town and one of the best. It's a Belle Epoque dining palace, resplendent with brass and stained glass and a fine place to give children a taste of old-school dining. A children's menu introduces them to traditional fish and meat dishes (salmon, sea-snails, mini portions of foie gras, veal steak in cream sauce). Desserts are delicious and usually include chocolate sauce. For grown-ups popular traditional choices are *sauerkraut* and *sole meunière*, or roasted leg of lamb with fondant of artichoke hearts and parsley purée. Weather permitting, you can dine on an outdoor terrace.

Open *Noon–3pm, 6.30pm–1am Mon–Fri; noon–1am Sat–Sun and public holidays.* ***Main Courses*** *15€–35€).* ***Fixed-price menu*** *34€.* ***Credit*** *AmEx, MC, V.* ***Amenities*** *limited disabled access (toilets non-adapted for wheelchairs), children's menu 13.50€, terrace. Reservations recommended.*

INEXPENSIVE

Breakfast in America ★★

4 rue Mahler, 4th arr., ☎ 01 42 72 40 21; ***www.breakfast-in-america.com****. M° St-Paul.*

Crispy bacon, sausages, eggs, chilli hotdogs, burgers, steaks, pancakes, maple syrup, and golden crispy fries are what you get in this tiny but wonderful American diner. It's so popular with Parisian families, queuing is inevitable (if you can't get in there's a larger second branch at 17 rue des Ecoles, 5th arr., M° Cardinel Lemoine or Jussieu). If counting calories, chips can be replaced with tomatoes, coleslaw, or green salad, and fruit or

Two Fine Veggie Addresses

The Pain Quotidien chain (18–20 rue des Archives, 4th arr., M° St-Paul. ☎ *01 44 54 03 07;* ***www.lepainquotidien.com***) has good vegetarian options, or try the tiny totally veggie **Potager du Marais** (22 rue Rambuteau, 4th arr., M° Rambuteau. ☎ *01 42 74 24 66*).

Tea Down to a 'T'

For a family cuppa in the Marais, try the cosy Le Loir dans la Théière (named after Alice in Wonderland's dormouse in the teapot) with its mismatched furniture and Alice in Wonderland murals (3 rue des Rosiers, 3rd arr., M° St-Paul, *01 42 72 90 16*). For somewhere relaxed, there's **Café Suédois** in the **Centre Culturel Suedois** (p. 129). And for a traditional tearoom with more than 500 teas from around the globe and waiters in black-and-white suits, give **Mariage Frères** a whirl (30–32 rue du Bourg-Tibourg, 4th arr., M° St-Paul, *01 42 72 28 11.*

yogurt rather than dessert, though the banana split and hot chocolate are winners. With young children, bring pens to draw on the paper placemats.

***Open** 8.30am–11pm daily. **Main Courses** 7€–10€. Desserts: 2.20€–6€. **Credit** MC, V (no cheques). **Amenities** disabled access, student's menu 7.50€ Mon–Fri 12pm–3pm (with valid ID), Fixed-price menu 9.95€ Mon–Fri 12–3pm. Toilets on ground floor.*

L'Autobus Impérial ★

*14 rue Modétour, 1st arr., 01 42 36 00 18; **www.autobus-imperial.fr.** M° Les Halles.*

Smack-bang in the middle of Les Halles, this stately restaurant is a foodie's hotspot with quality brasserie cuisine at bistro prices with *parmentier* of ham (rather like a shepherd's pie) with a fricassee of wild mushrooms, sea bass roasted in thyme, and a sticky tart from the dessert trolley. Your family could also stop by for a peaceful afternoon tea in the airy salon (free WiFi), where the fancy pastries (particularly strawberry tart) and hot chocolates (plain or orange, cinnamon or caramel flavoured) go down a treat.

***Open** 12pm–3pm, 7pm–10.30pm Mon–Sat. Lunch menus 13.50€–17.50€; evening-menus 24€–30€. **Credit** MC, V. **Amenities** disabled access, toilets on the ground floor, children's menu on request (evenings only).*

7 From St Germain-des-Prés to Luxembourg & Montparnasse

ST-GERMAIN TO MONTPARNASSE

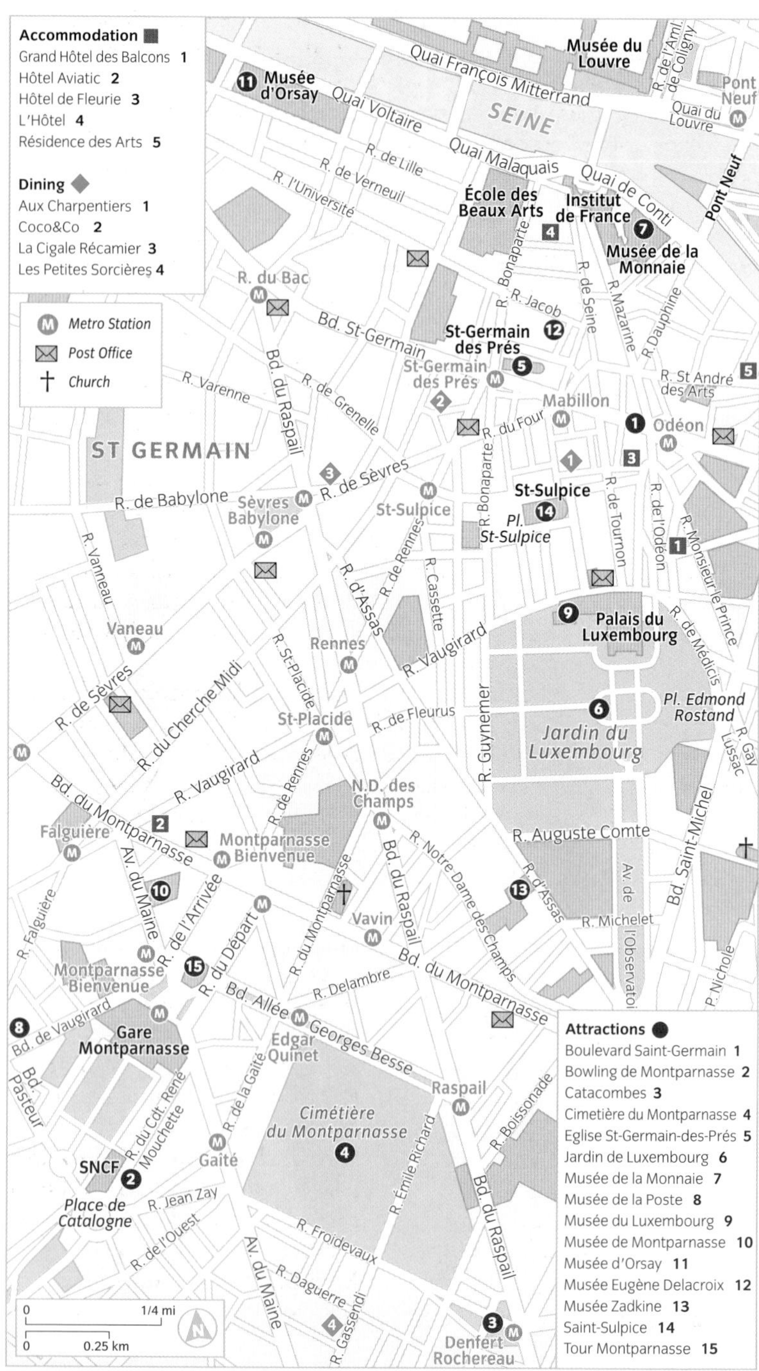

Wandering St-Germain-des-Prés district, there's no getting away from the legacy of generations of artists, thinkers, and writers who made the Left Bank their home in the first half of the 20th century. Past celebrities like Jean-Paul Sartre, Simone de Beauvoir, Picasso, Modigliani, and Ernest Hemingway still draw crowds to the cafés they used to frequent (Café des Deux Magots, Café Flore, and Closerie des Lilas p. 170), which, despite the high prices, have kept their intellectual edge (look out for the literati reading serious tomes on the terrace).

As with the Right Bank, here the 19th-century architect Haussmann (p. 110) replaced much of medieval Paris with his signature boulevards (like Boulevard St-Germain (p. 159), Rue de Rennes and Boulevard de Montparnasse). However, between the avenues, vestiges of the Middle Ages live on in narrow, cobbled streets and wonky ancient buildings. Though thoroughly gentrified (converted into chic housing, designer boutiques, and gourmet food shops) they still capture the charm of yesteryear.

After World War II, Montparnasse was the first part to modernise. In the '60s and '70s streets and housing (including many of the old artists' ateliers) were cleared to make way for the modern mainline train station (Gare SNCF-Montparnasse) and controversial Tour Montparnasse (p. 159) skyscraper. Some hail the tower as 'architectural blasphemy' though it does provide some of the best views over Paris from its rooftop viewing terrace.

In sharp contrast, the Luxembourg quarters, dominated by the striking Jardin du Luxembourg (p. 160 – a must for children) and its sumptuous palace (the government's Senate and Musée du Luxembourg p. 157), are a haven of peace. This is where many Parisians would like to live if they could afford the rent – amid unspoilt streets, old gateways, bookshops, and greenery.

ORIENTATION

The main thoroughfare parallel to the river is Boulevard Saint-Germain, which links the Latin Quarter to the Pont de la Concorde (and therefore to the bottom of the Champs-Elysées). The districts of St-Germain-des-Prés, Luxembourg, and Montparnasse make up a large chunk of the Left Bank, touching on four arrondissments (6th, 7th, 14th, and 15th). The good news is that these areas can be covered on foot quite easily (St-Germain and Montparnasse to Luxembourg is 15 minutes, St-Germain to Montparnasse is 10 minutes) and when the going gets tough on tiny feet, taxis are usually easy to find. Métro line 4 runs underneath Rue de Rennes (between St-Germain and Montparnasse), as does bus number 95. Line 4 is also a handy and direct route to Châtelet (from where you can catch the RER to Disneyland) and Barbès-Rochechouart near Montmartre. The Louvre and Notre-Dame are all easy walking distances from these districts too.

GETTING AROUND

The principal bus routes are no. **95,** which links Montparnasse to St-Germain, the Louvre, Opéra, and Montmartre; no. **38**, which travels along Boulevard St-Michel on the east of the Jardin du Luxembourg; no. **89** also goes to the gardens after a quick stint on rue de Rennes; no. **68** travels along boulevard de Raspail past the Cimetière de Montparnasse; and no. **63** covers most of Boulevard St-Germain. A handy **Batobus** stop is **Saint-Germain-des-Prés**.

INSIDER TIP

RER B from Denfert-Rochereau or Luxembourg is direct to the Gare du Nord and the Charles-de-Gaulle (north) and Orly (south) airports.

VISITOR INFORMATION

There aren't any Tourist Offices in this area so stock up on information or bring this guide with you. The nearest office is in the Carrousel du Louvre (99 rue de Rivoli, 1st arr., M° Palais-Royal-Musée du Louvre. *08 92 68 30 00*; ***www.parisinfo.com***).

WHAT TO SEE & DO

Children's Top 5 Attractions

❶ **Sailing** toy boats in the Jardin du Luxembourg (see p. 160).

❷ **Learning** how coins are minted in the Musée de la Monnaie (see p. 152).

❸ **Starting** or adding to your stamp collection in the Musée de la Poste (see p. 153).

❹ **Spying** on the whole of Paris 59 floors up on the Tour Montparnasse (see p. 153).

❺ **Navigating** a spooky maze of bones and skulls in the Catacombes (see p. 162).

Culture & Museums

Musée de la Monnaie ★★

AGES 8 AND ABOVE

11 quai de Conti, 6th arr., 01 40 46 56 66; ***www.monnaiedeparis.com****. M° Odéon, Pont Neuf or St-Michel, RER Band C St-Michel.*

In the gorgeous, Neoclassical *Palais Conti* on the Seine (circa 1770s) is the minting museum – a fantastic place if your children love collecting shiny new coins and medals. Hi-tech exhibits trace the history of global and local coinage from pre-Roman times to today and good audio guides in English (for 10s and above) are available for individual tours. The Workshop tour (Wed–Fri 2.15pm, 3€) shows families how the minting process takes place, with reducing lathes, striking of the coins, and final chiselling and polishing.

Open *11am–5.30pm Tues–Fri, noon–5.30pm Sat–Sun.* ***Admission*** *5€ adults, free under-12s.*

Musée de la Poste ★★

AGES 8 AND ABOVE

34 boulevard de Vaugirard, 15th arr., 01 42 79 24 24; ***www.museedelaposte.fr****. M° Montparnasse, Pasteur, or Falguière.*

Stamp collectors rejoice, this one's for you: 15 rooms on five floors entirely devoted to the history of the postal service with uniforms, carriages, letter boxes, waxwork figures, pistols, official documents, and, of course, stamps – hundreds of them – all documenting French and international philately. As your children look at the exhibits, they'll also pick up interesting historical titbits: for instance, during the 1870s' Prussian invasions, Parisians used carrier pigeons and hot-air balloons to communicate with the outside world, along with contraptions called *boules de Moulin* – balls filled with letters that they floated down the Seine in the hope that someone would find them. Some of the best parts for under-10s are in rooms 9 to 12, with exhibition cases filled with rare stamps from China, Canada, Germany, and the USA, and corresponding postmen's uniforms.

Open *10am–6pm Mon–Sat. Closed most bank holidays.* ***Admission*** *5€ adults, 3.50€ 19–26s, free under-18s.*

Musée de Montparnasse ★

AGES 13 AND ABOVE

21 avenue du Maine, 15th arr., 01 42 22 91 96; ***www.museedumontparnasse.net****. M° Montparnasse or Edgar Quinet,*

In the early 20th century, Montmartre's reputation as a centre for art caused its prices to rise and its impoverished artists to move south to the more reasonably priced Montparnasse district. Here they created workshops and theatres, frequented the cafés, and turned the whole area into a thriving artistic and literary centre. The Musée de Montparnasse, set down an exquisite cobbled lane surrounded by modern-day artists' ateliers, was the former workshop of artist Marie Vassilieff who used it as a canteen for needy artists. Braque, Modigliani, Léger, Picasso, Matisse, and Cocteau all ate here – as did Trotsky and Lenin, which caused problems with the police. Nowadays it documents Montparnasse's extraordinary and often debauched golden age in an endless series of temporary exhibitions (photos, paintings, letters, and sculptures). The **Espace Krajcberg** gallery next-door (open 2pm–6pm Tues–Sun) is a joint venture between France and Brazil, promoting modern art and the importance of respecting the environment, often in weird and wacky exhibits which appeal to young children.

Open *12.30pm–7pm Tues–Sun.* ***Admission*** *5€ adults, 3€ students, free under-12s.*

Musée d'Orsay ★★

AGES 5 AND ABOVE

1 rue de Bellechasse or 62 rue de Lille, 7th arr., 01 40 49 48 14; ***www.musee-orsay.fr****. M° Solférino. RER: Musée d'Orsay.*

The Musée d'Orsay, in the old Orsay train station, is one of the world's top museums and a must for all families. There's something magically incongruous about seeing so much art in a place that looks like it should hold steam-engines, and your children will be intrigued by the huge arching glass roof, which lets in floods of light.

Like the Louvre, there are so many exhibits it's vital to decide what to see first.

The Orsay's astounding collection covers 1848 to 1914, with a treasure trove by the big names plus lesser-known groups (symbolists, pointillists, realists, and more). The 80 galleries also include furniture, photographs, objets d'art, and architectural models.

Choose a theme such as dancing, getting your smaller children to find pieces linked to performing, or exhibits showing people dancing. Older ones can try and understand the underlying ideas. Examples include:

❶ **Carpeaux's *La Danse*** (ground floor central alley). Commissioned by architect Charles Garnier for the Opera House in 1865, it shows laughing women, allegories of bacchanal dancing, and carnal pleasures. When revealed on the face of the Opera House (a copy is still visible today, see p. 101), it was considered so shocking one person threw an ink bottle at it.

❷ **Miniature street plan of the Opéra district** (ground floor). Sunk into the floor, with a glass top, children can pretend to be giants walking on top of the streets, houses, and domes, including the Opera House. See if they can find it.

Outside the Musée d'Orsay

TIP Which Floors?

Works from the mid to late 19th century are on the ground floor; Art Nouveau art and paintings and sculptures from the late 19th century and early 20th century are on the middle floor; and a breathtaking collection of Impressionist and neo-Impressionist works is on the top floor.

❸ **Degas' *Ballerina*** (petite danseuse de 14 ans) on the upper floor. The little 14-year-old dancer, lifting her chin into the air, is one of Degas' most famous works. Like Carpeaux's *La Danse*, the sculpture was deemed scandalous, daring to represent the underworld of the Opera – a place where, to survive, young ballerinas often became courtesans. The surrounding works include bronze statuettes of Degas' study of dance movements, and famous paintings like ***Le Foyer de la Danse*** and ***Classe de Danse*** (dance class).

❹ ***La Danse au Moulin Rouge*** (upper floor). At end of the gallery you'll find Toulouse-Lautrec's famous depiction of the Moulin Rouge cabaret. Not long after Lautrec painted the scene, the lead cancan girl was forced to become a belly dancer at the Foire du Trône funfair (see p. 22).

Another great theme is Impressionism. But beware; the impressionist paintings are the ones that draw the hordes. Led by Manet, Renoir, and Monet, the Impressionists (see p. 83) shunned religious and mythological set pieces for a light-bathed Seine, faint figures strolling in the Tuileries, pale-faced women in hazy bars, and even ugly train stations like the Gare St-Lazare. The Impressionists were also the first to paint that most characteristic feature of Parisian life – the sidewalk café.

Highlights to point out are:

❶ Manet's 1863 ***Déjeuner sur l'herbe (Picnic on the Grass)*** in room 19; a forest setting with a naked woman and two fully clothed men, which sent

HISTORY A Quick History Lesson

With almost 10,000 visitors a day, the former Gare d'Orsay gets more attention today than it did as a railway station. Built for the World Fair in 1900, it connected southwest France to Paris until 1939, when modern trains could no longer use the station's short platforms. During the war it became a detention centre for prisoners of war, and then briefly housed the Renaud-Barrault theatre company before falling into disrepair. It was heading for demolition until president Valéry Giscard d'Estaing decided to turn it into a 19th-century art museum in 1977. It finally opened in 1986.

Statue-spotting in Front of the d'Orsay

Chances are you'll be queuing to get into the Musée d'Orsay. So if you're with small children, get them to name the animals in the statues in front of the main entrance. There's a horse by Pierre-Louis Rouillard, an ensnared elephant by Alfred Jacquemart, and a rhinoceros by Emmanuel Freimet. All were ordered for the 1878 World Fair and initially stood in the Trocadéro gardens (see p. 75). For older children, six statues along the Rue de Lille evoke the six continents. See if they can recognise which is which. From left to right they are: Europe, Asia, Africa, North America, South America, and Oceania.

shockwaves through respectable society when first exhibited.

❷ The ***Bal du Moulin de la Galette*** (1876) in room 32 is one of Renoir's most joyous paintings. You can see the real Moulin today in Montmartre – a restaurant in a converted windmill (see p. 103).

❸ The effect of changing light on ***Rouen Cathédrale*** (room 34) fascinated Paris-born Monet, and he brought its stone to life in a series of five paintings, the differences between them often appealing to children. There's also Monet's ***Houses of Parliament*** in the same room.
If you're there over lunch, grab a light bite in the self-service restaurant on the top floor, or opt for the pricier dining room just behind the station's old transparent clock. Even if you don't eat there, take the children to see the clock as there is something magical about being on the inside of a transparent timepiece that looks out over the city. In the summer a small terrace is also open.

Open *9.30am–6pm Tues–Sun (until 9.45pm Thurs).* ***Admission*** *7.50€ adults, 5.50€ 18–24s, free under-18s.* ***TIP:*** *Save your ticket and within eight days of your visit, get reduced entry to the Musée Gustave Moreau (p. 100) and the Palais Garnier Opera House (p. 100). Also buy a combined ticket for the Musée d'Orsay and Rodin museum for 12€.*

Musée Eugène Delacroix

AGES 13 AND ABOVE

6 rue Furstenberg, 6th arr., ☎ 01 44 41 86 50; ***www.musee-delacroix.fr****. M° St Germain-des-Prés.*

These collections will be lost on younger children (although they can enjoy the little garden), but if you want to show your teenagers where the leading nonconformist Romantic painter lived, worked, and died, this is worth at least an hour, ideally followed by a trip round the St Sulpice church (p. 158), where in Chapelle des Anges you can see the original murals Delacroix was working on when he lived here from 1857 to 1863.

A large arch on a courtyard leads to Delacroix's studio featuring sketches, lithographs, watercolours, and oils. Highlights of the passionate and highly coloured works are *Mary Magdalen in the Wilderness* (a mysterious lady with a mane of thick black hair); a rare self portrait (1821) dressed as Edgar Ravenswood, a character from Walter Scott's novel, *The Bride of Lammermoor*; and *Charles V at the Monastery of Yuste,* painted for his student and friend Marie-Elisabeth Boulanger-Cavé in 1837. Delacroix (1798–1863) is something of an enigma. Baudelaire called him 'a volcanic crater artistically concealed beneath bouquets of flowers'. Even his parentage is controversial. Many believe Talleyrand was his father and not Charles Delacroix who was married to his mother.

***Open** 9.30am–5pm Wed–Mon. **Admission** 5€ adults, free under-18s.*

Musée Zadkine

AGES 5 AND ABOVE

*100 bis rue d'Assas, 6th arr., 01 55 42 77 20; **www.paris.fr/musees/zadkine**. M° Notre-Dame des Champs or Vavin*

Near the Jardin du Luxembourg, in this small house with its conservatory, pigeonnier, and lovely garden, the Cubist sculptor Ossip Zadkine (1890–1967), lived and worked from 1928 to his death. Children of all ages will appreciate his 300 pieces of sculpture ranging from 'left wing' cubist extremism to his later classical works, displayed in the museum and dotted about the charming garden. The garden is one of the finest places to relax in Paris on a sunny day.

***Open** 10am–6pm Tues–Sun. **Admission** free to permanent collections. **Exhibition admission** 4€ adults, 2€ under-26s.*

Culture in the Park – Musée du Luxembourg

*19 rue Vaugirard, 6th arr., 01 42 34 25 95; **www.museeduluxembourg.fr**. M° St-Sulpice.*

The Palais du Luxembourg (today's French Senate) and its famous gardens (a fabulous park for children, see p. 160) were originally built for Marie du Médici (widow of Henri IV) to remind her of her native Florence. Before the Revolution, in 1750, a small wing of the palace became France's first public gallery. Today, regular art exhibitions – usually one-offs of some of the world's most famous artists – are held here. Reserve in advance (online or at Fnac or Virgin Megastore) and to jump the queues and maximise the time the children can spend in the park, book a '*coupe-file*' (queue jumper) ticket choosing your time of visit. There's a lovely little café (Café Médicis) on the way in.

***Open** 10.30am–10pm Mon, Fri, Sat. 10.30am–7pm Tues–Thurs, 9am–7pm Sun (during school holidays from 9am daily). **Admission** 11€ adults, 9€ 10–25s, free under-10s.*

4 Roues sous un Parapluie

Treat your family to an unusual sightseeing tour in a real French 2CV Citröen, with **4 Roues sous un Parapluie**, a unique company offering a range of excellent themed driving tours (Secret Paris, Eternal Paris, Paris à la Carte) around town and out into Versailles (Paris Outskirts). Children find it wholly novel and you don't have to worry about confronting mad Parisian drivers. Prices from 54€ to 238€ per person (max. 3 per car). *0800 800 632* (within France), *+33 6 67 32 26 68*; (from overseas); ***www.4roues-sous-1parapluie.com***.

Places of Worship

L'Eglise St-Germain-des-Prés ★★

3 place St-Germain-des-Prés, 6th arr., 01 43 25 41 71. M° St-Germain-des-Prés.

Dating from the 6th century when a Benedictine abbey was founded here by Childebert, son of Clovis, the marble columns in the triforium are all that remain from the period. But if your family enjoys visiting old buildings you won't be disappointed by the wholly medieval atmosphere inside. There's a Romanesque nave and an exquisite Gothic choir, plus the tombs of Descartes (his heart, at least) and Jean-Casimir, the king of Poland who abdicated his throne and later became abbot here. Topping it all is a Romanesque tower with a 19th-century spire, visible across the city. For a real treat, take your children to one of the regular classical music (often Gregorian) concerts – the church boasts fantastic acoustics. For booking details buy the *Officiel du Spectacle* or *Pariscope* from a press stand, or check the ticket office in a Fnac or Virgin Megastore.

Open *8am–7.45pm Mon–Sat, 9am–8pm Sun.* ***Admission*** *free.*

Saint-Sulpice ★★

Rue St-Sulpice, 6th arr., 01 46 33 21 78. M° St-Sulpice.

Dan Brown's *Da Vinci Code* wrongly said that the St Sulpice's gnomon (a type of sundial) and obelisk were part of Paris's meridian line. However, if your children enjoyed *The Da Vinci Code*, they'll take pleasure in

Saint Sulpice

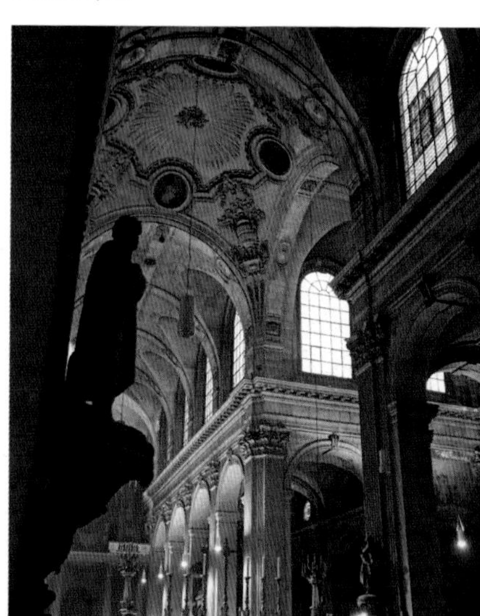

seeing where some of the critical scenes took place. Work on the church began in 1646 and it features Delacroix frescoes in the **Chapelle des Anges (Chapel of the Angels),** the first on your right as you enter. Look for his muscular Jacob wrestling with an effete angel. On the ceiling, St Michael is having some troubles with the Devil, and another mural depicts Heliodorus being driven from the temple.

Open *7.30am–7.30pm daily.* ***Admission*** *free.*

Streets & Monuments

Boulevard Saint-Germain

The 3km-long Boulevard St Germain is one of Paris's most celebrated and busy thoroughfares, cutting through three districts from the Pont de la Concorde in the 7th arr. to Ile St-Louis in the 4th arr. Its intoxicating atmosphere inspired the writings of many authors including Ernest Hemingway. It witnessed the birth of Jean-Paul Sartre's existentialist philosophy (see box below), and it has even given its name to one of France's most popular electro-jazz music bands (St Germain) – a group with enough street-cred to interest teenagers (as well as mums and dads). Check out their CDs in Fnac or Virgin Megastore.

Tour Montparnasse ★★

ALL AGES

33 avenue du Maine, 15th arr., 01 45 38 52 56; ***www.tourmontparnasse56.com****. M° Montparnasse-Bienvenue.*

Completed in 1973, the 210m Montparnasse tower was denounced by some as 'bringing Manhattan to Paris' and the city soon passed an ordinance outlawing any further structures of this size in the heart of Paris. However, it's an exciting place to bring children, with a big underground shopping centre and a lift to the 56th floor that moves so fast your ears pop. There you'll find a panoramic café and excellent restaurant with its own piano

Mum, Dad what's Existentialism?

Although it had forerunners in earlier centuries, existentialism is a philosophical movement that attracted a great following in France and Europe after World War II. It considers each person a unique being responsible for his own actions and an actor in his own destiny. The writer and philosopher Jean-Paul Sartre along with his partner Simone de Beauvoir and the author Albert Camus (famed for his 1942 novel *L'Etranger* (*The Stranger*)) are given credit for its widespread popularity. For them, and their many followers, existentialism wasn't only defined by their way of life, but also by where they lived – in this case, St-Germain-des-Prés, where they deliberated human existence and politics in its many cafés and jazz clubs.

FUN FACT Tour Montparnasse

- It weighs 120,000 tonnes.
- Its lifts are the fastest in Europe, moving 6m/second (that's 38 seconds for the 196m tall lift shaft).
- There are 30 sq km of shops inside the whole structure (mostly underground).

bar (Ciel de Paris, *01 40 64 77 64*. Average 80€), and an indoor viewing point with a few interactive exhibits aimed at families. Three flights of stairs above, the roof terrace affords dramatic vistas over Paris (some 40km on a clear day), taking in virtually every important monument. Don't forget to point out the helipad marks on the floor of the terrace: the seven-year-old I took found it very exciting to think that helicopters sometimes land here.

If you visit towards the end of December, there are family Christmas treasure hunts and other activities on the top floors, (no reservations required. 9.50€ adults; 4€ 7–15s; free for under-7s).

***Open** 9.30am–11.30pm daily Apr–Sept, 9.30am–10.30pm Sun–Thurs, 9.30am–11pm Fri–Sat and the eve of public holidays Oct–Mar. Last lift 30 min before closing. **Admission** 9.50€ adults, 7€ students 16–20, 4€ 7–14s, free under-7s.*

Parks & the Outdoors

Jardin du Luxembourg ★★

FIND ALL AGES

*Main access: 2 rue Auguste Comte, 6th arr., **www.paris.fr**. M° Notre-Dame-des-Champs, RER B Luxembourg.*

This is one of Paris's best parks for families. Its handsome 25

Wooden boats for hire, Jardin du Luxembourg

hectares are arranged around a large fountain (*Le Grand Bassin*), with rectangular alleys radiating from the centre, plus a stunning terrace and regal statues sprinkled about the grounds. There are also fun activities, plenty of little ice cream and drinks stands, and lovely shaded benches on hot sunny days.

In the summer (Apr–Sept) miniature **wooden boats** sailed on the Grand Bassin are a hit with toddlers and under-10s alike, who poke them around the water with long sticks and occasionally try to sink their neighbour's vessels. Under-6s can make sandcastles in the **sandpits**, walk on the **lawns**, play on the swings, and for 7–12s there's an **enclosed play area. Ponies and donkeys** are there all year round ready to take youngsters on a ride. There's **boules** (a sort of lawn bowling) dominated by old, moustached, Gitanes-smoking regulars; and on a hot day, whizz-kids can try their hand at a game of **chess** with elderly men who wear black berets and sit at rickety tables that look like they haven't been moved for 70 years – and probably haven't. The best activity, however, has to be the Guignol puppet show in the **Théâtre des Marionnettes** (*01 43 26 46 47* or *01 43 29 50 97*; ***http://guignolduluxembourg.monsite.orange.fr***. Open Wed, Sat–Sun, bank holidays and daily during school holidays. Tickets: 4.50€ each adult and child). In the middle of the garden, this is a family-run institution that has been performing French Punch and Judy shows since 1933. Even if you don't understand French, the shows (often based on universal fairy stories like the Three Little Pigs or Red Riding Hood), held in the biggest puppet theatre in France (300 seats) are visual enough to be understood and very funny.

Get there 30 minutes before the performance to grab the best seats. **Tip:** On your way in or out of the gardens, look out for

History – A Lady's Park

Marie de Médici, wife of Henri IV, ordered the **Palais du Luxembourg** to be built on this site in 1612, shortly after she was widowed. Alas, the queen didn't get to enjoy the palace, as her son, Louis XIII, forced her into exile when he discovered she was plotting to overthrow him. She died in poverty in Cologne.

Built for one lady, the park also honours another – Paris's patroness, St. Geneviève. Parisians believed that her prayers saved Paris from attacks by Attila the Hun (he struck Orleans instead). She is represented in a beautiful statue by Michel-Louis Victor (1845), with long plaited pigtails. See if your children can find it in the park. It's on the right-hand side of the palace (looking at it), just up the flight of stairs to the right of the Grand Bassin.

Hemingway's Pigeon Eating

During the poverty-stricken days of the author Ernest Hemingway, the Jardin du Luxembourg was his preferred hunting ground. He wheeled a baby's pram through the garden (known 'for the classiness of its pigeons'), and when the gendarme went across the street for a glass of wine, would eye his victim, preferably a plump one, lure him with corn, 'snatch him, wring his neck', and hide him under the blanket. 'We got a little tired of pigeon that year,' he confessed, 'but they filled many a void.'

the ever-changing photo exhibitions on the walls. They are usually both thought-provoking (previous exhibits have included shots of the environment and 20th-century photography) and attractive to young eyes.

Open *8am to nightfall daily.* ***Amenities*** *WC chalet 0.40€ with padded changing table.*

Spooky Paris

Catacombs ★★

AGES 13 AND ABOVE

1 place Denfert-Rochereau, 14th arr., ☎ 01 43 22 47 63; ***www.paris.fr****. M° and RER B Denfert Rochereau.*

Not for the faint-hearted, the catacombs are Paris's spookiest museum and young children might get frightened by the dark corridors of anonymous bones, skulls, and altars, but teenagers, especially those harbouring gothic tendencies, will be mesmerised by the 910m long tunnel, 18m underground, where the walls are entirely made from more than six million ghoulishly arranged skull-and-crossbones skeletons. (The catacombs actually cover 11,000 sq m, but only this small portion can be visited legally).

First opened to the public in 1810, this 'empire of the dead' is now illuminated with electric lights. In the Middle Ages, it was the site of quarries, but by the end of the 18th century, overcrowded cemeteries were becoming a menace to public health (some people's cellars had bones poking through the walls). City officials decided to use the tunnels as a burial ground, and move the bones of several million people from graveyards across the city. Nowadays more than 160,000 visitors face their fear here every year. Don't worry, there really is nothing to be afraid of; and as you leave, you'll walk underneath two wonderful *cloches de fontis* (vaulted ceilings, created during the quarrying process) that are some of the finest examples open to the public. **Tip:** Bring a torch to get a good look at the bones, and footwear that you don't mind getting dirty, as the ground is often wet and chalky.

Open *10am–5pm Tues–Sun (last ticket sold at 4pm).* ***Admission*** *7€ adults, 3.50€14–25s, free under-13s.*

FUN FACT The Catacombs

1. In World War II, they were the headquarters of the French Resistance.
2. Before that, in 1871, they were the scenes of bloody battles of the French Commune.
3. On 2 April 1897, 45 musicians played an illegal concert of Chopin and Beethoven's Funeral Marches among the bones.
4. *Cataphile* is the name given to those who enter the catacombs illegally (since 1955); the problem has become so great that special police march underground.

Shopping

The area around St-Germain-des-Prés and Montparnasse is often overshadowed by the reputation of the Opéra's department stores (see p. 114), however this is where you'll find the locals doing *le shopping*, nipping in and out of designer shops and one-off clothes boutiques (on **Boulevard St Germain,** around **St Sulpice, Rue du Bac,** and **Marché St Germain**), high-street chains such as Fnac, Zara, and H&M (below the **Tour Montparnasse** and along **Rue de Rennes**) and some of the capital's gourmet food stores (see below). **Galeries Lafayette** has a branch beneath the Tour Montparnasse (22 rue Départ, 15th arr. M° Montparnasse-Bienvenuë), and Paris's oldest department store, opened in 1848, is **Le Bon Marché**, (24 rue de Sèvres, 7th arr. ***www.lebonmarche.fr*** M° Sèvres-Babylone) with its global designer labels, swish Balthazar Men's section, and women's pampering area known as the Théâtre de la Beauté. Its **Grande Epicerie de Paris** is fabulous for families who are self-catering or looking for a posh snack, with a never-ending array of luxury foodstuffs.

Books

Paris wouldn't truly be Paris without its iconic, little green bookstands, **Les Bouquinistes**, which follow the banks of the Seine along the Left Bank (Quai de la Tournelle, 5th arr., to Quai Malaquais, 6th arr.) selling secondhand editions of classical and unusual books. Children may be

Off with their Heads at no. 9 Cour du Commerce St-André!

Everyone thinks that Dr Guillotin invented the guillotine used in the Revolution. However, all he did was perfect it. Here at 9 cour du Commerce St-André (6th arr. M° Odéon) the real inventor was the Paris surgeon Dr Louis, and the first guillotines used during the *Terreur* were called *Louisettes*.

Window gazing at Galeries Lafayette

lucky enough to find some old fairy stories and for the older ones, there are retro-style posters, postcards, and photos. If your children are studying French, **La Hune** (170 boulevard St Germain, 6th arr. M° St Germain-des-Prés) is a Left Bank literary institution with a huge selection of books on art and design and French literature.

Food

The best place to take children of all ages is **Poilâne** (8 rue du Cherche-Midi, 6th arr. M° Sèvres-Babylone or St-Sulpice), a bakery selling delicious country *miches* (loaves), tarts and shortbread, run by the 24-year-old Apollonia Poilâne who had to take over the family business aged just 18 when her parents died in a helicopter accident. They've been making the same organic bread here (enjoyed by celebrities like Robert De Niro who has his loaves sent to the USA via Fedex) since Apollonia's grandfather opened the shop in 1933. If you come when it's quiet you can to go downstairs to see the traditional bread oven. **Fromagerie Quatrehomme** (62 rue de Sèvres, 7th arr., M° Vaneau) is an award-winning cheese shop, famed for its ripe St-Marcellin cheeses and truffle-filled brie. **Pierre Hermé** (72 rue Bonaparte, 6th arr., M° St-Sulpice) is a pastry superstar loved by children and adults

Quick Shopper's Snack

Just next door to Poilâne, their sister café, **Cuisine du Bar** (8 rue du Cherche-Midi, 6th arr. M° Sèvres-Babylone or St-Sulpice), is a handy spot for a quick sarnie on some wholesome Poilâne bread.

Getting Chocolatey Fingers on the Left Bank

There are numerous chocolate shops around Saint-Germain but here are four of the best your family can try and compare:

1 **Christian Constant** – delicious *ganaches* flavoured with jasmine, cardamom, and verbena (37 rue d'Assas, 6th arr., M° St-Placide or Rennes).
2 **Debauve and Gallais** – tea, honey, and praline-flavoured chocolates, sold in a former 19th-century pharmacy (30 rue des Saints-Pères, 7th arr., M° St Germain-des-Prés or Rue du Bac).
3 **Jean-Paul Hévin** – audacious chocolates filled with cheeses and even aphrodisiac chocolates. (3 rue Vavin, 6th arr., M° Vavin)
4 **Pierre Marcolini** – 44 ganache flavours and chocolate cakes considered to be edible sculptures (89 rue de Seine, 6th arr., M° Mabillon).

alike for his lip-smacking, sculpted creations. The most original cakes in town can be bought in the Japanese patisserie **Sadaharu Aoki** (35 rue de Vaugirard, 6th arr., M° St-Placide) which combines traditional French techniques with Japanese flavours like green tea. The **Huilerie Artisanale Leblanc** (6 rue Jacob, 6th arr. M° St Germain-des-Prés) is a fantastic family-run oil shop selling all sorts of varieties from unusual pistachio nut oil to traditional olive oils. Mums and Dads should also stop in at **Ryst Dupeyron** (79 rue du Bac, 7th arr., M° Rue du Bac), an Ali-Baba's cave of Armagnac (with some bottles dating from 1848), ports, and more than 200 bottles of Bordeaux wines.

Just for children

For that ultimate Parisian child look, **Coquelicot-Paprika** (99 rue du Bac, 7th arr., M° Rue du Bac or Sèvres Babylone) sells simple, elegant children's clothes for babies and under-12s. There are also toys strewn around the shop to occupy young children while parents look around. Other good French children's clothes stores are **Bonton** (82 rue de Grenelle, 7th arr., M° Rue du Bac) a mini concept store for youngsters and their trendy parents with colourful clothes and accessories; **Jacadi** (73 rue de Sèvres, 6th arr., M° Sèvres-Babylone) where pretty dresses, trousers, and shoes are a hit with Parisian mums; and for shoes, **Six Pieds Trois Pouces** (223 boulevard St-Germain, 7th arr., M° Solférino) which stocks children's and teen brands from Aster and Little Mary to Reebok and Camper. For a whole range of toys, games, and teddies for newborns to 12-year-olds, **FNAC Junior** (19 rue Vavin, 6th arr., M° Vavin) is unbeatable on the Left Bank.

Fashion Titbits

Older teenage girls may like to visit the boutique of **Corrine Sarrut** (4 rue du Pré-aux-Clercs, 7th arr., M° Rue du Bac), who dressed the actress Audrey Tautou for her role in *Amélie*. **Le Mouton à Cinq Pates** (138 boulevard St-Germain, 6th arr., M° Odéon) is a great vintage store for unusual designer wear. If you have any family weddings coming up, **Marie Mercié** (23 rue St Sulpice, 6th arr., M° Odéon) designs some beautiful hats; and for utterly wearable, older boy's and men's rags, **APC** (4 rue de Fleurus, 6th arr., M° St-Placide), with its simple cuts and cool accessories is the place to see and be seen in.

Markets ★★
At the **Marché Raspail**, on Boulevard Raspail, between Rue du Cherche-Midi and Rue de Rennes (6th arr., M° Rennes; 7am–2.30pm Tues–Fri) you can smell the cheeses, admire the fresh produce, and allow your family to experience a truly Parisian market. It turns into an organic market on Sundays (9am–3pm). The **Marché Couvert St-Germain** is a lovely (if expensive) covered market, open all week (8am–1pm, 4pm–8pm Tues–Fri, 8am–1.30pm, 3.30pm–8pm Sat; closed Mon).

Nightlife

Bowling de Paris Montparnasse AGES 5 AND ABOVE

25 rue du Commandant Mouchotte, 14th arr., 01 43 21 61 32; ***www.bowling-amf.com****. M° Gaïté.*

Going bowling probably isn't the first activity that springs to mind in Paris, but after dinner or if it's raining, this light and well looked after bowling alley will entertain the troops with 16 competition-sized bowling lanes, pool tables, video games, and a snack bar. Bowling balls are provided and shoes can be hired. Special barriers can also be installed in the lanes to help small children. Ask about their student (*étudiant*) and night (*nuit*) packages, which offer two games, shoe hire, and a drink at the bar for 11€ and 16€ respectively.

Open *10am–2am Sun–Thurs, 10am–4am Fri, 10am–5am Sat.* ***Admission*** *4.50€ Mon –Fri before 8pm and Sat–Sun until 2pm; 6.30€ after 8pm Mon–Fri and after 2pm Sat–Sun.*

FAST FACTS

Internet Café **Milk**, 5 rue d'Odessa, 14th arr., *08 20 00 10 00*; M° Montparnasse. Open 24/7. **Haagen Dazs**, 12 rue de Buci, 6th arr., M° Odéon or Mabillon, *01 44 41 00 05*. Open 9.30am–midnight Sun–Thurs, 9.30am–2am Fri–Sat

Pharmacy **Pharmacie Saint Germain Des Prés**, 19 boulevard Haussmann, 9th arr.,

01 43 26 52 92, M° St-Germain-des-Prés. Open 9am–midnight daily.

Post Office **La Poste** 53 rue de Rennes, 6th arr., *01 44 39 28 20*. M° Saint-Germain-des-Prés. Open 8am–7pm Mon–Fri, 8am–noon Sat or **La Poste** 24 rue de Vaugirard, 6th arr., *01 42 34 99 20*. M° Odéon or RER B Luxembourg. Open 8am–7pm Mon–Fri, 8am–10am Sat.

Supermarket **Monoprix**, 50 rue de Rennes, 6th arr., *01 45 48 18 08*. M° Saint-Germain-des-Prés. 9am–10pm Mon–Sat.

FAMILY-FRIENDLY ACCOMMODATION

VERY EXPENSIVE

L'Hôtel ★★

*13 rue des Beaux-Arts, 6th arr., 01 44 41 99 00; **www.l-hotel.com**. M° St-Germain-des-Prés*

Cosy, romantic, opulent, and exuberant – this is a gem of a hotel, tucked away on a quiet street between St-Germain and the Seine. There's decadent 19th-century-style décor, a pool, sauna, and a list of VIPs that includes Johnny Depp (he likes the bar). You'd be forgiven for thinking that children aren't accepted, but the hotel welcomes families with extra beds and cots that can be fitted into some rooms on request, babysitters can be ordered, and staff are happy to heat babies' bottles for you if necessary. Children love the unusual spiral staircase that looks out on to the circular hall (classed as a national monument), and literature fans appreciate staying in the hotel where Oscar Wilde died penniless, on the ground floor. One of the rooms (Chambre Oscar Wilde) recreates his living room in England. The restaurant, run by rising star chef Philippe Bélissent, has just received its first

L'Hôtel

Michelin star, and is the perfect setting for an intimate family treat (average 80€). Lifts are small, which may mean you have to leave your buggies downstairs, but it's a small price to pay for such a lovely establishment.

***Rooms** 20. **Rates** 345€–640€ doubles, 640€–740€ suites; extra bed and cot (free).**Credit** AmEx, MC, V. **Amenities** A/C, bar. **In room** safe, TV, Internet plug.*

EXPENSIVE

Hôtel de Fleurie ★ FIND

*32–34 rue Grégoire-de-Tours, 6th arr., 01 53 73 70 00; **www.hotel-de-fleurie.fr**. M° Odéon or Mabillon*

Off Boulevard St-Germain on a colourful little street, the Fleurie is perfect for families, with thoughtfully appointed rooms. Many are connecting and others large enough to contain an extra bed for one or two children. Its statuary-studded façade recaptures 17th-century elegance, and the stone walls in the salon have been exposed. Many of the guest rooms have elaborate fabrics and antique reproductions, and the location is very central, so you can explore much of the Left Bank on foot. **Tip:** This is popular with families, so book well in advance.

***Rooms** 29. **Rates** 250€–350€ doubles, 450€ family rooms. Children under 12 stay free in parents' room. **Credit** AmEx, DC, MC, V. **Amenities** bar; babysitting on request; laundry service; dry cleaning; rooms for those with limited mobility. **In room** A/C, TV, Internet plug, safe.*

Résidence des Arts ★

*14 rue Git-le-Coeur, 6th arr., 01 55 42 71 11; **www.hotelresidencedesartsparis.com**. M° St-Michel or Odéon.*

This 16th-century residence is a family favourite, filled with handsomely decorated rooms and apartments for three to four, smack-bang in between St-Germain-des-Prés and St Michel in the Latin Quarter. Regular doubles feature shower-only bathrooms, but each suite and apartment offers a large sitting room with a hide-a-bed, separate bedroom with a king-size bed, and bathrooms with tub and shower. They also come with a kitchenette equipped with microwave, fridge, electric hobs, utensils, and crockery should you wish to save money by self-catering. The furnishings are tasteful and comfortable, and the service first-rate. The next door bistro, the Café Latin, is a great place to dine if you don't want to go far for a hearty French meal.

***Rooms** 11. **Rates** 225€ doubles, 350€ family suites. **Credit** AmEx, MC, V. **Amenities** AC, restaurant; bar; babysitting; laundry service. **In room** A/C, TV, WiFi, kitchenette, safe.*

MODERATE

Hôtel Aviatic ★★ FIND

*105 rue de Vaugirard, 6th arr., 01 53 63 25 50; **www.aviatic.fr**. M° Montparnasse or St-Placide*

Nestled on a quiet street behind Montparnasse, just a 10-minute walk to St-Germain-des-Prés and with a direct bus route at the end of the road to the Louvre, Opéra, and Montmartre (no. 95), this lovely, boutique hotel is a hit with families who come for the warm welcome and rooms adapted for three to five people. At the back of the hotel, families can reserve entire floors with two rooms per floor. Picnics can be prepared for use when out sightseeing – perfect for lunch in the nearby Jardin du Luxembourg. The décor is warm and tasteful with lots of deep reds, greens, and lemons; the bistro-style breakfast room with its old Parisian posters will appeal to young eyes, while the plump croissants and pains-au-chocolat will appeal to their stomachs. There are lifts to all floors, babies' bottles can be heated day or night, babysitters can be booked on request, there's private parking, and transfers to and from the airports can be arranged. It's one of the loveliest places to stay around Montparnasse.

Rooms *43.* ***Rates*** *149€–199€ doubles, 199€–310€ triples and suites. Cot free. Under-16s stay free in their parents' room. Check the website for promotional rates. A Sunday night's stay is often 50% of the standard price.* ***Credit*** *AmEx, MC, V.* ***Amenities*** *lift, A/C, Internet, concierge booking facilities.* ***In room*** *TV, safety box. Small animals permitted.*

INEXPENSIVE

Grand Hôtel des Balcons ★★

3 rue Casimir Delavigne, 6th arr., ☎ 01 46 34 78 50; ***www.balcons.com****. M° Odéon*

Baudelaire used to stay in this fine budget hotel, embellished with original Art Nouveau features (on the ground floor), just a 10-minute walk from the Jardin du Luxembourg. All rooms are simply decorated with patchwork touches. Triple rooms are suitable for families of three or four, and some of the doubles have twin beds should you decide to let the children sleep in

Hôtel Aviatic

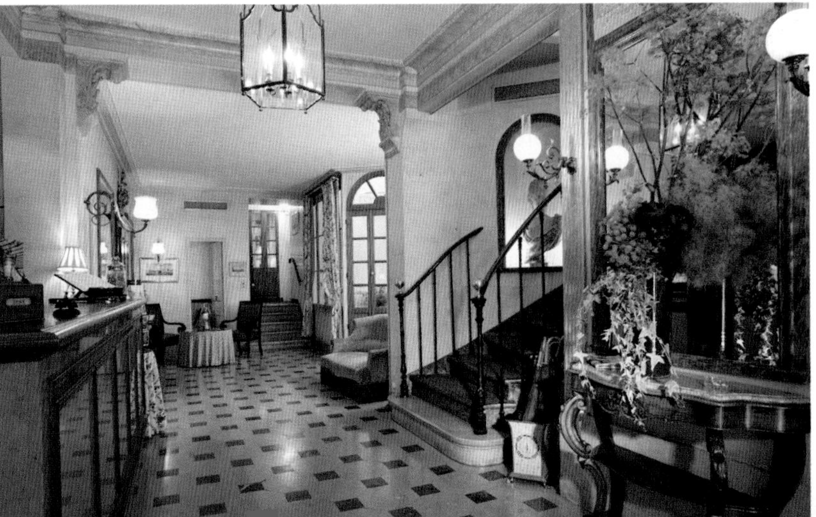

a separate bedroom. At breakfast, a giant self-service buffet serves an abundance of bacon, sausages, scrambled eggs, and French pastries, including little pastry balls covered in sugar crystals called chouquettes.

***Rooms** 50. **Rates** 85€ singles, 110€ doubles, 200€ triples. Extra bed and cots free. **Credit** MC, V. **Amenities** WiFi. **In room** TV, safety box.*

FAMILY-FRIENDLY DINING

Café life is an enduring cliché of Left Bank life. For Parisians these are everyday venues and meeting places. For visitors they are where avant-garde intellectuals and literary figures defended their visions of the world and plotted a few changes or two of their own. For your family they are perfect spots for soaking up the atmosphere and giving your children a taste of daily Parisian life.

The oldest café in Paris is **Le Procope** (13 rue de l'Ancienne-Comédie, 6th arr. M° Odéon), which opened in 1689 and has seen the likes of Voltaire, Benjamin Franklin, and the young Napoleon Bonaparte, who reportedly left his hat as security while he searched for the money to pay his tab. Today it's a good restaurant, decorated in 19th-century style. The most famous café duo, however, has to be **Les Deux Magots** (6 place St-Germain-des-Prés, 6th arr., M° St-Germain-des-Prés) and **Café de Flore** (172 boulevard St-Germain, 6th arr., M° St-Germain-des-Près), which both still trade on their reputations as the literary cafés where Simone de Beauvoir, Jean-Paul Sartre, Ernest Hemingway, and other philosophers and writers used to meet. Just opposite, the **Brasserie Lipp** (151 boulevard St-Germain, 6th arr., M° St-Germain-des-Prés) is an Alsatian café that has been serving sauerkraut, coffee, and beers since the 19th century. **La Coupole** (102 boulevard de Montparnasse, 14th arr., M° Vavin) in Montparnasse is still a fine spot for breakfast, lunch, coffee, or dinner with its Art Nouveau dining room loved by clients such as Josephine Baker and Roman Polanski. Hemingway fans, however, should head to the **Closerie des Lilas** (171 boulevard de Montparnasse, 14th arr., M° Vavin), where he spent six weeks writing *The Sun Also Rises* on its terrace. Much of the action in the book takes place in the restaurant. Older children might like to read the novel before visiting.

EXPENSIVE

La Cigale Récamier ★★

4 bis rue Récamier, 7th arr., ☎ 01 45 48 87 87, M° Sevres-Babylone

Soufflés, soufflés and more soufflés are the fluffy sustenance on offer in this chic but fun address. Whether you stop by for lunch after shopping in and around Le Bon Marché (see p. 163), or come for an evening meal (a real treat in summer when the terrace opens on to an exquisite side street), one thing is for sure: you need to be hungry. Children will not need a starter, and adults may well struggle to down a dessert – a shame because they're damned delicious (think salted caramel and sticky chocolate soufflé with a ball of melting ice cream). As an adult, you'll most certainly be impressed at the way all the soufflés (which need varying times to cook) are served at the same time. Children, on the other hand, will simply enjoy the destructive element of cutting open the soufflé's pastry hat to see what's inside before gobbling it up.

***Open** Noon–2.30pm, 7.30pm–10.30pm Mon–Sat. 3-course average: 50€. **Credit** AmEx, MC, V.*

MODERATE

Aux Charpentiers

10 rue Mabillon, 6th arr., ☎ 01 43 26 30 05. M° St-Germain-des-Prés or Mabillon.

This old bistro, which opened more than 130 years ago, attracts those seeking the Left Bank of yesteryear. It was once the rendezvous spot of the master carpenters whose guild was next door, and in true tradition all the original woodwork has been preserved. Nowadays, it's a fine place for a French meal with all the family (ex-president Chirac celebrated his 60th birthday here). Starters include pâté of duck and rabbit terrine served with a big clay pot of gherkins. Recommended as a main course is roast duck with olives and port. Other *plats du jour* recall French home cooking: salt pork with lentils, *pot-au-feu,* and stuffed cabbage. There's a fine selection of red and white wines, especially Bordeaux; and children enjoy the low-key atmosphere and uncomplicated dishes.

***Open** Noon–3pm and 7–11.30pm daily. 3-Course Average: 35€, fixed-price menu at 28€ evening only. **Credit** AmEx, DC, MC, V. Reservations required.*

Les Petites Sorcières ★

2 rue Liancourt, 14th arr., ☎ 01 43 21 95 68; M° Denfert Rochereau.

The *petites sorcières* (little witches) at this restaurant are the owner's three daughters. There are, however, a few 'real' petites sorcières hanging from the ceiling, amusing younger children as you tuck into delicious dishes like *blanquette de veau* (veal casserole), exceptionally tender magret of duck served in a Sichuan sauce, and impeccable crèmes-brûlées and fruit crumbles. If you're looking for a large lunch after a trip around the catacombs (also at Denfert-Rochereau, see p. 162) this restaurant is in a useful spot just off the main square; it's also easily reached (10 to 15 minute walk or direct metro) if staying in Montparnasse.

***Open** 8pm–10pm Mon and Sat, noon-2pm, 8pm–10pm Tues–Fri. **Average** 40€. **Credit** MC, V.*

Organic Choco-Fix

If you're a fair-trade conscious family of chocoholics, Chocolatitudes ★★ (57 rue Daguerre, 14th arr., ☎ *01 42 18 49 02*; ***www.chocolatitudes.com***) is a must. It doesn't look much from the outside and is off the beaten track, but inside you'll find a minimalist chocolate shop run by a passionate ex-cocoa bio-technician (Laurence Allemano), who not only spoils her clients with some of France's purest chocolate, she educates them. Fresh hot chocolate is made every day using vegetable milks, so you don't have to worry about cow milk allergies. For children's birthdays, Laurence organises two-hour-long workshops in English (for 6 to 8 youngsters) on the origins of chocolate and makes a special chocolate birthday cake (18€ per person).

INEXPENSIVE

Coco&Co ★★

11 rue Bernard Palissy, 6th arr., ☎ *01 45 44 02 52;* ***www.cocoandco.fr****. M° St-Germain-des-Prés.*

For children, this has to be Paris's most 'eggciting' restaurant, serving nothing but chicken eggs in the form of omelettes (more than 22 varieties), *oeufs-en-cocotte* (baked eggs in cream or wine), boiled eggs with soldiers, plus scrambled and fried varieties, in a sleek, modern, egg-themed dining area. Choose between the comfy banquette in the downstairs room, behind which a farmyard scene is nestled under the low roof, or take the narrow wooden steps up to the mezzanine area and get a bird's eye view of the clients tucking into Europe's favourite comfort food. To keep the children occupied, there are tiny buckets of chalk on the slate tables. The set *formule* is excellent value, offering an *oeuf en cocotte* with salad and a drink for just 8€.

Open *10am–8pm Tues–Sun.*
Average *20€.* ***Credit*** *MC, V.*

Chocolatitudes

8 Île de la Cité, Île St-Louis & the Latin Quarter

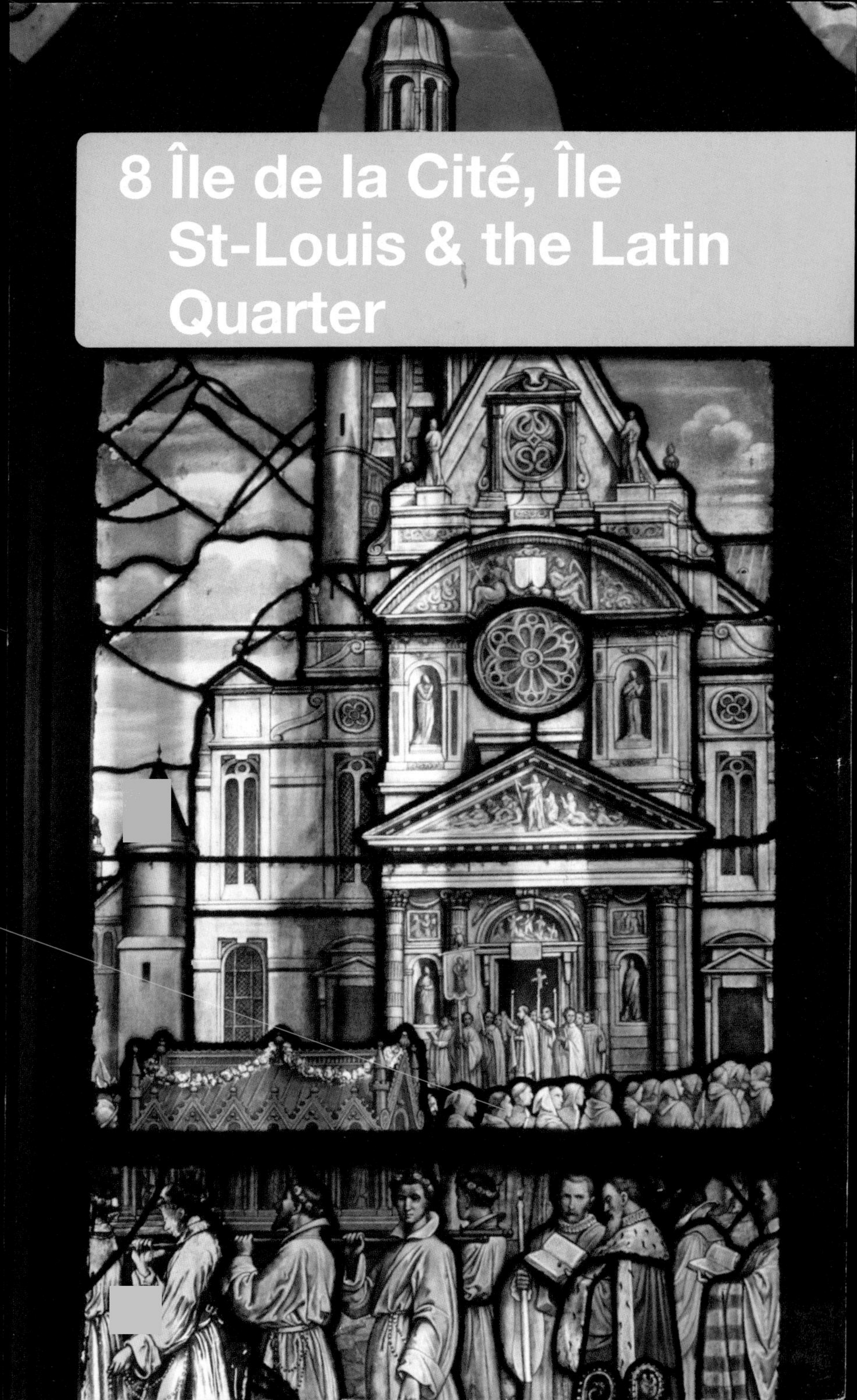

ÎLE DE LA CITÉ & ÎLE ST-LOUIS

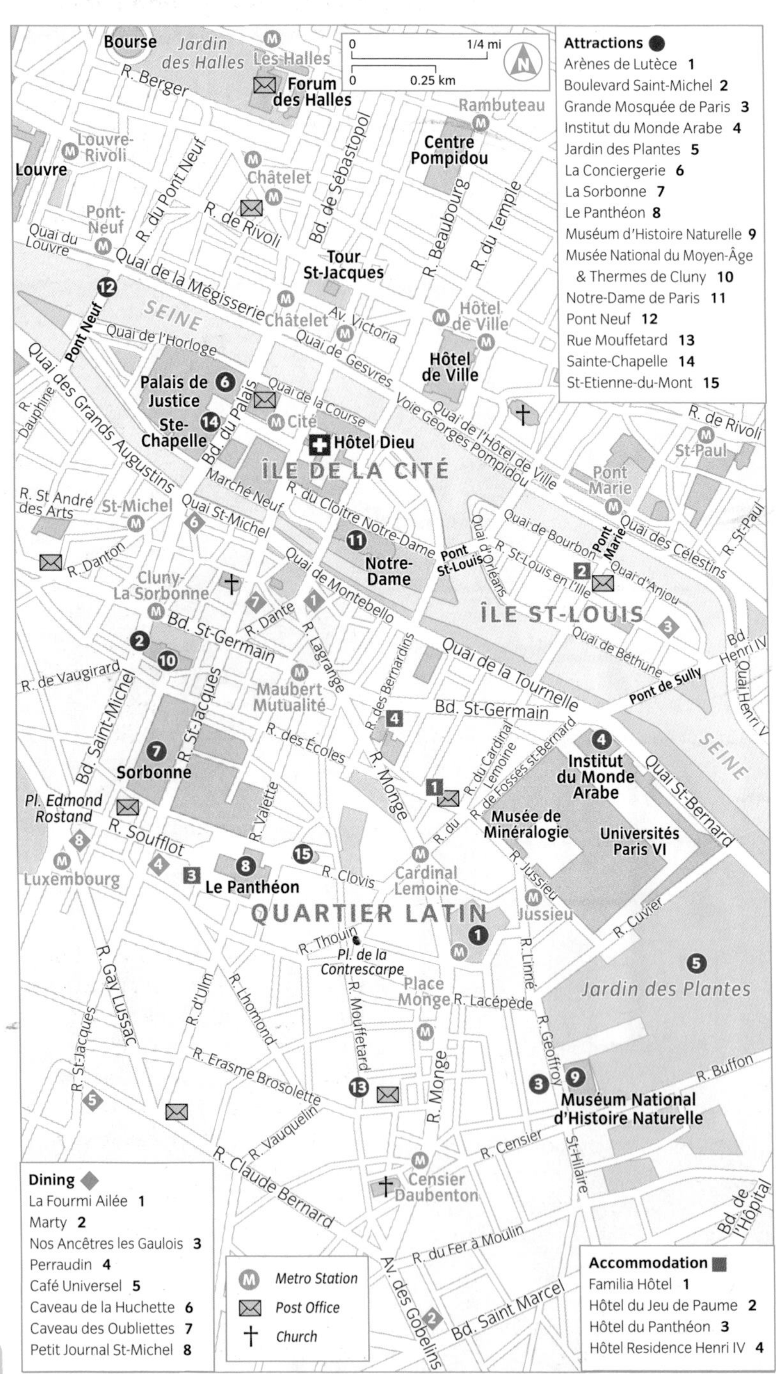

The River Seine is the life-force of Paris and the very reason the city exists today. As the river meandered its way north through the Île de France (Greater Paris) towards the sea, it carved two islands, Île de la Cité and Île St-Louis. Easy to defend, they became the capital of Celtic Gaul, home of the Parisii tribe. Romans conquered in 52 BC, building a temple to Jupiter (under today's Notre-Dame p. 186), baths (still visible in the Musée de Cluny p. 182), amphitheatres (see Les Arènes de Lutèce p. 191), and civil buildings (partly visible in the Crypte de Notre-Dame p. 189) on the Île de la Cité and in the Latin Quarter.

When the empire fell, the islands became the centre of royal power, with a medieval castle and a chapel (the Conciergerie and la Sainte-Chapelle p. 182) and Christian edifices, such as Notre-Dame. Remnants of these eras, plus more, in the Conciergerie including the Revolution, are still visible today. Together they make these quarters a veritable treasure trove for history-loving children and their parents.

Between the river and the Luxembourg gardens, the *Quartier Latin* (Latin Quarter) is a bustling district dominated by the Sorbonne University (p. 190). For more than 800 years, it has been a place of learning – so much so that the area takes its name from the early Latin-speaking students. Before then, the Romans created one of the city's first roads – the Rue St-Jacques – and over the last century, it has attracted artists, jazz musicians, and intellectuals. It has also been the scene of political unrest, both in 1871 when Place St-Michel was the centre of the Paris Commune, and in May 1968 when students rioted. Nowadays it's a fine destination for families, with cobbled streets, tree-lined quays, cafés, shops, and, for young children, the Jardin des Plantes (p. 192, Louis XIII's botanical garden) which also contains a small zoo (La Menagerie p. 192) and a Natural History Museum (p. 180).

ORIENTATION

Five small bridges link the Île de la Cité and Île-St-Louis to the Right Bank and five others link them to the Left Bank. Both Pont Neuf (western tip) and Pont de Sully (eastern tip) span the entire river. The main thoroughfares are Rue de la Cité (linking the Hôtel de Ville to Rue St-Jacques on the Left Bank) and Boulevard du Palais (linking Châtelet to Boulevard St-Michel).

The main road on Île St-Louis is Rue St-Louis en l'Île, lined with boutiques, food-shops, hotels, and cafés. The Latin Quarter is where Boulevard St-Germain commences in the east (parallel to the river) and where Boulevard St-Michel runs south towards the Luxembourg gardens. The islands and the Latin Quarter make up the 4th and 5th arrondissements, touching on the 13th in the east where new developments provide unexpected family activities (box p. 187). Everywhere can be covered on foot (St-Michel to Jardin des Plantes is 20 minutes and Luxembourg 15 minutes). Taxis are easily flagged down on all main roads, and Métro 4 runs through Île de la Cité from Montmartre (north) and Montparnasse (south). Métro 10 runs east–west through the middle of the Left Bank; and Métro 7 links the Jardin des Plantes with Châtelet and Parc de la Villette (p. 246).

GETTING AROUND

The principal bus lines are no. **24** (along the quays), no. **38** (along Boulevard St-Michel), no. **47** (down Rue Monge), no. **85** and **58** across Île de la Cité, and no. **67**, **86**, and **87** (along Boulevard St-Germain) across Île St-Louis. No. **89** passes between the Jardin des Plantes and the new Bibliothèque quarters. A good **Batobus** stop is **Jardin-des-Plantes**. **Tip:** Châtelet-les-Halles with direct lines to Disneyland (RER A) and the airports (RER B) is within walking distance.

VISITOR INFORMATION

The nearest Tourist Office is the Carrousel du Louvre, 99 rue de Rivoli, 1st arr., M° Palais-Royal-Musée du Louvre. *08 92 68 30 00*; ***www.parisinfo.com***.

WHAT TO SEE & DO

Children's Top 5 Attractions

❶ **Seeing** dinosaur bones and learning about evolution in the Musée d'Histoire Naturelle (see p. 180).

❷ **Discovering** Marie-Antoinette's prison cell in the Conciergerie (see p. 177).

❸ **Spotting** gargoyles and Quasimodo's bell in Notre-Dame cathedral (see p. 186)

❹ **Enjoying** a family picnic on the banks of the Seine (see Square du Vert-Galant, p. 200).

❺ **Sampling** delicious oriental pastries in a working mosque (see Grande Mosquée de Paris, p. 184).

Culture & Museums

Institut du Monde Arabe ★★

AGES 6 AND ABOVE

1 rue des Fossés St-Bernard, 5th arr., 01 40 51 38 38; ***www.imarabe.org****. M° Jussieu, Cardinal Lemoine or Sully-Morland.*

This bastion of Arab intellect and aesthetics is a fascinating and insightful way to introduce your family to the age-old culture of countries too often overshadowed by international politics. From the Crusades onwards, France has had trade links with Arab countries, and ruled some of them as colonies in North Africa – one reason for the large Arab population in France today. Designed in 1987 by architect Jean Nouvel and funded by 22 different countries (mostly Arab), the museum covers all of this plus calligraphy, decorative arts, architecture, and photography from the Arab/Islamic world, plus insights into its religion, philosophy, and politics. The building's shuttered windows, inspired by Moorish palaces, open and close like camera apertures, depending on the level of sunlight. And don't miss the roof terrace with views encompassing Notre-Dame, l'Île de la Cité, and Sacré-Coeur.

The excellent ground-floor bookshop, a replica of a medina, sells high-quality gift and art objects, and for a bite to eat, your family can choose between the self-service café (**Le Moucharabieh**, 11.30am–3pm Tues–Sun), the **Café Littéraire** (literary café, 11am–7pm Tues–Sun) or the gastronomic and panoramic **Ziryab** Moroccan restaurant on the roof (11am–11.30pm, *01 55 42 55 42*. Tues–Sun lunch)

***Open** 10am–6pm Tues–Sun. **Admission** roof terrace and café free. Admission to permanent exhibitions 5€ adults, 4€ students, free under-12s. Temporary exhibits vary.*

La Conciergerie ★★ FIND

AGES 5 AND ABOVE

*2 boulevard du Palais, 1st arr., 01 53 40 60 97; **www.monuments-nationaux.fr**. M° Cité or St-Michel, RER St-Michel/Notre-Dame*

London has its Bloody Tower, and Paris has its Conciergerie – a haunting monument to medieval and revolutionary history. The building (which shares space with the *Palais de Justice* law courts, *La Sainte-Chapelle* p. 182 and police offices) had a long regal history before the French Revolution, and certain

La Conciergerie

parts remain as they were in the Middle Ages. Others have been forever stained by the Reign of Terror and live on as infamous symbols of the time when carts hauled off fresh victims for Dr. Guillotin's grisly invention.

Excellent guided tours in English can be arranged three weeks in advance, or if you go it alone, pick up a leaflet in English and split your visit in two.

1 Medieval Conciergerie

Much of the Conciergerie was built in the 13th and 14th centuries as the royal Palais de la Cité and during the reign of Philippe Le Bel it was considered the most sumptuous château in Europe. Walk from Pont Neuf (p. 190) along Quai de la Mégisserie on the Right Bank and you'll fully appreciate the majesty of the building.

Back on the island, you approach through its landmark twin towers, the **Tour d'Argent** (where the crown jewels were once stored) and **Tour de César** (which adjoined Philippe Le Bel's private apartments). Once inside, your children will be wowed by the Gothic **Salle des Gens d'Armes** (Guard Room, see Fun Facts p. 179). At 64m long, 28m wide and 8.5m high, it was used as a refectory for the king's servants and could contain 2,000 people. Up to 500 watchmen slept here on the floor, warmed by the monumental chimneys. On the right, the two-storey **Cuisine** (kitchen) was built in 1353. The ground floor was used for cooking and the king would dine upstairs.

During the Middle Ages the Conciergerie also became an administrative and judiciary centre. On the wall (on the left) is a fragment of a black marble table used by the king when judging his subjects in the *Salle Haute* (High Room). On such occasions, he usually used the **Salle des Gardes** (on the right) as an antechamber.

Even when the royal residents moved out to the Louvre, the Conciergerie kept its judicial role and in time became synonymous with death and torture. Few, however, endured tortures as severe as those imposed on Ravaillac, who assassinated Henry IV in 1610. In the Tour de César he had hot lead and boiling oil poured on him like bath-water before being quartered in front of the Hôtel de Ville (p. 137).

2 The French Revolution

During the Revolution the whole Conciergerie was presided over by Paris's most hated man, the prosecutor Fouquier-Tinville, who condemned many to death by guillotine. One of the most moving parts for children is a reconstitution of Marie-Antoinette's cell with a waxwork figure of the queen. After being seized by a crowd of peasants who stormed Versailles, she and Louis XVI were brought here to await their trials. In failing health and shocked beyond grief, *l'Autrichienne* ('the Austrian,' as she was called with malice) had only a small screen (sometimes not even that) to

FUN FACT People of Arms

The word for the French police, '*gendarmes*', dates back to the time when the king's guardians, the 'Gens d'Armes' (literally 'people of arms', as in the *Salle des Gens d'Armes* in the Conciergerie) assured his majesty's security.

protect her modesty from the gaze of guards stationed in her cell. Shortly before noon on the morning of 16th October, 1793 her executioners came for her, cutting her hair, as was the custom for guillotine victims. Her official cell was converted into the **Chapelle Expiatoire** under Louis XVIII (during the Restoration era).

Not everyone was important enough to have a large cell however. On the first floor, three **cachots** (cells) no bigger than 5 sq m show where poor prisoners were kept. Further round, your children can also see a real guillotine hanging on the wall.

Back downstairs, outside, is the **Cour des Femmes** (women's courtyard), used by female prisoners for exercise, washing and, across the grates, saying farewell to their male relatives before execution.

Open *9.30am–6pm daily 31 Mar–Oct, 9am–5pm 1 Nov–Feb.* ***Admission*** *6.50€ adults, 4.50€ 18–25s, free under-17s. Combined tickets can be purchased for the Conciergerie and Sainte-Chapelle for 10€.*

Le Panthéon ★

AGES 8 AND ABOVE

Place du Panthéon, 5th arr., ☎ 01 44 32 18 00. ***http://Panthéon.monuments-nationaux.fr.*** *M° Maubert-Mutualité and Cardinal-Lemoine or RER B Luxembourg.*

Some of the most famous men in French history (Victor Hugo for one) are buried here on the crest of the mount St. Geneviève (the patron saint of Paris). In 1744, Louis XV vowed that if he recovered from a mysterious illness, he'd build a church to replace the Abbaye de Ste. Geneviève. He recovered, but it wasn't until 1764 that he allowed Madame de Pompadour's brother to hire Soufflot to design a church in the form of a Greek cross with a dome reminiscent of St. Paul's in London.

After the Revolution, the church was converted to a 'Hall of Fame' and became a Panthéon for the great men of France. Voltaire's body was exhumed and placed here. In the 19th century, the building changed roles so many times – a church, a Panthéon, a church again – that it was hard to keep up. After Hugo was buried here, it became a Panthéon once again. Other notable men entombed within are Rousseau, Soufflot, Zola, and Braille. Only one woman has so far been deemed worthy of placement here: Marie Curie (who discovered Radium).

There is also Foucault's pendulum (the original is in the Musée des Arts et Métiers p. 131) which hangs 67m up in the air. It was here that Foucault

Poor Marie-Antoinette

'Let them eat cake,' is what Marie-Antoinette supposedly uttered when told the peasants had no bread. The comment added fuel and fury to the revolutionary campaign. However, in the 18th-century, cake flour was less expensive than bread flour, so it would have made sense. Often criticised for her naïvety and (by some) idiocy, Marie-Antoinette still showed real dignity when taken to be guillotined.

originally demonstrated the Earth's rotation to Napoleon in 1851.

Energetic children will love the climb (some 206 steps) to the viewing galleries round the dome (summer only), which give 360 degree panoramas over Paris.

Tip: With small children, good behaviour in the Panthéon is easily rewarded by an hour or so in the Jardin du Luxembourg at the bottom of the hill (p. 160).

Open *10am–6.30pm daily 1 Apr–30 Sept, 10am–6pm daily 1 Oct–31 Mar (last entrance 45 min before closing).* ***Admission*** *7.50€ adults, 4.80€ 18–25s, free under-17s.*

Muséum d'Histoire Naturelle (Natural History Museum) ★★

AGES 11 AND UNDER

56 rue Cuvier, 5th arr., 01 40 79 54 79; ***www.mnhn.fr****. M° Jussieu or Gare d'Austerlitz.*

The Natural History Museum was founded in 1635 by Guy de la Brosse, physician to Louis XIII, to research science and nature. London's Natural History Museum considerably outclasses it, but it's still worth seeing with younger children who will appreciate the big displays on dinosaurs, endangered and vanished species, plus galleries on palaeontology, anatomy, mineralogy, and botany. Within the museum's grounds (the Jardin des Plantes see p. 192) you'll find **winter gardens** containing tropical plant life, and a **menagerie** with small animals to coo over, p. 192.

❶ Grande Galerie de l'Evolution

36 rue Geoffroy Saint Hilaire, 5th arr., 01 40 79 54 79

Two giant skeletons of **whales** greet your children as you enter the ground floor sea-life department. The biggest skeleton (30m long) is of the mighty Blue Whale, the largest animal known on Earth. Further along, the **North and South Poles** are represented with baby albatrosses and elephant seals (named after their trunk-like noses). Also don't miss the **Narwhal** whose giant horn was poached in medieval times and sold as a unicorn horn.

Upstairs the visit continues into the **African savannah**. African elephants stand alongside giraffes, rhinos, and gazelles. Next up, in the **Salle des Espèces Menacées et Disparues** (endangered and extinct species room) is a stuffed **Dodo** (a non-flying relative of the cuckoo, killed off by man in the late 17th century) and a **giant egg**, bigger than a dinosaur egg, belonging to the extinct Madagascan Ostrich. As for the **Mountain Gorillas** (the inspiration for King Kong), there are only about 400 left between the Congo and Rwanda – a strong message to children about man's role in protecting the environment.

Open *10am–6pm Wed–Mon.* ***Admission*** *8€ adults, 6€ 4–13s, free under-3s.*

❷ Galerie de Paléontologie du Muséum

Jardin des Plantes, 2 rue Buffon, 5th arr., 01 40 79 56 01

A stegosaurus statue guarding the gallery entrance sets the theme for your visit; go past the anatomy section and up the creaky wooden stairs to the realm of fossils and dinosaurs, where there's a **25m-long Diplodocus** skeleton looming overhead, along with a **giant crocodile**, ready to snap and an **Iguanodon** with nasty-looking hooks behind its legs. Also look out for the ***Allosaurus fragilis***, which marks the evolution from dinosaurs to birds. Towards the bottom of the gallery, your children will gradually get to the **early carnivores** (around at the same time as prehistoric man) such as lions, wolves, and cave bears – much more frightening than their modern-day cousins. Next to these, giant dinosaur eggs and woolly mammoth skeletons finish off their prehistoric journey.

Open *10am–5pm Wed–Mon.* ***Admission*** *6€ adults, 4€ 4–13s, free under-3s.*

❸ Galerie de Minéralologie du Muséum

36 rue Geoffroy St-Hilaire, 5th arr., 01 40 79 56 01

This is the world's oldest collection of rocks and minerals and a treat for children interested in geology. Regular temporary exhibitions on unrelated subjects can both disturb and embellish your visit, but either way your little ones will be wowed by the giant crystal collection – the only one of its type – with colossal agates and geodes from mines in Brazil. The **Salle du Trésor** (treasure room) below, displays more than 2,000 precious items given to the kings of France including

Giant skeletons at the Natural History Museum

FUN FACT **Where does 'Paris' come from?** 

When Paris was under Roman rule it was called Lutecia. Before that it was inhabited by Celtic river-traders called the Parisii, from whom the city takes its name today.

bars of gold and the Saint-Louis Emerald. **Tip:** Call to check it is open – problems with air-conditioning means it closes on hot days.

Open *10am–5pm Wed–Mon.* ***Admission*** *7€ adults, 5€ 4–13s, free under-3s.*

Musée National du Moyen Age & Thermes de Cluny ★★

VALUE **AGES 5 AND ABOVE**

6 place Paul-Painlevé, 5th arr., 01 53 73 78 00; ***www.musee-moyenage.fr****. M° Cluny–La Sorbonne, Saint-Michel, or Odéon.*

For medieval history fans of all ages this museum is a must-see, and downstairs are Roman baths – one of Paris's few visible Roman ruins. Audio guides in English can be hired for 1€.

Open *9.15am–5.45pm Wed–Mon.* ***Admission*** *free as part of a government trial scheme. After June 2008 entry may be charged.*

Sainte-Chapelle ★★

AGES 5 AND ABOVE

Palais de Justice, 6 boulevard du Palais, 1st arr., 01 53 40 60 97; ***www.monuments-nationaux.fr****. M° Cité, St-Michel, or RER: St-Michel/Notre-Dame*

This jewel-box of a medieval chapel (the best-preserved in Europe), all decorated in deep blues, golds, reds, and greens, is just the sort of place would-be princes and princesses can live out their fantasies. For adults and older children, it's quite simply one of the most breathtaking chapels you'll ever see. Countless writers have tried to describe the 'light show' cast on the interior when the sun shines through the stained-glass windows; but few

Sainte-Chapelle

Garden Fix by the Cluny Museum

If you're with young children, you might need to take them outside for some fresh air. The **Jardin Medieval du Musée du Moyen Age** (medieval garden), is a lovely spot, entirely reconstituted to look like an authentic medieval garden. All the plants, many aromatic, would have been used either for food, perfume, or medicine in the Middle Ages. Get your children to rub the lavender and rosemary and smell the fragrance on their hands.

Corner of Boulevard Saint-Germain and Boulevard Saint-Michel, 5th arr., M° Cluny-La Sorbonne or St-Michel. ***Open*** *9am–5.50pm daily (until 9pm in summer).*

have managed to capture its beauty.

You approach the church through the **Cour de la Sainte-Chapelle** (see box below p. 186) of the **Palais de Justice**. If it weren't for the chapel's 33m spire (dating from 1853 after five others either burned down or were destroyed), the law courts would almost swallow it up.

Begun in 1246, the two-level chapel was built to house relics of the True Cross (now in Notre-Dame Cathedral p. 186), including the Crown of Thorns acquired by St. Louis (the Crusader king, Louis IX) from the emperor of Constantinople.

You enter through the **Chapelle Basse (lower chapel)**, used by the palace servants; it's supported by flying buttresses and ornamented with fleur-de-lis designs. The king and his courtiers used the **Chapelle Haute (upper chapel)**, one of the greatest achievements of gothic art and reached by visitors up a narrow spiral staircase. Small children may need to be carried.

The walls are almost entirely glass – some 670 sq m, which had to be removed for safekeeping during the Revolution and again during both world wars. On a bright day, the 15 stained-glass windows glow with Chartres blue and deep reds. They depict stories from the Bible. With the rose window behind you, the first image on the left, for example, shows Genesis including the Garden of Eden.

Guided visits in English can be arranged 21 days in advance or leaflets in English are provided.

In the summer, the Sainte-Chapelle stages regular classical music **concerts** – a wonderful setting (tickets usually cost 20€–30€ ☏ *01 53 40 60 97* for details).

Open *9.30am–6pm daily Mar–31 Oct; 9am–5pm daily Nov–28 Feb.* ***Admission*** *7.50€ adults, 4.80€ 18–25s, free under-17s or combined ticket with the Conciergerie 10€.*

Condensed History of the Hôtel de Cluny for Children

Built as the mansion of a rich 15th-century abbot, on the ruins of a Roman bath, by 1515 the Cluny was the residence of Mary Tudor, widow of Louis XII and daughter of Henry VII and Elizabeth of York. Seized during the Revolution, it was rented in 1833 to Alexandre du Sommerard, who adorned it with medieval artworks. After his death in 1842 the government bought the building and the collection.

Enter through the cobblestoned **Cour d'Honneur** (Court of Honour), where you can admire the flamboyant Gothic building with vines, turreted walls, gargoyles, and dormers with seashell motifs.

Highlights for children include:

1. The blue **'Mille Fleurs'** (thousand flower) tapestries in the first room after the entrance, which depict the life of a noble medieval gentleman: ladies sit around sewing while the men go hunting with falcons.
2. In the next room, **red velvet drapes** embroidered with golden leopards were used to cover the thrones of English kings during knights' tournaments.
3. **Stained-glass windows** in the Gothic room are handily displayed at child-level. An easy one to explain is the yellow and grey *Joueurs d'échecs* (chess players, 1430s), a metaphor for the way medieval men wooed their ladies. She is very fashionable with a shaved forehead and horn-like head-dress, and he is tastefully dressed with cloaks and a floppy turban.
4. In the Marble room (*Salle des Marbres*) children love looking at the 'real' **unicorn horn,** actually p. 180 the horn of a narwhal, an endangered seal-like sea-creature with a long horn rising straight out of the middle of its head. The horns were much prized in the Middle Ages.
5. In the next room, youngsters love the fact that most of the exhibits were fished out of the Seine and can see items like square **medieval**

Places of Worship

Grande Mosquée de Paris ★★ ALL AGES

*2 place du Puits-de-l'Ermite, 5th arr., 01 45 35 97 33; **www.mosquee-de-paris.net**.*

This beautiful Hispano-Moorish mosque was built in 1922 to honour the North African countries that had helped France during World War I. Today, it's the spiritual heart of the city's North African-dominated Muslim population and an excellent place to bring your family. Short tours of the building, its stunning central courtyard and Moorish garden, give an insight into Islamic beliefs and practices. There is also a working hammam (sauna, body-scrub, and massage) on site

shoes, combs engraved with romantic words like '*tu es belle*' (you are beautiful), and **games of chess**.

6. During the Revolution, Notre-Dame Cathedral was sacked and most of its statues beheaded. Your children can count **21 heads** (dating from 1220 and corresponding to the Kings of Judah) only rediscovered in 1977 when workmen were building a car park. They'd been secretly buried in the courtyard of a royalist mansion.
7. Before you head up to the first floor, Harry Potter fans should scrutinise the walls to find the **epitaph of Nicolas Flamel**, maker of the philosopher's stone (see p. 134.)
8. Most people come to see **The Lady and the Unicorn Tapestries** ★★★, mysterious tapestries discovered only a century ago in Limousin's Château de Boussac. They depict the five senses: from left to right, taste, hearing, sight, smell, and touch (see if your children can guess which is which). The sixth is embroidered with the words '*A Mon Seul Désir*' (my only desire) meaning that the beautiful woman is ready to forsake worldly riches for the pleasure of the senses. The background forms a rich carpet of spring flowers, fruit-laden trees, birds, rabbits, donkeys, dogs, goats, lambs, and monkeys for youngsters to pick out.
9. Downstairs are the ruins of the **Roman baths** from around 200 A.D. The best-preserved section is in room X, the frigidarium, where Romans used to bath in cold water. It used to measure 21m by 11m, rising to a height of 15m, with stone walls nearly 1.5m thick. Your children might notice that the ribbed vaulting rests on consoles that look like ships' prows. This is because the builders of the baths were Paris boatmen. The column to Jupiter now on view in the court was found beneath Notre-Dame's chancel (see p. 186) and is called the 'Column of the Boatmen'. It is believed to be the oldest sculpture created in Paris.

serving men and women at different hours of the day (not recommended if pregnant) (✆ *01 43 31 18 14*; 15–35€). However, most locals come for the delicious couscous, sweet mint tea, and sticky north-African pastries, served in the authentically decorated **Restaurant de la Mosquée de Paris** (open noon–3pm, 7pm–10.30pm daily, ✆ *01 43 31 38 20*), and its pretty blue and white tiled patio – a relaxing spot, favoured by crumb-hunting sparrows and families with children.

Tip: The mosque is ideally combined with a trip to the Natural History Museum and the Jardin des Plantes over the road.

Tours *9am–noon, 2–6pm Sat–Thurs. Closed Muslim holidays.* ***Admission*** *3€ adults, 2€ 7–25s, free under-6s.*

Notre-Dame de Paris ★★

ALL AGES

6 parvis Notre-Dame, Place Jean-Paul II, 4th arr,. ☎ 01 42 34 56 10; ***www.cathedraledeparis.com****. M° Hôtel de Ville, St-Michel, or Cité; RER B and C Notre-Dame/St-Michel. Towers: Rue du cloître Notre-Dame, 4th arr., ☎ 01 53 10 07 07;* ***http://notre-dame-de-paris.monuments-nationaux.fr****.*

Notre-Dame de Paris is the heart of Paris and even of France. It is also, for children who have read Victor Hugo's The Hunchback of Notre-Dame or seen Disney's adaptation of it, the realm of Quasimodo, his bells and Esmeralda, the innocent gypsy maiden whose life is ruined by the murderous priest Frollo.

With children, it is best to divide your visit into three parts, beginning with the section that will take the most time to get into – **the towers**. Or you could come along for a **free guided tour in English** on Wed and Thurs (2pm) and Sat (2.30pm) which begins underneath the great organ pipes.

❶ **Towers** ★★ If you and the family can climb the 387 stairs you'll find the entrance to the 68m-high twin towers on the left of the cathedral, outside. At the top awaits a menagerie of **gargoyles** ★★ (many copied by Disney) designed by Viollet-le-Duc. Some hobgoblins blow raspberries, other hybrid beasts and fantastic birds pull their tongues. Quasimodo's bell, **Le Bourdon**, is still in place, poised to chime, and further along, a spiral staircase leads to the South tower from where you can see the whole of Paris.

Tip: To avoid queues, come when the towers open or just before last entry. If the inevitable happens, save time by taking it in turns to visit inside the cathedral while someone stays in the queue.

❷ **The inside** The main body of the church is typically Gothic, with slender, graceful columns. In the **choir** (rebuilt in the 18th century by Robert Le Cotte), medieval stone reliefs depict biblical scenes your children might recognise like the Resurrection (south) and the Nativity (north). The paintings by Charles Le Brun in the side chapels are known as '**Mays**' because they

FUN FACT Romans under the Sainte-Chapelle 

In the same way that the site of Notre-Dame has long been occupied by a religious building (a Roman temple and an early Christian church), the sites of the Conciergerie and the Sainte-Chapelle were formerly occupied by a Roman palace of justice. In 1847, archaeological digs underneath the *Cour de la Sainte-Chapelle* revealed fragments of Roman columns and inscriptions. The building would have been colossal, with stone walls covered in murals rather like those in Pompeii. That the kings chose to build on this spot was not an accident. It showed that the power of Rome had died and Gaul now had its own rulers.

Family Fun in New Quarters: Bibliothèque (13th)

To the east of the Latin Quarter, on the Left Bank near the Bibliothèque François Mitterrand's triple towers (the national library), Paris is undergoing a revolutionary facelift. Between the Gare d'Austerlitz (train station and Métro) and Boulevard Masséna, brand new apartments, offices, a university, a school of fashion, as well as restaurants, bars, and activities for families, have been mushrooming for the last five years. It's not finished but here are family attractions you can already try:

1. **Paris's newest bridge** – Passerelle Simone de Beauvoir, inaugurated in 2006, links the redeveloped Bercy quarters to the Bibliothèque François Mitterrand. For budding photographers it's an ideal spot to create new views of the most photographed city in the world.
2. **Piscine Joséphine Baker** – In the summer this open-air, floating swimming pool with a sun-deck (Quai François Mauriac, 13th arr. M° Quai de la Gare. *01 56 61 96 50*) is a fun place to swim (bring suncream).
3. **Cinéma MK2** – The Blibliothèque branch of this Parisian cinema chain specialises in both arthouse films and Hollywood blockbusters. For screenings of English-language films, look for VO (version originale). Film-buff little ones can use the excellent specialist bookshop. The morning programme usually includes films for small children. (128–162 avenue de France, 13th arr., *08 92 69 84 84*; ***www.mk2.com***, M° Bibliothèque or Tolbiac).
4. **La Dame de Canton** – This converted river-boat has something for everyone with fairy stories, music concerts, or puppet shows in French (2.45pm Wed) for over-3s (puppet shows are without text), evening rock, folklore, jazz concerts (8.30pm) and after-hour discos for over-18s. Port de la Gare, 13th arr., *01 44 06 96 45* (concerts), *06 10 42 34 46* (children's show); ***www.damedecanton.com***, M° Bibliothèque or Quai de la Gare.
5. **Paris-Plage** – Each August when the banks of the Seine become a beach, this area is jam-packed with activities and water games for children (see Festivals p. 24)

were donated to the cathedral by the guilds on May Day each year. Near the southeast pillar of the transept stands the 14th-century **Virgin and Child**, highly venerated among Paris's faithful. Near the altar is a dominating statue of **Louis XIII**. After years without an heir, he promised to redecorate the east chancel in honour of the Virgin if a son was born to him. The birth of Louis XIV answered his prayers in 1638, but the works weren't carried out until 60 years later. Inside the **treasury** are displayed

Mémorial des Martyrs Français de la Déportation de 1945 (Deportation Memorial)

Approached through a garden behind Notre-Dame on the tip of Île de la Cité is this poignant underground memorial commemorating the French citizens (mostly Jews) who were deported to concentration camps during World War II. Carved into stone are these blood-red words (in French): 'Forgive, but don't forget.' It is a solemn, moving place to bring children old enough to understand about Hitler and World War II, and for those whose great-grandparents fought in the War.

***Open** 8:30am–nightfall Mon–Fri (from 9am at weekends). **Admission** free.*

vestments and gold objects including crowns, and the pride of the cathedral, the **True Cross** and the **Crown of Thorns**, which long sat in the Sainte-Chapelle (p. 182).

❸ **The outside** You need to walk all around the cathedral to fully appreciate the 'vast symphony of stone.' Better yet, drag the children over the Pont au Double to the Left Bank, and view it from the quay.

The **Parvis de Notre-Dame** (the square immediately in front of the entrance, recently renamed Place Jean-Paul II) is the best place to see the three sculpted 13th-century portals. On the left, the **Portal of the Virgin** depicts the signs of the zodiac and coronation of the Virgin, an association found in dozens of medieval churches. (See if your children can name all 12 signs of the zodiac). The restored central **Portal of the Last Judgement** depicts three levels: the first shows Vices and Virtues; the second, Christ and his Apostles; and above that, Christ in Triumph after the Resurrection. Over it is the remarkable **West Rose window** (9.5m wide), forming a show-case for a statue of the Virgin and Child. On the far right is the **Portal of St. Anne,** depicting scenes like the Virgin enthroned with Child. It's Notre-Dame's best-preserved and most perfect piece of sculpture. Finally, on

Notre-Dame de Paris

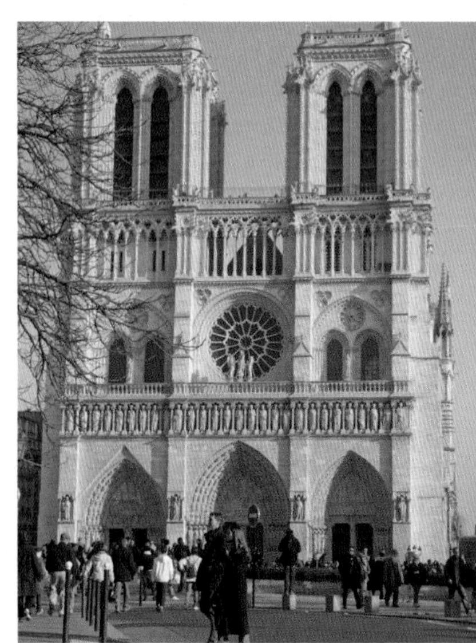

FUN FACT Kilomètre Zéro

At the far end of the Parvis de Notre-Dame in front of the cathedral, a circular bronze plaque marks **Kilomètre Zéro,** from where all distances from Paris to all parts of France are calculated**.**

the Seine side of Notre-Dame, the **Portal of St. Stephen** traces that saint's martyrdom.

Open *Cathedral year-round 8am–6:45pm daily. Towers 10am–6.30pm daily Apr–Sept (until 11pm Sat–Sun and June–Aug); 10am–5.30pm daily Oct–Mar.* ***Admission*** *free to cathedral. Admission to Towers 7.50€ adults, 4.80€ 18–25s, free under-17s.*

St-Etienne-du-Mont ★

1 place St-Geneviève, 5th arr., ☎ 01 43 54 11 79. M° Cardinal Lemoine or RER B Luxembourg.

This chocolate-box church, tucked in a corner behind the Panthéon, was built between 1492 and 1626 and is a mishmash of Gothic and Renaissance styles. Possibly the prettiest in Paris, it used to adjoin the abbey church of Ste-Geneviève, founded by Clovis and named after the patron saint of Paris whose prayers are believed to have saved the city from Attila the Hun in 451. The interior is tall and light and contains the only surviving Renaissance rood screen in Paris, with its double spiral staircase and splendidly ornate stonework.

Holding up the wooden pulpit children might recognise Samson, clutching a bone in one hand, with a slain lion at his feet – a scene from *Samson and the Lion.*

Open *10am–7pm Tues–Sun.* ***Admission*** *free.*

Streets & Monuments

Boulevard Saint-Michel

The Latin Quarter's main meeting point is the huge Davioud fountain with a bronze statue by Duret showing St Michael slaying

Crypte Archéologique du Parvis de Notre-Dame

Paris has more layers than a giant club sandwich, and nowhere is it more evident for children than in the little-known archaeological crypt in front of Notre-Dame. Here bits and pieces of Roman ramparts, quaysides, medieval shops, pavements, an 18th-century hospital, and part of a 19th-century sewer are revealed – a mishmash you'll have trouble distinguishing, but showing how the city has developed.

Open *10am–6pm Tues–Sun. Closed most public holidays.* ***Admission*** *3.30€ adults, 1.60€ 13–26s, free under-12s.*

Parvis Notre-Dame - Place Jean-Paul II, 4th arr., ☎ 01 55 42 50 10;. M° Cité, RER Notre-Dame/St-Michel.

MOMENTS **Fire-eaters & more . . .**

In the summer, on the Pont Louis (4th arr.), which links Île de la Cité with Île St-Louis, fire-eaters, magicians, acrobats, and the occasional body-popper entertain the crowds and sometimes invite children to join in.

the dragon, on Place St Michel. This busy hub, lined with bookshops (see Shopping, p. 193), marks the beginning of Boulevard St-Michel, 'Saint-Mich' to locals (5th arr., M° St-Michel, Cluny La Sorbonne, RER St-Michel-Notre-Dame) – a long avenue, created in 1869, once famed for its literary cafés. With your children, look out for a plaque on the wall near the fountain that commemorates the many students who died here in 1944, fighting Nazi invaders.

La Sorbonne

France's most famous university was at the centre of the Latin Quarter's intellectual activity from 1253 when it was created by Robert de Sorbon, Louis IX's confessor, until 1968, when students occupying the building were stormed by riot police during massive social unrest that led Charles de Gaulle to dissolve the government and hold emergency elections. After this episode the university was dispersed but this section still houses the Faculté des Lettres (faculty of arts and literature).

La Sorbonne

Pont Neuf ★

The name of Paris's oldest bridge ironically translates as 'new bridge'. It was begun in the reign of Henri III and Catherine de Médici in 1578 and took 30 years to complete. Its arches are lined with funny, grimacing faces that will amuse younger children who can try to copy them. They are supposed to be caricatures of Henri III's courtiers. The bridge's centrepiece is a beautiful statue of Henri IV. The 1635 original was melted down to make cannons during the Revolution, so this one was put up in 1818.

Rue Mouffetard ★

Hemingway's description of the oldest street in Paris and the original road to Rome as 'that wonderful narrow crowded market, beloved of bohemians' is

St-Louis-en-L'Île

On the Île-St-Louis, near the Hôtel de Lauzun is the church of **St-Louis-en-l'Île** (19 bis rue St-Louis-en-l'Île, 4th arr.) where the interior is one of the finest examples of Jesuit baroque, built between 1664 and 1726. It's a favoured spot for weddings – in fact the white stone and gilt makes you feel like you're inside a wedding cake – and a 1926 plaque reads 'In grateful memory of St. Louis, in whose honour the city of St. Louis, Missouri, USA, is named'.

way out of date. Rue Mouffetard still exudes charm but has been taken over by rows of cheap shops, bistros, crêperies, Lebanese takeaways, and Greek restaurants, offering tourists and locals some of the city's cheapest fare: great news if you're eating on a budget but not if you're seeking Left Bank tranquillity. Your family can still enjoy the street market on the lower half, however, which joins a market more frequented by locals at Place Monge (see p. 195). The best reason to come is for the ice cream at **Gelati d'Alberto** (no. 45, open 12.30pm–12.30am daily). Each scoop is formed into the shape of a petal: the more flavours you choose, the bigger your ice-cream flower.

Parks & the Outdoors

Arènes de Lutèce ★

Corner of Rue Monge and Navarre, 5th arr., M°Jussieu.

Discovered and partially destroyed in 1869, this amphitheatre is Paris's most important Roman ruin after the baths in the Musée de Cluny

Gargoyles on Pont Neuf

The Narrowest House in Paris

Take your family to see 22 rue St-Séverin, the narrowest house in Paris – barely wide enough for two windows. It's the former residence of Abbé Prévost, the author of the book *Manon Lescaut,* later turned into a Puccini opera.

(p. 182). It's popular with children playing soccer, parents pushing buggies down the paths, and nannies grabbing a breath of fresh air. It's another ideal spot for a picnic – bring some games for the children and treat yourselves to a bottle of wine.

Open *8am–10pm daily May–Sept, 8am–5.30pm daily Oct–Apr.* ***Admission*** *free.*

Jardin des Plantes ★★ FIND

ALL AGES

www.mnhn.fr

This is a lovely park for a stroll, a play, and to see birds, mammals, and reptiles.

❶ La Menagerie

3 quai Saint-Bernard or 57 rue Cuvier, 5th arr., 01 40 79 37 94; ***www.mnhn.fr****. M° Gare d'Austerlitz or Jussieu.*

As heads rolled during the Revolution, royal and noble collections of exotic animals needed new homes. This mini-zoo was the unlikely solution. Today, certain parts still need a revamp, but renovations are gradually breathing life and comfort into many of the animals' compounds. Kangaroos, wallabies, little black pigs, camels, llamas, and the famous Przewalski horse (so rare it disappeared from the

Jardin des Plantes

wild 40 years ago), will win children's hearts. Being small makes the zoo ideal for very young ones. A table is placed in front of the panthers' cage, so you can sit and watch the couple at play, making an ideal spot for a family snack. Further round are boas, anacondas, geckos, and pythons or for those less daring there are cute monkeys, including the orang-utan Lingga, born in 2005, and a little male red panda, soon to be given a mate.

***Open** 9am–6pm daily Apr–Oct, until 5pm Nov–Mar. **Admission** 7€ adults, 5€ 4–13s, free under-3s. See Muséum d'Histoire Naturelle for info on combined tickets p. 180.*

❷ The Trees

*Enter between Rue Cuvier and Geoffroy-Saint-Hilaire, 5th arr., ✆ 01 40 79 56 01; **www.mnhn.fr**. M° Jussieu.*

The main park was created as a botanical garden in the 17th century by order of Louis XIII who wanted a place to cultivate medicinal plants. It's been used as a centre for research ever since. Begin your trail at the foot of the **petit labyrinth** (little maze) near the *Grande Serre* (winter garden, which by 2009 should be filled with tropical plants). Look out for a rare oriental plane tree planted in 1785 (**Plane de l'Orient**) and by the statue of the chemist Chevreul, the *desespoir des singes* (monkey's despair or, in English, monkey puzzle tree) so-called because the spikes would make it hard to climb. Along the **Allée du Grand Labyrinth**, young children may be tempted by the bright red yew berries but be warned, they are highly toxic. Nearby is a 20m-high **cedar tree.** The 17th-century botanist Antoine de Jussieu bought it back as a sapling from England in his hat. The trunk now measures 4m in circumference and, if conditions are right, it could live up to 2,000 years. Towards the Seine, the **acacia** propped up by a metal frame is the garden's oldest tree, planted in 1635.

***Open** 8am to nightfall daily. **Admission** free.*

Shopping

The Latin Quarter and islands aren't renowned for their shops, but these are the quarters where

Walk Around Île-St-Louis ALL AGES

Île St-Louis is a wonderful world of tree-shaded quays, townhouses with courtyards, restaurants and antique shops. It has always been primarily residential (nearly all the houses were built from 1618 to 1660), lending the island a remarkable architectural unity. In the summer it throngs with tourists, but is still a fine place to stroll.

Tip: After a trip around the island, treat the family to an ice cream from **Berthillon** (29–31 rue St-Louis en l'Île, 4th arr., ✆ *01 43 54 31 61* M° Pont Marie.), supposedly the best *glacier* (ice-cream maker) in Paris.

Ramps for Skates & Boards

If your children can't go anywhere without their wheels, the pretty **Jardin Tino Rossi**, sandwiched between the Seine and the Institut du Monde Arabe (p. 176) has enough ramps and flat bits for your skaters to twist and turn to their heart's content. There's also a pretty open-air sculpture museum you can walk round while you wait. On summer evenings impromptu dance classes are held near the Seine – also a nice spot for a family picnic.

Quai St Bernard, 5th arr., M° Gare d'Austerlitz or Jussieu.

your family is most likely to come across a little-known boutique that thrives thanks to a handful of devoted regulars. For these, along with gourmet food shops, head to the islands. Boulevard St-Michel is a centre for books.

Books

The place for every Left Bank student is **Gilbert Jeune**, with 8 branches around Place St-Michel (5th arr., M° St-Michel and RER St-Michel/Notre-Dame) selling new and used books on every subject under the sun. For **literature,** try 10 place St-Michel; **secondhand** tomes at no. 2; **general reading**, cards, postcards, and Paris-related books in English are at no. 5; and for **children's books** try 27 quai St-Michel.

The one-stop English secondhand bookshop, once frequented by Hemingway, is **Shakespeare & Co** ★★ (37 rue de la Bûcherie, 5th arr., ☎ *01 43 25 40 93*; ***www.shakespeareco.org***. M° St-Michel. Open 10am–11pm daily), a fabulous treasure chest of floor-to-ceiling books. The legendary owner, George Whitman, is in his 90s so his young daughter Silvia runs the shop, organising regular literary debates in English and signings with authors – the staple diet of many Left Bank ex-pats living their literary dream in Paris.

Food

For a scrumtiddlyumptious baguette, or one of baker Dominique Baibron's famous

Shakesphere & Co

organic sourdough loaves, head to the **Boulanger de Monge** ★ (123 rue Monge, 5th arr., ☎ *01 43 37 54 20*; ***www.leboulangerdemonge.com***. M° Monge. 7am–8.30pm Tues–Sun). For marinades, fajitas, dried chillis, and all things Latin American, **Mexi & Co** (5 rue Danton, 5th arr., ☎ *01 46 34 14 12*, M° Cluny la Sorbonne. noon–midnight daily, cash only) doubles as a cheap Mexican restaurant and a *traiteur* (delicatessen). At **51 rue St-Louis en l'Île** (4th arr.) two shops, a gift shop for foodies (L'Epicerie), and a butcher selling wonderful cuts, joints, and cold meats provide extra special items for a picnic basket.

Just for children

If the little ones are crying out for a wooden toy, a teddy, or a puppet, or you're looking for a present for someone who's just had a baby, you need a trip to **L'Epée de Bois** (12 rue Epée de Bois, 5th arr., ☎ *01 43 31 50 18*. M° Jussieu. Open 10.30am–7.30pm Tues–Sat, 11am–1.30pm Sun, 1.30pm–7.30pm Mon) – a toy shop favoured by the Latin quarter's mums and nannies. For older children, **L'Oeuf Cube** (24 rue Liné, 5th arr., ☎ *01 45 87 28 83*; ***www.oeufcube.com***. M° Jussieu. Open 10.15am–7pm Mon–Sat) sells a range of fantasy and Sci-Fi role play games, strategic games, board games, figurines, and collector's cards.

Arche de Noé – *Noah's Ark* – (70 rue St-Louis en l'Île, 4th arr., ☎ *01 46 34 61 60*. M° Pont Marie. Open 10.30am–7pm daily) is great for the little'uns with wooden toys, finger puppets, and jigsaws.

Markets

The most famous markets in central Paris are the **Marché aux Fleurs** (flowers, 8am–7.30pm daily) and **Marché aux Oiseaux** (birds, 8am–7pm Sun) on Île de la Cité. The setting is indeed idyllic; right between the Right and Left Banks; the flowers too are very pretty and worth purchasing; however, I have always felt uncomfortable about the Marché aux Oiseaux (which also sells hamsters, mice, and rabbits). The animals are kept in clean spaces, but they don't always look very healthy. If you have teenagers sensitive to animal rights issues, it's best to avoid the area. For foodstuffs, **Marché Monge** (Place Monge,

Quick Shopper's Tea Break

For the ultimate tea experience with your family, the **Maison des Trios Thés** ★ is run by one of the world's leading tea experts, Yu Hui Tseng, who'll teach your children how to make a proper brew. More than 1,000 teas are on offer, all costing a small fortune. However, after tasting them, Tetley won't ever be the same again. 1 rue St-Médard, 5th arr., ☎ *01 43 36 93 84*. M° Monge. 11am–7.30pm Tues–Sun. Closed Aug.

5th arr., M° Monge; 7am–2.30pm Wed, Fri, 7am–3pm Sun) is handily situated near the bottom of **Rue Mouffetard's** street market.

Nightlife

Jazz Clubs

Paris was synonymous with jazz during the post-war era. French and European musicians were joined by the big names of the USA, who came to play in the city's vaulted basements and smoky dens which, unlike in the States, allowed blacks and whites to appear together. It was a golden age in musical history, and the legacy lives on in a spattering of clubs. While many of the Latin Quarter's venues have closed, you can still bring older children to institutions such as the **Caveau de la Huchette** (5 rue de la Huchette, 5th arr., *01 43 26 65 05*; ***www.caveaudelahuchette.fr***. M° St-Michel. 9.30pm daily) a typical bar cum jazz club, **Caveau des Oubliettes** (52 rue Galande, 5th arr., *01 46 34 23 09*; ***www.caveaudesoubliettes.com***. M° Cluny la Sorbonne. Concerts from 10pm daily), which doubles as a pub from 5pm; and the **Petit Journal St Michel** (71 boulevard St-Michel, 5th arr., *01 43 26 28 59*; ***http://pages perso-orange.fr/claude.philips/index.htm*** RER Luxembourg. Open from 7.30pm Mon–Sat) which serves dinner and continues to produce top international jazz acts. **Le Café Universel** (267, rue St Jacques, 5th arr., *01 43 25 74 20*; ***www.myspace.com/cafeuniversel***. RER Luxembourg or Port-Royal. Concerts 9.30pm Mon–Sat) is one of Paris's youngest jazz clubs and attracts a young crowd.

FAST FACTS

Internet Café Milk, 17 rue Soufflot, 5th arr., RER Luxembourg and **Milk**, 53 rue de la Harpe, 5th arr., M° Cluny la Sorbonne. Both *08 20 00 10 00*. Open 24/7.

Pharmacy Pharmacie Saint Germain, 25 boulevard St Germain, 5th arr., *01 43 54 76 18*, M° Maubert-Mutualité. Open 8.30am–8pm Tues–Sat, 11am–8pm Mon.

Post Office La Poste 10 rue Epée de Bois, 5th arr., *01 55 43 77 00*. M° Censier Daubenton. Open 8.30am–8pm TuesSat, 11am–8pm Mon.

Supermarket Champion, 34 rue Monge, 5th arr., *01 53 73 00 60*. M° Monge. 8.30am–10pm Mon–Sat.

FAMILY-FRIENDLY ACCOMMODATION

VERY EXPENSIVE

Hôtel du Jeu de Paume

54 rue St-Louis en l'Île, 4th arr., 01 44 41 99 00; ***www.jeudepaumehotel.com*** *M° Pont Marie.*

From the moment your family steps through the old carriage

entrance, you can tell this hotel is steeped in atmosphere. Lots of establishments call themselves a home away from home, but few pull it off as well as this place – all cosy and warm with its wooden beams and ancient stone walls and fireplaces, yet ultra-modern with its steel spiral staircase, transparent lift, and glass balconies overlooking the lobby. Two self-catering apartments (five-night minimum stay) offer the height of luxury with spacious family living areas, fully furnished kitchens, and three or two bedrooms sleeping four to six. Cots are available on request. If you're staying for under five nights, the suites sleep up to three people, and adjacent rooms can also be reserved. This is a great place for a family who will appreciate the games and billiard rooms, the sauna and sports centre. There is even a little garden.

Rooms *32.* ***Rates*** *275€–350€ doubles, 385€–545€ suites; 600€–900€ apartments (five-night min); extra bed and cot Free.* ***Credit*** *AmEx, MC, V.* ***Amenities*** *A/C, soundproofing, WiFi and Internet room, bar, babysitting on request, library, music room. Small pets permitted.* ***In room*** *safe, TV, Internet plug, fully-fitted kitchen in apartments.*

MODERATE

Hôtel du Panthéon ★

19 place du Panthéon, 5th arr., ☎ 01 43 54 32 95; ***www.hoteldupantheon.com****. RER Luxembourg.*

This Provençal-style hotel has views into the Panthéon and is wonderfully situated for both the Latin and Luxembourg quarters. In fact if your children have energy they need to run off, the Luxembourg gardens are just 100m away. Most rooms can be converted into triples and some cater especially for families. If you choose a deluxe room, your family can enjoy breakfast on the balcony with views across Paris to the Sacré Coeur. The furnishings are stylish and comfy, and the service is excellent. Cots can be added to some rooms if requested when you book.

Hotel du Jeu de Paume

Rooms *36.* ***Rates*** *90€–255€ doubles, 150€–275€ triples, 180€–470€ family suite.* ***Credit*** *AmEx, MC, V.* ***Amenities*** *babysitting on request; Internet.* ***In room*** *TV, WiFi, safe.*

Hôtel Residence Henri IV

50 rue des Bernardin, 5th arr., ☎ 01 44 41 31 81; ***www.residencehenri4.com****. M° Maubert Mutualité*

This small, Belle-Epoque-style hotel, ideally situated between the Panthéon and the river, is popular with families looking for self-catering accommodation, with five furnished apartments that can house up to four, including tots. The nine other rooms are big enough to take an extra child's bed or cot if necessary. The concierge is happy to recommend places of interest and book restaurants for you.

Rooms *14.* ***Rates*** *90€–310€ doubles, 180€–340€ apartments. Cot free. Book online for discounted rooms and check last-minute offers which can include 40% off the rack room price.* ***Credit*** *AmEx, MC, V.* ***Amenities*** *lift, A/C, Internet, concierge booking facilities.* ***In room*** *TV, safety box.* ***In apartment*** *TV, safety box, microwave, fridge, hobs, crockery.*

INEXPENSIVE

Familia Hotel

11 rue des Ecoles, 5th arr., ☎ 01 43 54 55 27; ***www.hotel-paris-familia.com****. M° Jussieu or Maubert-Mutualité.*

As the name implies, this hotel has been family-run for decades and is very welcoming to families with children of all ages, offering both triple and quadruple rooms. Many personal touches make the place unique. Children especially like the fine frescoes of Parisian scenes on the walls of 14 rooms. Some rooms boast balconies with delightful views over the Latin Quarter. The dynamic owners renovate regularly.

Rooms *30.* ***Rates*** *99€–129€ doubles, 167€ triple, 179€ quadruple.* ***Credit*** *AmEx, DC, MC, V.* ***Amenities*** *parking 20€, free breakfast; limited room service.* ***In room*** *TV, dataport.*

FAMILY-FRIENDLY DINING

Historically linked with the 'financially challenged' (AKA penniless) students of the Latin Quarter, St-Michel is one of Paris's cheapest areas for dining. If your family is on a low budget, the sidestreets around **Rue de le Huchette** (5th arr., M° St-Michel) are touristy, but offer cheap and respectable food. Here you'll find rows of Greek restaurants, pizzerias, and crêperies. On the other side of Boulevard St-Michel, also try **Rue St André des Arts**.

MODERATE

Marty ★★

20 avenue. des Gobelins, 5th arr., ☎ 01 43 31 39 51; ***www.marty-restaurant.com****, M° Gobelins.*

Charming, with an authentically 1930s stone-trimmed décor and lots of Jazz-Age memorabilia scattered around, this is a fine address for sophisticated but unpretentious family dining. Set right on the southern edge of the Latin Quarter, food is satisfying, and unfussy (think guinea fowl with vegetable moussaka, grilled squid and strips of red mullet, or fried scallops with garlic butter sauce) and children are welcomed with a special menu – mains usually including a beefburger or tuna steak, with vegetables or chips. Dessert for both adults and children might include a soup of red fruits, ice cream, chocolate mousse, or crème brûlée. Views from the mezzanine tables take in the loud, large, and animated scene below.

Open *Noon–3pm and 7–11pm daily.* ***Main Courses*** *19€–27€ Set menu 34€. 3-course average 50€.* ***Credit*** *AmEx, DC, MC, V.* ***Amenities*** *terrace, highchairs, children's menu 19€. Reservations recommended.*

Nos Ancêtres les Gaulois ★ FIND

39 rue St Louis-en-l'Île, 4th arr., ☎ 01 46 33 66 07; ***www.nosancetreslesgaulois.com*** *M° Pont Marie.*

If your children like Astérix the Gaul and his super-human sidekick Obélix, a meal in this Gaulois-themed restaurant is a must. It's a bit like stepping into a medieval banquet hall with long wooden tables, deer heads on the stone walls, vegetable baskets with raw carrots and celery, all-you-can-eat buffets of cold meats and sausages, beef, lamb, and chicken steaks, Corbières wine poured straight from wooden barrels, and giant Gaul-sized cheeseboards and desserts. Troubadours occasionally serenade the tables with very cheesy songs, and a relaxed, party atmosphere reigns. If you think your children will never be able to eat it all, you're wrong! An under-10s version is available for 15€ and includes all you-can-drink soft drinks.

Open *7pm–2am daily, noon–3pm Sun.* ***Fixed-price*** *39€.* ***Credit*** *AmEx, DC, MC, V.* ***Amenities*** *ground floor toilets. Children's menus 15€. Reservations required.*

INEXPENSIVE

La Fourmi Ailée ★

8 rue du Fouarre, 5th arr., ☎ 01 43 29 40 99; ***www.premiumwanadoo.com/parisresto/Fourmi/MenuFourmi.php*** *M° St-Michel or RER B St-Michel/Notre-Dame.*

The 'flying ant' is an all-day tearoom that doubles as a library and, despite being in a handy spot near Notre-Dame, manages to retain a 'local' feel with Parisian couples, groups of students, and local families all popping in for tea, salads, a hot dish, or a dessert. The café has been around for centuries and at one time was used by students of the Sorbonne, who would take lessons sitting on bales of hay. Throughout the day, the café serves delicious quiches, salads, and *tartines* (toasted sandwiches) as well as hot dishes, including their signature *blanquette de veau* (creamy veal and mushroom casserole served with rice). For children in need of familiar food, the menu also offers pasta dishes including a rather scrumptious lasagne. For small appetites, there is also a children's dish (usually tagliatelle in a creamy

Picnic Time in the Square du Vert-Galant

On the tip of Île de la Cité lies one of the most picturesque spots for a family picnic: the **Square du Vert Galant** and the **quaysides** below, (access by the statue of Henri IV on Pont Neuf), look out on to the river so your family can wave to the passing boats and relax along the water's edge. Bring some colouring pencils, mini-board games, cards, a blanket and a picnic basket. Square du Vert Galant, 4th arr., M° Châtelet or Pont Neuf.

sauce) at 5€. Ice creams and hot apple crumbles complete the experience.

***Open** Noon–midnight daily. Average 20€. **Credit** MC, V. **Amenities** toilet up two steps. Children's menu 5€.*

Perraudin ★

*157 rue St-Jacques, 5th arr., ☎ 01 46 33 15 75; **www.restaurant-perraudin.com**. M° Cluny–La Sorbonne. RER: Luxembourg.*

Everything about this place – red and white tablecloths, zinc-topped bar, cuisine, prices, and service – attempts to duplicate an early-1900s bistro. This one was built in 1870 as an outlet for coal and wine. It evolved into the wood-panelled bistro you see today, where little has changed since Zola was buried in the Panthéon nearby. The charming owner and chef, Madame Rameau, will feed your children half portions if necessary, otherwise items on the menu suitable for smaller children include pâtés, steak and chips, sausages with potato purée, and, egg mayonnaise. For adventurous youngsters there are plump, garlicky snails as starters. Reservations are only accepted for 7 to 8pm – or wait at the bar (tables turn over quickly.)

***Open** Noon–2:15pm and 7–10pm Mon–Fri. Closed 3 weeks in Aug. Fixed-price lunch 18€, fixed-price evening menu 28€. **Main Courses** 15€–23€ **Credit** DC, MC, V. **Amenities** child-sized portions on request. One highchair. Ground-floor toilets (one step up).*

Find a picnic spot in the square du Vert-Galant

9 Disneyland® Resort Paris

DISNEYLAND® PARK & WALT DISNEY STUDIOS® PARK

Disneyland® Park

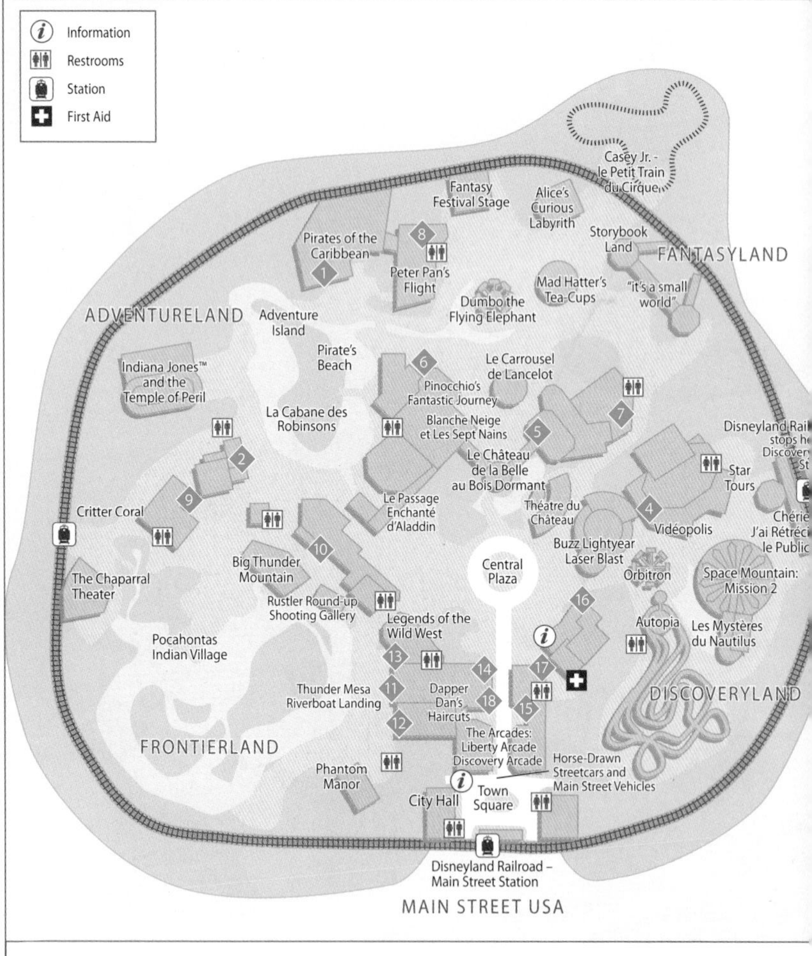

Dining ◆

Adventureland
Blue Lagoon Restaurant 1
Colonel Hathi's Pizza Outpost 2

Discoveryland
Buzz Lightyear's Pizza Planet Restaurant 3
Café Hyperion 4

Fantasyland
Auberge de Cendrillon 5
Au Chalet de la Marionnette 6
Pizzeria Bella Notte 7
Toad Hall Restaurant 8

Frontierland
Cowboy Cookout Barbecue 9
Fuente del Oro Restaurante 10
Last Chance Café 11
Silver Spur Steakhouse 12
The Lucky Nugget Saloon 13

Main Street, U.S.A.
Casey's Corner 14
Market House Deli 15
Plaza Gardens Restaurant 16
Victoria's Home-Style Restaurant
Walt's—an American Restaurant

Walt Disney Studios® Park

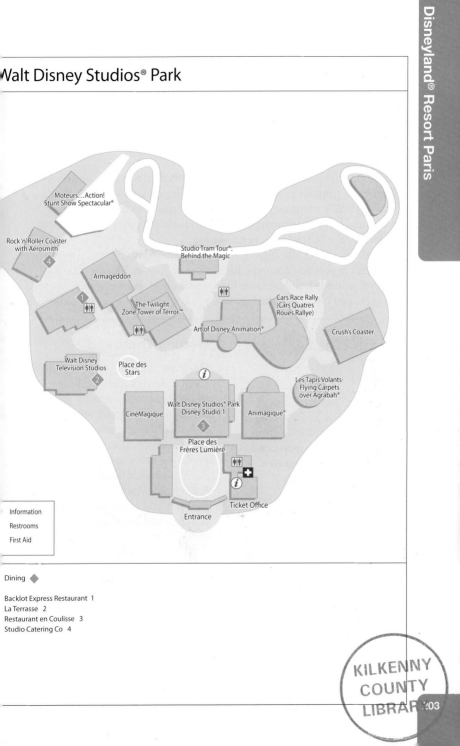

Moteurs…Action! Stunt Show Spectacular®

Rock 'n' Roller Coaster with Aerosmith 4

Studio Tram Tour®: Behind the Magic

Armageddon

1

The Twilight Zone Tower of Terror™

Cars Race Rally (Cars Quatres Roues Rallye)

Art of Disney Animation®

Crush's Coaster

Walt Disney Television Studios 2

Place des Stars

Les Tapis Volants- Flying Carpets over Agrabah®

CinéMagique

Walt Disney Studios® Park Disney Studio 1 3

Animagique®

Place des Frères Lumière

Ticket Office

Entrance

Information

Restrooms

First Aid

Dining

Backlot Express Restaurant 1
La Terrasse 2
Restaurant en Coulisse 3
Studio Catering Co 4

In recent French history, nothing has provoked such enthusiasm and controversy as the multimillion-euro Disneyland Paris, situated on a humongous site in the suburb of Marne-la-Vallée. Opened in 1992, it's one of the world's most lavish theme parks, conceived on a majestic scale, and covering ground about one-fifth the size of Paris. Despite initial worries that America's cultural imperialism would be the death knell of French civilisation, Disneyland Paris actually transposes itself nicely into French culture. For your children, this means everything looks, tastes, and feels like the Disney parks in California and Florida, but they get the novel bonus of ordering *'un'* cheeseburger *'avec frites'*.

In 2002, the park added **Walt Disney Studios**, focusing on the role of movies in popular culture and tricks of the trade in cartoon animation. This was a smart move as your family can now counterbalance the dream-like enchantment of the main park with more fast-moving and spectacular special-effects rides.

Take one day for the highlights, two or three days for more depth, but whatever you do, don't spend all of your time at Disney. Yes, it's a fun destination for children, and yes, every child will want to experience it at least once; but the city of Paris is also a living theme park.

ESSENTIALS

Address

Disneyland® Resort Paris, Marne-la-Vallée 77705. *08 25 30 60 30 or 0870 503 0303* from UK; ***www.disneylandparis.co.uk*** or ***www.disneylandparis.com***. RER A Marne-la-Vallée.

Opening Times

Opening times vary throughout the year, but generally the Disneyland® Park is open 10am–8pm daily Sept–mid-July and 9am–11pm mid-July–Sept. The Walt Disney Studios® Park closes slightly earlier with hours from 10am to 6pm in winter and 9am to 7pm in summer.

Getting There

By Train Eurostar operates one service per day from **London St Pancras International** (departure usually 8.53am), stopping at **Ashford International** (departure usually 9.27am) to **Marne-la-Vallée station** (arrival 12.27pm). Return trains usually leave from Marne-la-Vallée at 7.35pm and arrive at Ashford at 8.36pm and London St Pancras at 9.23pm.

If you've booked an inclusive Disney package with a tour operator, you can opt for the **Disney Express Service**, which allows you to complete your hotel check-in and get your Disney Park tickets on board. There's also a luggage service that takes your bags straight from the train to the hotel, so you can go straight to the park.

Parking

If you're staying in Hôtel l'Elysée Val d'Europe, Radisson SAS Hotel, Vienna International Dream Castle Hotel, Holiday Inn®, MyTravel's Explorers Hotel or Hôtel Kyriad, you have free parking at the hotel and in the Disneyland Parks® (show your check-in card). There is also parking at the Résidence Pierre et Vacances Val d'Europe but at a charge. If you're not staying in a Disney hotel, parking per day (Disneyland Park and Toll Plaza near the entrance to the Disney Village) is 5€ for motor-bikes and sidecars, 8€ for cars, 13€ for coaches and campervans.

Tip: note where you leave the car (each section is named after a Disney character), otherwise you'll spend an eternity trying to find it again.

Once in your seats, all children get activity packs and some of Disney's staff move through the carriages to help you plan your visit. Journey time is under three hours. *08705 18 61 86* from the UK or check ***www.eurostar.com***.

Other Eurostar services go to Brussels and Paris via Lille, from where you can catch a direct **TGV** (France's high-speed trains) connection to Marne-la-Vallée without going into Paris. See ***www.sncf.com***.

By Car Disneyland® Resort Paris is about 32km east of **Paris** and is well signposted from the centre. On the *Périphérique* (Paris's ring road), at the Porte de Bercy exit (southeast), follow the A4 motorway direction Metz/Nancy. Exit at junction 14 (Val d'Europe, Parc Disneyland®) for the parks. If you're staying in the Davy Crockett Ranch, take exit 13 'Provins/Serris'.

From **Roissy Charles de Gaulle Airport** (north), follow signs for Marne-la-Vallée until the A104 (a road called *La Francilienne*). After 27km join the A4 motorway following Metz/Nancy (see above for relevant junction exits).

From **Orly Airport** (south), head for Paris and then follow signs for Créteil on the A86. After 11km join the A4 (direction Metz/Nancy) and exit as above.

If arriving from elsewhere in France, the A1 (coming down from the Channel ports), the A6 (heading up from the Riviera, Italy, and Switzerland) and the A10 (from around Bordeaux, Spain, and Portugal), you will probably join La Francilienne (A104 and N104), from where you should follow signs to Marne-la-Vallée until you join the A4 (dir. Metz/Nancy) and exit as above.

By Public Transport The RER *(pron. Ehr-urr-ehr)* suburban commuter network (Line A) has a stop within walking distance of the park. Board the RER in Paris at Charles-de-Gaulle-Etoile, Châtelet-Les Halles, Nation or anywhere along the A line. Only one branch of RER A terminates at Marne-la-Vallée/Chessy so check the destinations board on the platform (bulbs light up next to the destinations covered by the arriving train) and make sure your family is on the right train (not direction Boissy-St-Léger). The journey takes 45 minutes from central Paris and costs 6.30€ each way for an adult and 3.15€ for a child (see age restrictions at the ticket desk). Trains run daily every 10 to 20 minutes from 5.30am (direction Disneyland®) to midnight (from Disney direction Paris).

Tip: You can buy a one-day Disney Pass at the same time as your transport ticket for quicker access into the parks: 47€ adults and 39€ 3–11s, free under-3s.

By Air Most international flights arrive at either Roissy-Charles-de-Gaulle airport (north) or at Orly (south) (special Paris Airports (ADP) number *39-50*). **Shuttle buses** (*01 72 30 10 25*; ***www.vea.fr***) connect both airports with each hotel in the Disneyland® resort (except Davy Crockett Ranch). They depart every 20 to 45 minutes from 8.30am to 7.45pm. One-way transport to the park from either airport is 17€ for adults, 13€ for children aged 3–11. E-tickets can now be bought online.

Tip: If you're catching a plane home straight after your trip to Disney, take a Vea coach at least 2½ hours before your check-in time.

Disabilities: The shuttle buses aren't adapted for those with reduced mobility, but an adapted vehicle can be reserved *01 53 48 39 38* or email ***E: veaventes@aol.com***.

Orientation

Disneyland® Resort Paris is one enormous resort with two separate theme parks: **Disneyland® Park** is devoted to the magical world of Disney, and **Walt Disney Studios® Park** is based on film production. There's also an entertainment centre, the **Disney Village**, which is open to non-ticketholders, with nightclubs, shops, restaurants, and bars. The resort also contains multiple hotels, a campsite, championship golf course, large artificial lake and canal, and traffic-free promenades linking the hotels to the Parks.

Disneyland® Park

This main theme park is split into five different worlds:

Main Street, USA is the gateway to the other themed lands, designed to look like a turn of the 20th century small-town street with horse-drawn carriages, pretty architecture, shops, and arcades. This is also the main embarkation point for the steam-powered railway car (Main Street Station), which takes you to all lands except Adventureland.

A Grand Canyon diorama leads to **Frontierland**, the largest of the five lands, with its paddle-wheel steamers reminiscent of Mark Twain's Mississippi river. Other attractions are the Critter Corral, where your children can pet the animals, Big Thunder

Mountain, one of the fastest rides around, the spooky Phantom Manor ghost train, and the Pocahontas Indian Village playground for little children.

North of Frontierland is **Adventureland**, with its swash-buckling pirates, Swiss Family Robinson tree house, knuckle-whitening Indiana Jones™ rollercoaster, and the immensely popular Pirates of the Caribbean ride. **Fantasyland**, just next door is a favourite for families with small children and is where you'll find the **Sleeping Beauty Castle** *(Le Château de la Belle au Bois Dormant),* whose pinnacles and turrets are an idealised interpretation of a French château. In its shadow are the gentler rides of *Blanche Neige et les Sept Nains* (Snow White and the Seven Dwarfs), Peter Pan, Dumbo, Alice in Wonderland, the Mad Hatter's Tea Cups, and Sir Lancelot's Magic Carousel (*Le Carrousel de Lancelot).*

Visions of the future are in **Discoveryland** (right off Main Street USA and south of Fantasyland) where tributes to invention and imagination draw from the works of Leonardo da Vinci, Jules Verne, H. G. Wells, and the *Star Wars* films series. This is also where the Lion King show takes place at Vidéopolis.

As you wander around the five areas you'll see characters from *Aladdin*, *The Lion King*, *Pocahontas*, *Snow White*, *Cinderella*, and *Toy Story*; and as Disney continues to churn out animated blockbusters, look for the newest stars, such as those from Ratatouille.

Walt Disney Studios® Park

Walk past the Disney Village opposite the entrance to Disneyland® Park to get to this smaller, yet fun-packed, theme park, which takes your family on a behind-the-scenes interactive discovery of film, animation, and television.

Once through the main entrance (Studio Services), you get to the **Front Lot** with Disney Studio 1 – an elaborate sound stage complete with hundreds of film props and filled with souvenir boutiques and restaurants.

The **Toon Studio** is the best district for young children, where your family can learn the trade secrets of Disney animators, sing Disney songs (in the Animagique® theatre), and fly magic carpets over Agrabah (*Les Tapis Volants*).

Production Courtyard lets you look behind the scenes of film and TV production. On the Studio Tram Tour® at Catastrophe Canyon your family gets plunged into the heart of a special-effects shoot, with towers of flames and floods of water. This is also where Disney's newest adrenalin ride, The Twilight Zone Tower of Terror™, takes adults and older children on a hair-raising trip round an old Hollywood hotel.

Finally, the **Back Lot** is home to special effects and stunt workshops such as a live stunt show (Moteurs... Action!) featuring cars, motorbikes, and jet skis; the Rock 'n' Roller Coaster, featuring the music of Aerosmith, that combines rock memorabilia with high-speed scary twists and turns (completely in the dark); and an intense reconstruction of one of the explosion scenes in the Hollywood action film *Armageddon.*

Which Ticket?

Ticket prices per day decrease the longer you stay. However, it is worth remembering that spending one day in each park (with separate tickets) is cheaper than buying a two-day, two-park Hopper ticket. If you book your stay at Disney with a tour operator, your entry to the parks may also be included in the price of your room. Also consult the website for special offers. The Disney Village is accessible without a ticket. Two- to five-day Hopper tickets are valid for one year after purchase.

- 1-day, 1-park Hopper: 47€ adults, 39€ 3–11s
- 1-day, 2-park Hopper: 57€ adults, 49€ 3–11s
- 2-day, 2-park Hopper: 105€ adults, 89€ 3–11s
- 3-day, 2-park Hopper: 131€ adults, 111€ 3–11s
- 4-day, 2-park Hopper: 152€ adults, 129€ 3–11s.
- 5-day, 2-park Hopper: 163€ adults, 138€ 3–11s

Children under three: free entry.

Note: These prices may have risen by the time of publication.

FASTPASS®

The **FASTPASS®★★** is a handy way of cutting down queuing times for popular attractions. On indicated rides (see below), insert your normal park admission ticket into the FASTPASS® machine (at the entrance of the ride) and a second ticket will pop out indicating a return time. While you wait, visit other attractions and then come back at the time indicated on your ticket and board via the FASTPASS® priority entrance.

Tip: The passes are subject to availability (many rides run out of them before lunch time). Only one FASTPASS® ticket can be used at a time per person. It is only valid with a park admission ticket for the same day; and you can only get a second pass once the first one has been used.

Those staying as a *Suites* or *Castle Club* guest at Disneyland® Hotel, Disney's Hotel New York®, Disney's Newport Bay Club® or Disney's Sequoia Lodge® receive a VIP FASTPASS® which gives unlimited access to all FASTPASS® lines. One FASTPASS® per day per person is also available to all guests staying at the Disneyland® Hotel.

FASTPASS® rides are:

Adventureland

- Indiana Jones™ and the Temple of Peril

Discoveryland

- Space Mountain: Mission 2

- Buzz Lightyear Laser Blast®
- Star Tours

Fantasyland

- Peter Pan's Flight

Frontierland

- Big Thunder Mountain

Children's Facilities

In the Hotels If you stay in a Disney hotel, most establishments have on-site play areas for children. Disney characters regularly pop by to meet your youngsters (souvenir photos can be purchased – ask at the hotel) and all children get given a souvenir badge. Cots (on request) are free of charge (except in Résidences Pierre et Vacances Val d'Europe) and baby-bottle warmers and basic accessories are also available. Babysitters can also be hired so that mums and dads can sneak out for a slice of after-hours magic.

In the Parks Children's facilities are well indicated throughout the parks.

Buggies can be hired (*location de poussettes*) by the day in Town Square (Disneyland® Park) or near Studio Services (Walt Disney Studios® Park). You can also bring your own buggies into the whole resort.

Microwaves, bottle warmers, rocking chairs, and baby-changing tables are available in the **Baby Care Centres** (*Coin Bébés*) (between the Central Plaza and Main Street USA in Disneyland® Park or next to Studio Services in Walt Disney Studios® Park). Nappies and baby food can also be purchased here (in the Studio Photo boutique in Walt Disney Studios® Park), but bring your own towels. All toilets also have changing facilities.

If your children get lost, they will be taken to the **Lost Children Point** (*Rendez-vous Enfants Perdus*) where they will be comforted and looked after until you find them.

A useful, free facility for families with toddlers or children of mixed ages is the **Baby Switch service**. It allows parents and older children wishing to try the larger rides to take it in turns with their partner or parents, without having to queue twice. Ask the Cast Member (Disney employee) at the entrance to the ride about this.

In the Restaurants Children's menus for 3 to 11s can be requested in all restaurants. Specially adapted menus for under-3s are also available in waiter-service restaurants. Most eateries provide bottle warmers for parents with babies.

Restrictions

Here is a quick list of ride restrictions. Bear in mind that most rides in both parks are unsuitable for babies and that specific age restrictions are mentioned on information panels at the entrance to each attraction. Avoid jolting rides if you are pregnant, have heart problems, high blood pressure, neck or back problems, or any other illness likely to deteriorate on the attraction (see health restrictions, p. 210). For ride descriptions see 'What to See & Do'.

Key

DP = Disneyland® Park
WDSP = Walt Disney Studios® Park

Height Restrictions

La Plage des Pirates (DP, Adventureland) – playground for 3–6s and 7–9s, max. height 1m 40.
Indiana Jones™ and the Temple of Terror (DP, Adventureland) – min. height 1m 40.
Big Thunder Mountain (DP, Frontierland) – min. height 1m 02.
Space Mountain: Mission 2 (DP, Discoveryland) – min. height 1m 32.
Autopia (DP, Discoveryland) – min. height 81cm, max. height (for driving without a parent) 1m 32.
Rock 'n' Roller Coaster with Aerosmith (WDSP, Backlot) – min. height 1m 20.
The Twilight Zone Tower of Terror™ (WDSP, Production Courtyard) – min. height 1m 02.
Crush's Coaster (WDSP, Toon Studio) – min. height 1m 07

Health Restrictions

The following rides are not advised for those suffering from illness (including motion sickness) or anybody who is pregnant:
Indiana Jones™ and the Temple of Terror (DP, Adventureland)
Big Thunder Mountain (DP, Frontierland)
Star Tours (DP, Discoveryland)
Space Mountain: Mission 2 (DP, Discoveryland)
Autopia (DP, Discoveryland)
Armageddon Special Effects (WDSP, Backlot)
Rock'n'Roller Coaster with Aerosmith (WDSP, Backlot)
The Twilight Zone Tower of Terror™ (WDSP, Production Courtyard)
Crush's Coaster (WDSP, Toon Studio)

Frightening for Young Children

You will know your own children best but depending on their age and sensitivity, the following rides could be scary:
Pirates of the Caribbean (DP, Adventureland)
Phantom Manor (DP, Frontierland)
Honey I Shrunk the Audience (DP, Discoveryland)
Snow White and the Seven Dwarfs (DP, Fantasyland)
Les Voyages de Pinocchio (DP, Fantasyland)
Moteurs...Action! Stunt-Show Spectacular (WDSP, Backlot)
Cinémagique (WDSP, Production Courtyard)

Disabilities

If somebody in your family has a disability, a special booklet, the *Disabled Guest Guide*, is available at the main entrance to Disneyland® Park, City Hall, or Studio Services. There is wheelchair access across the resort, but guests will have to be lifted out of their wheelchairs to go on some of the rides (Disney staff are not legally allowed to help with this). If you're staying in a Disney hotel, all have designated disabled rooms, and special vehicles can be booked to help you get to the theme parks. If somebody in your family only needs a wheelchair occasionally, they can be hired in Town Square, Main Street USA or at Studio Services in the Front Lot. All shops, restaurants and toilets have disabled access. Special aids (including guides in braille) are also available for guests with sight impairments. Ask at City Hall, First Aid, or at Studio Services.

Information

There is a Tourist Office between the Marne-la-Vallée RER station and the Disney Village (Espace du Tourisme Seine et Marne, Place François Truffaut, Marne-la-Vallée, 77705 cedex 4) ☎ *01 60 43 33 33*; ***www.tourisme77.com***.

You can also get information on Disneyland® Resort Paris in Tourist Offices in Paris ☎ *08 92 68 30 00*; ***www.parisinfo.com***.

For general enquiries inside the Disneyland® Park, head to City Hall and in Walt Disney Studios® Park, go to Studio Services.

Medical Care

Fully trained nursing staff are in the **First Aid** (*Premiers Soins*) centres next to Plaza Gardens in Main Street USA, and in the Front Lot by Studio Services. Most hotels provide basic health supplies (plasters, painkillers, antiseptic sprays, etc.) but for serious problems alert any staff member in the parks or hotels. Remember ☎ *18* is Fire service/ Paramedics, ☎ *17* is Police and ☎ *15* is Ambulance. A medical centre can be found in nearby Esbly and there is an ER in Lagny.

Post Office

There is a post office near Marne-la-Vallée RER station (9am–7pm Mon–Sat), but you can buy stamps in many shops, and postboxes are dotted throughout both parks.

Useful Tips

Reservations

To reserve accommodation, rent cars (Hertz is an official Disney partner), or ask questions before you visit, call ☎ *08705 03 03 03* (from the UK); ☎ *01 60 30 60 30* or ***www.disneylandparis.co.uk*** and ***www.disneylandparis.com***.

Money-saving Tactics

It is hard to visit Disneyland on a budget: the prices inside the park are high, you are a captive audience, and everywhere you turn (shop, drinks stands, or even some rides which sell official photographs) there's something to entice you to spend. However, willpower and forward planning can go a long way.

- If you're coming for two days, save several euros by buying two separate one-day tickets and spend a day in each park. If you come for three days, however, the three-day Hopper is the best value as it allows free movement between parks and remains valid for up to one year after purchase, so you don't have to come for three consecutive days.
- Set yourself a souvenir budget and resist impulse buying of ice creams, soft drinks, T-shirts, mugs, pens, and mouse-ears. A couple of euros here and there mount up to a frighteningly large total during your stay.
- Bring a picnic to the designated picnic area between the guests' car park and the Disney® Parks. Food and drink aren't supposed to be brought into the parks, but bottles of water and baby food are justifiably tolerated.
- If a picnic isn't possible, embrace the prospect of artery-clogging junk food and choose a self-service restaurant rather than one with table service.
- If you're staying in an onsite hotel and know you'll be eating at least one meal a day in the park, enquire about the half-board deals which give up to 15% off some restaurants.
- Avoid the expensive, money-swallowing games arcades.
- Bring your own raincoats and umbrellas so you don't have to buy any here just in case it rains.

When to Come

Disney correctly boasts that there is something for everybody all year round. I visited on a freezing winter's day before Christmas and admit that the cold generously added to the experience by leaving real icicles on the outdoor attractions and making the whole park feel very festive. Generally speaking, however, with its many outside rides, a bright spring or autumn day is an ideal time to visit. Parades of Disney characters take place all year round, but Halloween, Christmas, and the Summer evening parades (when the Disneyland® Park stays open until late) are particularly impressive. The busiest times are during French school holidays (around Easter and Whitsun and from the end of June to early September).

You'll probably be tied to your children's school holidays however, so grinning and bearing the crowds is a philosophy best adopted. Also, arrive early when the queues tend to be shorter. Remember that mid-week – especially Tuesday – is usually quieter than weekends.

Don't Forget

It's all common sense, but here's a quick check-list:

- Come prepared for the weather, with suntan lotion, extra jumpers, rainwear, and comfortable shoes.
- Use the FASTPASS® service (see p. 208) wherever possible.
- Grab an Entertainment Programme from City Hall in Disneyland® Park or Studio Services in Walt Disney Studios® Park to find out which performances (see Entertainment, p. 229) are taking place and when. Get to these shows 30 minutes beforehand to make sure you can get in, especially the Lion King (see p. 225), which is very popular with families.
- Shoes and shirts must be worn at all times, even on very hot days.
- If you're staying in a Disney Hotel, the ID charge-card system (see p. 235) is very useful in shops and restaurants, as is the free shopping delivery service (p. 235).
- Save time by planning what you want to see, then choosing a district and trying all of the rides you want to go on there before moving on to the next district.
- If you would like a meal in a restaurant with table service, reserve in advance.
- Choose an emergency meeting point (the Sleeping Beauty Castle is visible from all over the park for instance) in case your children get lost. Or show them where to find the Lost Children Point (*Rendez-vous Enfants Perdus*).

WHAT TO SEE & DO

Key

DP = Disneyland® Park
WDSP = Walt Disney Studios® Park
DV = Disney Village

Top 5 Attractions

For young children

❶ **Finding** your way out of **Alice's Curious Labyrinth** (DP, Fantasyland, p. 220)

❷ **Taking** a musical cruise through the world of automated toys in **'it's a small world'** (DP, Fantasyland, p. 231).

❸ **Driving** your own 1950's car around town with **Autopia** (DP, Discoveryland, p. 223)

❹ **Helping** Buzz Lightyear to save the world from monsters using a laser-gun. (DP, **Buzz Lightyear Laser Blast**, Discoveryland, p. 223)

Alice's Curious Labyrinth, Fantasyland. ©Disney

❺ **Travelling** between Main Street USA, Frontierland, Fantasyland, and Discoveryland on the steam-powered **Disneyland Railroad** (DP, covers all lands, p. 215)

For older children

❶ **Destroying** the Empire's headquarters on the Death Star while dodging objects, planes, and asteroids (DP, **Star Tours,** Discoveryland, p. 224).

❷ **Facing** real special effects (smoke and balls of fire) as you play an extra on the **Armageddon** disaster movie (WDSP, Backlot, p. 227).

❸ **Marvelling** at the breathtaking motor stunts of a live film shoot. (WDSP, **Moteurs... Action! Stunt Show Spectacular**, Backlot, p. 227).

❹ **Shrinking** inside a 3D film in **Honey I shrunk the audience** (Chérie, J 'ai Rétréci le Public) (DP, Discoveryland, p. 223).

❺ **Watching** impressive, live special effects (fire and water) on the **Studio Tram Tour®** (WDSP, Production Courtyard, see p. 226).

For families

❶ **Seeing** your children's faces light up as they watch all their favourite characters in the **Disney Parade** (DP, Main Street USA, p. 230).

❷ **Swimming** with Nemo past Coral reefs and submarine wrecks in **Crush's Coaster** (WDSP, Toon Studio, p. 229).

❸ **Hakuna-Matata-ing** with characters from the Lion King

during a live musical-dancing performance in **Vidéopolis** (DP, Discoveryland, p. 225)

❹ **Tucking** into a hearty meal while watching **Buffalo Bill's Wild West Show**, live with horses, Cowboys, and Indians (DV, p. 234)

❺ **Experiencing** a ghostly pirate attack on **Pirates of the Caribbean** (DP, Adventureland, p. 220)

Key to the Attractions

To help you get the most out of the Disneyland® Park, the listings have been split into lands, and a key system (below) indicates the main target audience for the attractions. See Restrictions p. 209 for more specific information.

Y = Young children
F = Families
O = Older children
T = Thrillseekers

Disneyland® Park

Disneyland® Park aims to recreate on a majestic scale the magic that has enchanted so many generations of children and adults. Whether it succeeds or not is for you to decide – but you certainly won't be left indifferent. As you stroll down Main Street USA, excitement reigns at every turn as families hurry to reach the themed lands. Everywhere you go (come armed with the show programme and a map) you'll find musical extravaganzas, colourful parades, rides for the whole family, and opportunities to do everything from reliving the Wild West to becoming an explorer or an adventurer, flying through space, or seeing fairy-tales burst into life.

Main Street USA

The pastel-coloured, decorative architecture of the Disneyland® Park's hub is reminiscent of early 20th-century America, with the large pink Disneyland® Hotel spanning the entrance and streets lined with gaslamps, horse-drawn streetcars, old barber shops, ornate balustrades, and covered arcades. At **City Hall** on **Town Square** you can pick up maps and programmes and book restaurants and activities.

Disneyland Railroad – Main Street Station ★ Y F

Trains were one of Walt Disney's enduring passions and the Disneyland Railroad is a steam-powered train that gently choo-choos its way round the perimeters of the park, through woodland scenes and past the occasional live animal. On my visit with 7- and 9-year-old boys, one had taken the train on a previous visit and insisted it be the first thing we try this time round. It is also the only way to see the **Grand Canyon Diorama** – a hit with little children who like looking at the scenery of the Grand Canyon, recreated with Indian cliff dwellings, a stuffed fox, rat, rattlesnakes, racoons, and squirrels. Trains leave

FUN FACT **Far, Far Away**

When architects designed Main Street USA they cleverly graduated the top storeys of all the buildings so that Sleeping Beauty's Castle looks larger and further away than it really is.

roughly every ten minutes and take 20 minutes to get around the whole park.

Horse-Drawn Streetcars and Main Street Vehicles ★ Y F

Young children get very excited at the prospect of riding in an old-fashioned tram, pulled by friendly horses they can pet. If they want something more motorised, opt for one of the street vehicles opposite (police cars or fire-engines run by Hertz). You might even be lucky enough to share your seat with Mickey or Minnie.

The Arcades F

Two decorative, 19th-century-style covered passageways run up either side of Main Street USA. They're handy when it's cold or rainy, and give access to restaurants and shops. **Liberty Arcade** (left-hand side, facing the castle) contains an exhibition on the statue of Liberty in New York with plans, drawings, and photographs. **Discovery Arcade** (right side, facing the castle) is where children can look at cabinets containing blueprints for weird and wacky early 20th-century inventions.

Frontierland

Yee-Haa! Welcome to the town of Thunder Mesa in the Wild West, where an Arizona-inspired landscape provides a spectacular backdrop to a lake where you can take a relaxing cruise on a paddle-steamboat, test rides like Big Thunder mountain (one of the park's most famous roller-coasters), play in Pocahontas's Indian Village (if you're under 9 years old) and face your fear in the park's haunted house. This is the largest of the lands and looks surprisingly authentic thanks to genuine artefacts brought over from the States.

Big Thunder Mountain ★★ O T

Hold onto your hats! This is one of Disneyland's most fun white-knuckle rides (with queues to match). The route, in an Arizona landscape, rises to 36m, whizzing thrillseekers aboard a runaway train in and out of the rusting, rocky innards of a mine. Tearing through a mining camp and forest, you enter the mountain only to get caught in a dynamite explosion. The roof caves in and water washes away some of the track, but you make it back safely enough to either feel hungry for more, or adamant you'll never join the queue again!

Tip: Get a FASTPASS® ticket and don't board straight after eating.

Note: Not recommended for under-7s.

Big Thunder Mountain, Frontierland. ©Disney

Critter Coral Y F

Near the Disneyland Railroad Frontierland Depot, this mini-Western ranch is a hit with the little ones who come to stroke some of the real animals that include cows and goats.

Legends of the Wild West F

Pass through the old wooden gates of Fort Comstock (a replica of a log stockade built by early pioneers against Indian attacks) and climb all 135 steps to the top of the watchtowers for panoramic views over the park and to see an old cannon. The Indian Camp outside gives an insight into how native Americans would have lived, and, with a bit of luck, Buffalo Bill, Davy Crockett, and a Cheyenne Indian chief will be hanging around for a chin-wag and a photo. (No wheelchair access).

Phantom Manor ★★ F

Some parts could frighten little children but this ramshackle, haunted mansion is an exciting attraction with decent special effects and a genuine eerie atmosphere. A sinister host welcomes you into a circular room, which suddenly stretches downwards

Change Your Look

The last thing people come to Disneyland for is a haircut, yet in Main Street USA, **Dapper Dan's Haircuts** has been cutting and shaving visitors' locks for years. The service is at an extra charge, but if you or the children need a quick short back and sides, the whole place looks like a genuine olden-days barber's shop.

FUN FACT **Quiz**

Q: How many bricks and lightbulbs make up Main Street USA?
A: 580,000 bricks and 225,000 separate bulbs.

into the belly of the house where a carriage awaits to carry you on a journey through the haunted rooms. Watch out for the sobbing bride who pops out at intervals, the medium's head that appears in a crystal ball, and the old ballroom where holograms show wedding guests dancing then mysteriously disappearing.

Pocahontas Indian Village ★ Y

This charming spot is a reconstruction of the Algonquian princess's village and a great place for small children in need of time away from the queues and a good old play on climbing frames and slides.

Rustler Round-up Shooting Gallery F

Dads and sons (and some mums and daughters) may want to show off in this fun shooting gallery where you can take potshots at 74 moving targets such as cacti, a dynamite shack, and peeping tom, Peg-Leg Pete. **Beware:** This ride costs extra.

Thunder Mesa Riverboat Landing F

The *Mark Twain* and *Molly Brown* paddle boats were built especially for Disney as authentic reconstructions of vessels used on the Mississippi and Sacramento rivers during the Gold Rush. They can carry 400 people around Frontierland's lake, giving children a chance to glimpse Smugglers Cove, Wilderness Island where Joe and his barking dog sit watching the passing boats, an abandoned wagon next to two cow skeletons, and a water jet over dinosaur bones. The cruise lasts 15 minutes. Summer only.

Adventureland

The Caribbean islands, the Arabian desert and the Asian jungle are recreated in Adventureland – one of the most appealing areas for all age groups thanks to its water features, islands, vegetation, pleasant eating places, and opportunities to tackle pirates, speeding trains, and take to the trees with the Swiss Family Robinson.

Adventure Island Y F

If your littl'uns are intrepid adventurers, get them to cross the suspension bridges that lead to the secret hideout of swashbuckling pirates – Ben Gunn's Cave. There are six different, haunted entrances that drip with water and lead to a secret stash of treasure, guarded by bats and skulls. Don't go out of your way to see it, but if you're crossing the park this way, it's fun to stop by.

Indiana Jones™ and the Temple of Peril. ©Disney

Indiana Jones™ and the Temple of Peril ★ O T

Everybody's heard of the daredevil archaeologist Indiana Jones. Just like in his films, this high-speed rollercoaster slams its way through an ancient temple, past mummies, poisonous darts, bizarre statues, and precarious columns on an untamed ride that cumulates in a tummy-turning loop-the-loop.

Note: Not recommended for under-8s and if you don't want to see your ice cream again, eat it after the ride.

Tip: Use the FASTPASS® service.

Le Passage Enchanté d'Aladdin Y

This is a good one for under-7s who are fans of Aladdin, as miniature scenes are brought to life inside an Arabian Bazaar. Light and sound effects transport you through the City of Agrabah to a secret cave where Aladdin finds the magic lamp and its friendly genie.

Pirate's Beach Y

If your little shipmates feel the need to run around and tussle with a real pirate, Captain Hook's galleon moored on Pirate's Beach (overlooked by a skull-shaped waterfall) has a resident one for them to challenge. He looks fearsome (watch out for his hook), but he's warm at heart and always happy to let children have their photograph taken with him. There's also a snack bar down below (summer only). The

FUN FACT **Wild West**

The word Mesa (as in Thunder Mesa) means 'high desert plateau', evoking the Wild West rock formations around the rides.

beach itself is a children's play area (max. height 1.4m).

Pirates of the Caribbean ★★ Y F O

Even street-cred-conscious teens will like this blockbusting attraction based on the dastardly deeds of Captain Jack Sparrow. It's so packed with detail you could easily go through twice and notice different things each time. You pass the automated world of a pirate town, where buccaneers sing merry tunes and count piles of gold. Then suddenly, you're transported back to the 17th century in the middle of a pirate assault. Guns fire, cannons blast, and it all ends rather nastily, inside a ghost town, where dead pirates are forced to live in semi-transparent form.

The Swiss Family Robinson Tree-House (La Cabane des Robinsons) F

In the heart of Adventure Island, in a 28m-high fig tree, the Swiss Family Robinson has created the ultimate tree-top retreat using shipwreck timbers. Children enjoy counting the steps up to the top (all 176 of them), wandering in and out of the upstairs rooms and downstairs supplies stores (behind bamboo bars). Why not tell your youngsters that the first person to find the Robinson's shipwreck chooses the next attraction?

Fantasyland

Fantasyland is the ultimate land for families with young children. Teenagers may feel too cool to be seen there (at first), but the centrepiece, Sleeping Beauty's Castle, is both enchanting and a landmark when you get lost. It's also the setting for the open-air **Théâtre du Château** (on the right) where Disney characters sometimes perform live shows (great for getting your little and big children in the mood). As its name implies, Fantasyland's theme is fairy stories – a world where witches, princes and princesses, magic wishing wells, and surrealist labyrinths co-exist alongside gingerbread houses, flying elephants, giant teacups, and puppets that want to be boys. The Disneyland Railroad stops at **Fantasy Station** and if you're looking for a French meal, the **Auberge de Cendrillon** (Cinderella's Inn) p. 239 is one of the best restaurants in the park.

Alice's Curious Labyrinth ★ F

Watch out for the wicked Queen of Hearts who cries 'off with your head' in this fun, ivy-hedged maze, based on Alice in Wonderland. As your family twists and turns through the passages you'll see the Cheshire Cat grinning and rolling its eyes, watch the blue caterpillar smoking a hookah, catch the white rabbit running with his pocket watch, and enter a purple castle filled with optical illusions.

Casey Jr. – le Petit Train du Cirque Y

As a non-watery alternative for anyone over the age of 1, this gentle ride, modelled on the circus train in Dumbo the Flying Elephant, navigates small hills and bridges over the Storybook Land sets.

Dumbo the Flying Elephant ★ Y

This fairground ride is a great opportunity for parents to join their young children on a gentle but fun ride that takes you flying on the back of Dumbo the Elephant. If you're feeling brave, sit back and let your children control the height at which you soar.

'it's a small world' ★ Y

If your children like clockwork and automated toys, this ride may well be the highlight of Fantasyland. Dolls from around the world are joined by animals, toy soldiers, leprechauns, beefeaters, and flamenco dancers in one big, sugary musical display that will have you whistling the theme tune for the rest of the day. One part allows you to embark on a boat; other sections provide good opportunities for your children to pick out famous landmarks from around the world like Big Ben, the Leaning Tower of Pisa, the Eiffel Tower, and a windmill from Holland.

Lancelot's Carousel (Le Carrousel de Lancelot) Y

This is a traditional merry-go-round, coveted by young children who like to choose their steed while they queue, then rush up to it as quickly as possible so that nobody else can ride it.

Mad Hatter's Tea-Cups F

Spin around madly in giant pastel-coloured teacups (another tribute to Alice in Wonderland) that whirl around a giant covered roundabout. If your children want to get really dizzy, let them take the steering wheel to control the speed.

Peter Pan's Flight ★★ Y

If your children know all about the adventures of the boy who never grew up, they'll love this ride, where galleons sail over the rooftops of London to Neverland, past mermaids, Indians, and Captain Hook, forever trying to escape the crocodile's jaws.

Tip: Use the FASTPASS® system when queues are long.

Pinocchio's Fantastic Journey Y F

Whether your children have read Carlo Collodi's original story or seen the Disney version, they'll adore seeing the nose-growing puppet and his friend Jiminy Cricket re-enact their quest to turn Pinocchio into a real boy. Sit with your family in a little car that takes you through mountain landscapes and past numerous dangers before finishing back in Geppetto's toy-shop where his clockwork toys spring to action.

Sleeping Beauty's Castle ★ F

This might look like it's come straight out of a story book, but the architecture was, in fact, inspired by Mont St-Michel's island abbey-castle in Normandy (minus the pink cladding). Like a real fairytale château however, it is encircled by a moat and accessed across a drawbridge or via the side entrance next to a magic wishing well. Once inside,

FUN FACT

A Taller Sleeping Beauty

The Sleeping Beauty castle is 43m tall and was built using an architectural technique called 'forced perspective' that gives the impression the castle is even taller than it actually is.

make sure you look at the front window, which will wow children as its design changes from a rose into doves, as if by magic. Also head upstairs to **Sleeping Beauty's Gallery** (*La Galerie de la Belle au Bois Dormant*) to see displays on the famous story, admire the stained-glass windows and tapestries, and take in a sweeping panorama of the park from the balcony. Beneath the castle, venture, if you dare, into the **Tanière du Dragon** (dragon's den) where a fiery creature lurks, waiting to pounce.

Snow White and the Seven Dwarfs ★ Y F

Just outside the dwarfs' cottage, a diamond-mine car takes you through some of the film's most memorable scenes. Children can relive the moments when Snow White discovers the dwarfs' hut, when the wicked queen gazes into her magic mirror, when she poisons Snow White with an apple, and of course, when the handsome prince saves her at the end.

Storybook Land ★ Y

This is a canal cruise especially for young children who can watch miniature scenes from their favourite fairytales unfold before their eyes. Hansel and Gretel, Beauty and the Beast, and the Little Mermaid are all there, along with surprises inside Aladdin's cave.

Discoveryland

If you've been to Disneyland in the States, you'll recognise this as a European version of Tomorrowland. For the children I brought along, it was their favourite section (and probably mine too). They loved the retro-futurist architecture based on inventions by scientists and sci-fi writers like Jules Verne, H.G Wells, and Leonardo da Vinci. Space Mountain: Mission 2 genuinely gave them the willies. But Star Tours, based on the *Star Wars* films, was their 'absolute, definite favourite'; though they giggled with joy in Autopia, where they drove their own car like a grown-up. We all enjoyed the Honey I Shrunk The Audience (Chérie, J'ai Rétréci le Public) 3D show and the Lion King performance in Vidéopolis. Also, I'm pained to admit (because it's really for little children) that my favourite ride was the Buzz Lightyear Laser Blast, inside which I found myself genuinely competing with the youngsters to get the highest score when shooting the monsters. If you're on a budget, don't even enter the **Alpha** and **Beta** games arcades, which gobble your money faster than you can say 'not ten euros already'. The **Disneyland Railroad** stops here at **Discoveryland Station**.

Autopia ★★ Y

Your littl'uns don't have to wait for their 17th birthday to drive in Disneyland® Park. The retro-futurist city of Solaria (open high season only) has a special track for amateur drivers over 81cm tall. All your children have to do is steer and press the accelerator.

Buzz Lightyear Laser Blast ★★ Y F

Based on Pixar's *Toy Story 2*, the Evil Emperor Zurg has invaded the planet with wicked robots powered by batteries stolen from toys. Your family must help Buzz Lightyear save the planet by shooting the monsters' targets with your laser gun. The two-person space-cruisers take you through the galaxy and come with a joystick that lets you spin round 360° to assail the attackers from all angles. Your point score is displayed on a screen on the cruiser and tells you your rank: Star Cadet is the lowest, Galactic Hero (me) is the highest. On the way out, laugh at the screens displaying your souvenir photo.

Honey, I Shrunk the Audience (Chérie, J'ai Rétréci le Public) ★ F

Inspired by Disney's *Honey, I Shrunk the Kids* film, this 3D show runs every 20 minutes and allows you to attend the scientific awards ceremony where Professor Szalinski is demonstrating his incredible shrinking machine. But a problem occurs and he accidentally makes you shrink. Special glasses allow you to see the action as objects look bigger than ever before. Surround sound and touch sensations on the legs and face also make the whole ride seem real – especially when the professor shakes the theatre as if it's a doll's house.

Les Mystères du Nautilus F

Jules Vernes' famous mechanical submarine from *20,000 Leagues Under the Sea* is parked here in Discoveryland. It belongs to Captain Nemo, who enjoys playing the organ while gliding along the bottom of the sea. It's a good place to go for down time from the more interactive rides, with dimly lit rooms, a few surprises, and creaking sound effects that recreate an underwater atmosphere.

Orbitron ★ Y

This simple funfair ride allows your children to pilot one of 12 rocket ships around bronze, copper, and brass globes, changing height whenever they fancy by pulling on a control stick. As you queue (this could be for a while), watch out for the metal plaques depicting the signs of the zodiac and see if your children can recognise them.

Space Mountain: Mission 2 ★★ T

This is one of the park's most intense rides with a triple loop-the-loop and an acceleration of 14m/second – that's a

Orbitron® and Space Mountain Mission 2, Discoveryland. ©Disney

breathtaking G-Force of 1.3N. From the moment your spaceship catapults itself into the outer rim of the universe, it's a spine-tingling, adrenalin-pumping descent through pitch darkness, broken only by the flash of a planet or meteor, and the chilling sound of explosions.

This is not recommended for under-10s.

Star Tours ★★ Y F O

Star Wars' celebrities R2D2 and C3PO welcome you into their droid workshop as you queue up for the ride-of-your-life on a space shuttle heading for the Moon of Endor. The only problem is that your novice pilot doesn't know how to drive and accidentally takes you into the Empire's headquarters, where you have to join forces with the Jedi to destroy the Death Star. This is a virtual reality ride that bolts and jumps from side to side as a big screen makes you feel as though you're on some wild inter-galactic collision course. It's tremendous for anyone over the age of 3.

Tip: Use the FASTPASS®.

FUN FACT Space Mountain

The journey inside the 36m-high Space Mountain is 1km long and reaches a top speed of 70km/h.

Vidéopolis ★ F

Inside this vast auditorium, recognisable by the Hyperion airship parked in its roof, Disney's current live, family show is the **Legend of the Lion King**. Performers dance particularly well and the costumes and music will certainly excite your children's imaginations. Shows in French and English are scheduled at different times so make sure you check which is which and come at least 30 minutes before to queue. If you don't make it in, the Café Hyperion affords a view over the stage so you can grab a snack while you watch – although it's not the same as seeing it in the arena.

Walt Disney Studios® Park

The Walt Disney Studios® Park takes families on an interactive journey behind the scenes of Disney animation. It shares trade secrets on special effects, puts on live stunt shows, teaches children how cartoons are made and, since 2008, houses one of the scariest rides in the resort, the Twilight Zone Tower of Terror. Being much smaller than the Disneyland® Park, it is usually quieter, so queues are shorter for both the attractions and restaurants. Another advantage is that, unlike the Disneyland® Park, which aims mainly to recreate the dream of Disney, this park both thrills and educates. If your children are interested in film, it's a must-see – especially the special-effects rides Armageddon and Studio Tram Tour. As with anything linked to Disneyland, there are plenty of shops and restaurants for you to spend your hard-earned cash in too.

The Walt Disney Studios® Park is split into four lands: The **Frontlot** contains Studio Services and Studio 1, filled with boutiques and watering holes; **Toon**

Walt Disney Studios® Park. ©Disney

Key to the Attractions

Like in the Disneyland® Park, these listings are split into areas and the same key system indicates the main target audience for each ride.

Y = Young children

F = Families

O = Older children

T = Thrillseekers

Studio is good for smaller children with cartoon-related attractions; **Production Courtyard** looks into cinema and TV; and the **Backlot** is where thrillseekers will spend most of their time.

Frontlot©

The Frontlot© is the transition zone from the real world outside into the heart of the Seventh Art (the French nickname for film). Aside from the Mickey Mouse fountain outside **Studio Services** (information point, Baby Care Centre, toilets, and first aid), the main focal point is a water tower, topped by two recognisable black, round ears. These towers (without the ears) were the symbol of Hollywood studios during the golden era, used for extinguishing the fires that regularly occurred on sets.

Inside **Disney Studio 1** is Hollywood Boulevard – a covered street lined with shops and restaurants and decorated like a film set with hundreds of movie props.

Production Courtyard©

Charlie Chaplin welcomes you to this hub, where the secrets of film and cinema are divulged to wide-eyed audiences before a brand new ride plunges you 13 floors down a lift shaft, and an interactive show featuring the rascally alien Stitch replaces some of the attractions inside the former Disney TV Channel building.

CinéMagique F
This show lets your family relive the best moments in 100 years of cinema thanks to a poor guy trapped inside the screen, who gets transported from film to film. The 1,100-seat cinema is state-of-the-art (despite its 1930s' look) and the whole show offers some great surprises. It's also a fine spot in which to rest your weary legs.

Studio Tram Tour®: Behind the Magic ★★ Y F O
This special-effects ride is great for the whole family regardless of age. A tram takes you on a tour of the outside studios past film sets and props to Catastrophe Canyon® where you'll find yourselves in the heart of a special-effects shoot that projects flames and entire waterfalls over your vehicle. This is a great place for children to imagine what it would be like being an actor or a director on such a big film shoot.

The Twilight Zone Tower of Terror™ ★★ O T
In 1939 lightning struck the once glamorous and now eerie and abandoned Hollywood

Tower Hotel, causing the lift and all its passengers to plunge to their deaths 13 floors below. Nowadays the most remarkable building in the Walt Disney Studios® Park (new in Jan 2008) is a vertical rollercoaster cum ghost train where the drop to the bottom is faster than the speed of gravity. 'Drop in if you dare'.

Walt Disney Television Studios ★ F

This is the home of Disney Channel France, with some real production stages and a spattering of games, but the real attraction for families is the new **Stitch Live** interactive show, which, thanks to a satellite on top of the building, allows children inside to communicate with Stitch (somewhere in outer space) live on screen. Get your children to clear their throats and speak loud and clear – this will be their only opportunity to communicate in real time with the mischievous alien.

Backlot©

In movie-speak, the backlot is the place that doesn't get filmed – it's where special effects are invented and fine-tuned. True to its name this is where you'll see the most live action – red-hot special effects (literally), motor stunts, and the loudest and fastest rollercoasters in the resort. It's an ideal section for older children, teenagers, and thrillseekers.

Armageddon ★★ F

On this hard-hitting special-effects ride your family become the extras on the *Armageddon* disaster movie (a sci-fi movie on the Mir space station). A 10-minute introduction to the special effects used in the film isn't the most interesting part of the ride, but it will train you to scream loud enough so that once inside the space station (where the presenter tells you when to scream), you'll find some release from the life-like special effects that include real fireballs shooting out of the ceiling, water pouring down over the flames, and shaking walls. This could be scary for small children and claustrophobics.

Moteurs...Action! Stunt Show Spectacular® ★★ F

There's nothing like a live stunt show to make your heart beat faster – and believe me, it will, when you see the brave stuntmen defying death on motorbikes and high-performance cars. The show lasts for 45 minutes and is satisfyingly loud.

Tip: Queue at least 30 mins beforehand as it fills up very quickly.

Rock 'n' Roller Coaster with Aerosmith ★★ T

This is a spine-chiller with a sense of humour. After seeing Aerosmith play some tracks in the studio, the rollercoaster speeds up from 0–60mph in less than 3 seconds (with more G-force than an astronaut experiences) before hurtling screaming guests through unexpected

Moteurs....Action! Stunt Show Spectacular® ©Disney

turns, loops, and drops. 120 onboard speakers pump out Aerosmith's music throughout the ride, giving the feeling of being inside a giant amplifier.

Toon Studio©

Toon Studio© (formerly Animation Courtyard) reveals the secrets behind cartoon animation and thrills children with two new attractions based on Disney-Pixar films: Crush's Coaster, a white-knuckle ride with Nemo the fish, and Cars Race Rally, a roam around the world of *Cars* (the film). Except for Crush's Coaster, all attractions here are suitable for young children.

Animagique® Y
As if by magic, all your children's favourite Disney characters come alive in this avant-garde stage show that uses ultra-violet lights and fun special effects to draw you into scenes from classics such as *Pinocchio*, *Dumbo the Flying Elephant*, and *The Jungle Book*. Donald Duck hosts much of the show that, in true Donald style, doesn't always turn out the way he hopes.

Art of Disney Animation® Y F
This attraction aims to show you where Disney's 'magic' began. Your children can learn some of the tricks of the trade, especially in 'Drawn to Animation Theatre' where animated characters are brought to life by Disney artists. There is even one part that gives you a glimpse of scenes from the next Disney blockbuster, before its official release. At the end, children can try to create their own characters, using the interactive displays.

Cars Race Rally (Cars Quatres Roues Rallye) Y
In the sleepy town of Radiator Springs (an outside enclosure opposite Crush's Coaster), your children can pilot one of 12 cars and join the race for Route 66. Two plateaux move the vehicles around in a figure of 8, making you feel like you're dodging the other cars. It's a gentle ride that will particularly appeal to under-8s.

Crush's Coaster ★★ F T
For daredevil families this inventive ride plunges you into the watery world of Nemo (based on the film *Finding Nemo*) on the back of a friendly (spinning) turtle. Holograms and excellent special effects really make you feel like you're bobbing along in Nemo's animated underwater world, full of fish, coral reefs, submarine wrecks, and dangerous sharks, and although the ride doesn't jolt or move as quickly as Space Mountain or Big Thunder Mountain, it is arguably more impressive.

Les Tapis Volants – Flying Carpets over Agrabah® Y
Aladdin's Genie of the Lamp has selected you to be an extra in his film *Flying Carpets over Agrabah*. All your family has to do is climb on to one of 16 flying carpets, then sit back and enjoy the virtual-reality ride.

Entertainment

Dining with Entertainment
If you're with young children, the **Auberge de Cendrillon** (Fantasyland) offers family lunches in the company of Cinderella (55€ adults, 20€ 3–11s). For something cheaper and more boisterous, **The Lucky Nugget Saloon** (Frontierland) puts on a cheesy 30min story about a girl who strikes it rich and heads to Paris to meet her true love where they set up a dance troupe (30€ adults, 15€ 3–11s).

For evening entertainment with children of all ages, **Buffalo Bill's Wild West Show** in the Disney Village combines hearty food with a fast cowboy-themed spectacular twice-nightly at 6.30pm and 9.30pm (59€ adults, 39€ 3–11s).

Disney® Village
Although the Disney Village is open all day, it comes into its own at night when the main parks are closed, with 10 themed **restaurants**, four **bars, shops,** and **nightclubs** (some age restrictions apply). The **Gaumount Multiplex** is a 15-screen cinema showing the latest movies (in English at selected times – check the programme). Children also love the **IMAX cinema** which shows films in 3D.

The resort's best *diner-spectacle* is **Buffalo Bill's Wild West Show** (see Nightlife p. 234). **Billy Bob's Saloon** (also see Nightlife, p. 234) is very popular with families with teens, offering weekend **country music concerts**, and free rock 'n' roll, salsa, and line **dancing lessons**. On some Wednesday afternoons (3.30pm and 5.30pm) there are also free

storytelling sessions for young children (ask in City Hall, Studio Services, or in Disney Village).

Hurricanes Nightclub (see Discothèque, p. 234) is where over-18s dance until the wee hours, and the **Nex Game Arcade** (opposite the Vinci car park) is an indoor leisure centre for youngsters and families, offering bowling games, a football and basketball sports area, air-hockey, dancing games, flight simulators, and pool tables (3pm–1am Mon–Fri, 3pm–3am Sat, 3pm–11pm Sun: Tokens: 1 = 2€, 3 = 5€, 7 = 10€, 15 = 20€).

Parades & Fireworks

The Disney experience wouldn't be complete without its parades and fireworks. Dates and the themes of the parades can change according to the season, so pick up a programme. Regular parades include **The Wonderful World of Disney**, where all characters wave to the crowds from decorated floats; **Fantillusion**, an evening summer display whose twinkling lights are particularly enchanting; and in the Walt Disney Studios® Park, the **Disney Cinema Parade**, which pays tribute to the production side of the Seventh Art.

Fireworks are usually the climax of the day and are particularly impressive in summer when they shroud Sleeping Beauty's Castle in a blanket of ephemeral sparkle (June–Sept).

Shows ★★

For little children, nothing compares with seeing their favourite characters in the flesh. The line-up rotates weekly, so make sure you pick up a programme on your way in, but Winnie the Pooh and chums can usually be found in the **Théâtre du Château** next door to Sleeping Beauty's Castle and **Fantasy Festival Stage** (both in Fantasyland); **Vidéopolis** (Discoveryland) puts on a Lion King extravaganza; **The Chaparral Theater** (Frontierland) holds seasonal shows such as Mickey's Winter Wonderland or Tarzan™ (summer) and Walt Disney® Studios Park also shows performances such as Ciné Folies in **Disney Studio 1**.

Sports & the Outdoors

Boating

Aside from the boat rides inside the Disneyland® Park, the Disney Village's Marina Del Rey lake offers canoeing and water skiing opportunities (in summer, weather permitting).

Enquiries: 08 25 30 60 30 (from France) / 0870 503 0303 (from UK).

Cycling & Horse-riding

Bikes can be hired and pony rides reserved for guests staying at Davy Crockett's Ranch (see p. 237)

Golf

The 27-hole championship standard **Golf Disneyland®** is a few kilometres from the parks (conveniently close to Davy Crockett Ranch, p. 237). Golfers of all levels are welcome and the whole course has been landscaped to include lakes, hills, and waterfalls, plus the occasional Mickey Mouse-shaped green. The **Club House** by hole 18 has showers, a TV room, lockers and serves refreshments. **Goofy's Pro shop** sells and hires golf equipment. **Individual lessons** can be organised in English with professional golfers (*04 67 91 25 41*). You can also practise on the putting green and at 35 practice posts.

Allée de la Mare Houleuse, 77700 Magny Le Hongre. 01 60 45 68 90; ***www.disneylandparis.com;*** ***E: dlp.nwy.golf@disney.com****. Prices on request only.*

Health Clubs

The resort's four upmarket hotels (Disneyland® Hotel, Hotel New York®, Newport Bay Club®, and Disney's Sequoia Lodge) all pamper families with health clubs, gyms and saunas, massage spas, jacuzzis, and solariums. Disneyland® Hotel's **Spa Celestia** (*01 60 45 66 05*) is particularly relaxing. See Hotel Accommodation for more details, p. 234.

Hot-Air Ballooning

For more daytime fun, the **PanoraMagique**, by Lake Disney, is the world's largest captive balloon, carrying 30 passengers 100m above the ground. Although the whole experience only lasts six minutes, the 360° views are breathtaking (extra fee).

Ice Skating

In winter, the area in front of Hotel New York® becomes one big slippery ice rink. If your children fancy a slide, call *01 60 45 76 98* for more information. Hours are usually 2.30pm–6.30pm, 7.30pm–10pm. Cost 12€ adults, 9€ under-11s, 2€ reduction if you bring your own skates.

Jogging

Resort, hotel, and campsite guests can burn off all that junk food by jogging around two trails. One follows Lake Disney, the other meanders through the forest around Davy Crockett Ranch®.

Swimming

Don't forget your bathing costume if you're staying in Disneyland® Hotel, Hotel New York®, Newport Bay Club®, Sequoia Lodge, or Davy Crockett Ranch, which all have (smallish) heated swimming pools.

Tennis

You can hire rackets and balls to use the tennis courts at Hotel New York® (floodlit and can be used by any Disney hotel guest) and at Davy Crockett Ranch (hotel guests only).

Shopping

You are unlikely to find a bargain in Disneyland® Resort Paris. Most items are expensive and the park is arranged to provide you with as many spending opportunities as possible. However, buying Disney memorabilia (especially with younger children) can be a memorable part of the experience. The best shops are categorised below according to what they sell. The key below indicates their whereabouts in the parks.

Key

DP = Disneyland® Park
WDSP = Walt Disney Studios® Park
DV = Disney Village

Books

On Town Square (Main Street USA), lose your children in the **Storybook Store** amid rows of storybooks recounting (in several languages) the classic tales that have inspired Disney's many films. Tigger is usually on hand at the exit to stamp your children's books with the Disneyland logo.

Clothes

Children's clothing, including costumes, is sold in **Disney & Co** (DP, Main Street USA). Further down the street, **Main Street Motors** sells car-themed clothes and accessories. Irresistible mouse ears, along with other hats and headdresses are found in **Ribbons and Bows Hat Shop** (DP, Main Street USA). If your children fancy dressing up, **Le Coffre du Capitaine** (DP, Adventureland) has fully fledged pirate gear, and **Merlin l'Enchanteur** (DP, Fantasyland) has everything they need to become apprentice magicians. Beach attire can be purchased in **Legends of Hollywood** (WDSP, Front Lot). And the **Buffalo Trading Company** (DV) sells boots, hats, shirts, and bandanas for real 'yee-haaring' cowboys. Sports gear for all the family, including babies, can be bought in **Team Mickey** (DV).

Games, Teddies & Toys

La Bottega di Geppetto (DP, Fantasyland) takes children into the workshop that produced Pinocchio where they can buy all sorts of unusual wooden toys, puppets, music boxes, puzzles, and even cuckoo clocks. There are stuffed toys aplenty in **La Chaumière des Sept Nains** (DP, Fantasyland); **Constellations** (DP, Discoveryland) sells star-themed hi-tech toys; **The Disney**

Disney & Co. ©Disney

Store (DV) sells its usual fluffy and interactive fare for children; and the **World of Toys** (DV), as its name implies, has a huge range of costumes, games, puzzles, and teddies.

Gifts & Souvenirs

Disneymania climaxes in **Disneyana Collectibles** (DP, Main Street USA) where you can buy Disney-themed jewellery boxes, ceramics, limited edition books, and figurines. For men's watches, hats, Disney socks, ties, and a whole host of other accessories and souvenirs, head to **Emporium** (DP, Main Street USA). **Les Trésors de Schéhérazade** (DP, Adventureland) sells a variety of gifts including pretty wooden boxes and perfume bottles. For the ultimate Christmas decoration, **La Boutique du Château** (DP, Fantasyland) is an all-year-round Christmas shop. Weird souvenirs required by budding explorers are found in **Indiana Jones™ Adventure Outpost** (DP, Adventureland). Space-age children's gadgets, puzzles, and flashy badges are found in **Star Traders** (DP, Discoveryland). For music-themed memorabilia, **Rock Around the Shop** (WDSP, Backlot) has a good selection; and in Disney Village, King Ludwig's Store is an Ali Baba's cave of fantasy Bavarian delights such as beer mugs, swords, shields, and dragons.

Household

If you fancy keeping a bit of Disney's magic around the home, **Lilly's Boutique** (DP, Main Street USA) sells a range of tableware, and bathroom items (robes, towels) decorated with Disney characters. China, crystal, and hand-blown glass moulded into animal shapes are sold in **Harrington's Fine China and Porcelain** store (Main Street USA) behind an attractive stained-glass façade.

Photography

An array of photographic equipment is on sale in **Town Square Photography** (DP, Main Street USA) whether you need a quick repair, new batteries or an entirely new camera. (The

Out-of-Town Shopping

If you're looking for women's, men's, and children's fashion, plus a little something for your home, **La Vallée Village** is an excellent factory outlet shopping centre (over 80 brands with 30–70% knocked off retail prices) just a five-minute drive from the resort. If you're staying in a Disney hotel, a shuttle bus to and from the centre can be reserved for the whole family (10am–7pm Mon–Fri, 10am–8pm Sat, 11am–7pm Sun. Shuttle: 5€ adults, 2€ under-11s) discarded batteries can be left for recycling). Video cameras can also be rented here. Cameras and films are also on sale in **Studio Photo** (WDSP, Front Lot).

Sweets

Chocolate, fudge, toffees, marshmallow wands and lollipops are the delicious teeth-rotting naughties on sale in the **Board-Walk Candy Palace** (DP, Main Street USA). You could also treat your children to some sticky sweetness from **La Confiserie des Trois Fées** (DP, Fantasyland) – a pretty forest cottage cum sweetshop run by Cinderella's three fairy godmothers.

Nightlife

Billy Bob's Country Western Saloon ★ F O

Live Country and Western concerts, dance lessons (salsa, rock 'n' roll), beer, nachos, and nibbles make this three-level bar one of the resort's hottest nightspots.

Disney Village.

Buffalo Bill's Wild West Show ★★ F

In the Disney Village, this Western extravaganza sees Annie Oakley, a myriad of cowboys and Indians, stuntmen, horses, wagons, buffalos, and Buffalo Bill himself, perform a fast and furious tribute to the Wild West. Food (Tex-Mex kebabs on chilli for grown-ups, and roasted chicken or sausages with potato wedges for children) is served in your seat during the show.

Note: Not suitable for guests with asthma, other breathing problems, or allergies to any of the animals.

Disney Village. ***Shows*** *6.30pm and 9.30pm.* ***Prices*** *59€ adults, 39€ 3–11s, free under-3s. Duration: 1h 30.*

Hurricanes Discothèque O

Well-known European DJs are brought here to entertain the crowds who boogie into the wee hours with or without their children. Under-18s are allowed in but must be accompanied by a parent or guardian. Ladies get in free Friday and Tuesday nights before midnight. Thursday is free for all. Guests staying in Disney Hotels get in free when they show their ID pass (see p. 235).

Disney Village.

The Sports Bar F

If your trip to Disney coincides with an important sports event, you can catch it here on the big screen.

Disney Village.

FAMILY-FRIENDLY ACCOMMODATION

If you're planning to spend more than one day in Disney, there are advantages to staying inside the resort, not least that the price usually includes the facilities listed below. All Disneyland hotels are within walking distance of the parks, lakes, and Disney Village: only Davy Crockett Ranch requires personal transport.

If you can't stay in an official hotel, several nearby hotels are associated with the resort. They provide free transport to and from the parks and have good family facilities. For more information check ***www.disneylandparis.co.uk***.

If you're coming for just one day, it is very easy to drive to Disney, though you will need to pay for parking, or take the RER from central Paris (see p. 205).

Disney's® Hotels

To book any of these Disneyland hotels direct call *08448 008 898* from the UK or *08 25 30 60 30* from France. If you stay in a Disney hotel, you will be entitled to the following advantages:

- **Disney ID card**
  When you check in to your Disney hotel, you'll receive a Disneyland® Resort Paris Identity Card which gives free access to the Disney car parks, Hurricanes Discothèque in the Disney Village, and the pool or gym at your Disney hotel (where applicable). If you leave details of your credit card, you can also use the ID card for paying in shops and restaurants (ask the concierge for a list of participating venues).
- **Half-Board Option**
  You can opt for half board (lunch or dinner) which gives you access to either seven or 17 restaurants during your stay, depending on the package you choose. Ask your concierge to book you a table or call *01 60 30 40 50*. If you've already booked, but would like to turn your reservation into a half-board stay, call at least one day prior to arrival – *08705 03 03 03* from the UK or *33 (0)1 60 30 60 53* from other countries. Half-board meal plans have to be bought for your whole stay and for everyone in your party over 3 years' old.
- **Shopping Service**
  Disneyland® Resort Paris does everything in its power to make you spend. Before you know it, you're laden down with all sorts of fluffy memorabilia and toys that stop you getting on the rides. The solution lies in a free shopping delivery service, which transports your purchases directly to your Disney® hotel. Ask at the till.

Disneyland® Hotel ★★
This pink Victorian-style hotel is the first thing you see when you arrive and is as iconic as Sleeping Beauty's castle. It's one of the resort's plushest hotels (a piano plays in the large lobby and lounge and there are two lavish restaurants) and it's ideal for families. Several rooms can accommodate more than four people; there's a special children's breakfast during which your little ones can meet and be photographed with Disney characters, and the *Club Minnie* games room will take the children (4–11s) off your hands for an hour or so under the supervision of trained

entertainers. For older children and mums and dads, the Spa Celestia (☎ *01 60 45 66 05*) offers soothing massages and facials.

***Rates** from 320€ per adult.*
***Amenities** A/C, 24-hour room service, spa, two restaurants, bar, piano bar, FASTPASS® service, free entry to Hurricanes disco in Disney Village, valet parking, heated swimming pool, babysitting on request. **In room** cots, extra beds, TV. **Distance from the park** 3-min walk*

Disney's Hotel New York® ★

As its name implies, this post-modernist-style hotel tries to recreate scenes from New York, with bedrooms decorated in Art Deco styles and even bedside lights in the form of the Empire State Building. Family rooms are available and children enjoy this hotel for its games room (Times Square Games arcade) and outside children's play area (including a trampoline on sunny days). And, as at Disneyland® Hotel, breakfast is served in the company of Disney characters. In winter, this is very popular with families who come for the ice rink, right outside the front door.

***Rates** from 220€ per adult.*
***Amenities** A/C, 24-hour room service, spa, restaurant, bar, swimming pool, sauna, tennis courts, ice rink, FASTPASS® service, free entry to Hurricanes disco in Disney Village, valet parking, babysitting on request. **In room** cots, extra beds, TV. **Distance from the park** 10-min walk, free shuttle bus.*

Disney's Newport Bay Club®

This New England-style hotel overlooks Lake Disney and is reminiscent of a swish American beach club, with elegant communal areas and nautical-themed bedrooms. As with all Disney hotels, family rooms are available with extra beds and cots on request. Breakfast here is served alongside Mickey, and for evening dinner Pluto makes an entry. The Sea Horse club Game Arcade is full of video games for children; there is also a TV room and an outside playground. Before dinner, the Captains' Quarters and Fisherman's Wharf bars are relaxing spots for an aperitif.

***Rates** from 199€ per adult.*
***Amenities** A/C, room service (6.30am–10pm), gym, outdoor swimming pool, restaurant (with a children's buffet), bar, VIP FASTPASS® service (suites only), free entry to Hurricanes disco in Disney Village, babysitting on request. **In room** cots, extra beds, TV. **Distance from the park** 10-min walk, free shuttle.*

Disney's Sequoia Lodge® ★

This place aims to transport families into the heart of a Redwood forest. The trees are still a little young, but they're getting there. Family rooms are available (with cots and extra beds), and children feel particularly spoiled by the indoor swimming pool that has hot springs and a waterslide. As in the other Disney hotels there is a children's games arcade (Kit Carson's game arcade) and an outdoor play area. Rooms look like wooden cabins, with patchwork quilts.

***Rates** from 180€ per adult.*
Amenities** A/C, concierge, sauna, gym, buffet, restaurant, bar, VIP FASTPASS® service, free entry to Hurricanes disco in Disney Village, heated swimming pool. **In room

cots, extra beds, TV. ***Distance from the park*** *10-min walk, free shuttle.*

Disney's Davy Crockett Ranch® ★★

This activity-packed residence is a short drive from the parks, but has a lot going for it. Your family can rent a chalet in the middle of the forest, hire bikes, go swimming in the indoor pool, play tennis, sing karaoke in the bar, and test out the nearby Davy Crockett's Adventure (an activity centre in the trees where you and the children can swing between branches, see p. 242). Each bungalow has a convertible bed-settee in the living area, and a bedroom with a double bed and bunk beds. They also allow for self-catering with a fridge, microwave, hobs, crockery, and cooking utensils. A corner shop sells some foodstuffs, but a supermarket is cheaper. There's even a BBQ. Sheets and towels are provided. Just for children, there's an open-air Indian camp with teepees, a mini-zoo (Davy's Farm), a games and TV room, archery lessons, and pony rides. If you can't face cooking, Crockett's Tavern is a restaurant with children's menus.

Rates *from 150€ per adult.* ***Amenities*** *tennis and basketball courts, buffet grill, bar, heated swimming pool, bike hire, free parking.* ***Distance from the park*** *10-min by car, no shuttle. Free parking in the parks.*

Disney's Hotel Cheyenne® ★

If your children want to stay in the Wild West, this is the place for them – amid covered wagons and a check-in by the Hangman's tree. They can play at cowboys and Indians in the 'Little Sheriff's' corner, and there's an outside play area with Indian teepees and a place to become a buckaroo on the back of mechanical horses and bulls.

Disney's Hotel Cheyenne® ©Disney

Children and parents sleep in the same room – children on bunk beds and mum and dad in a double (no under-6s or children over 70kg on the top bunk). On a sunny day, the hotel's Chuck Wagon Café serves food outside.

Rates *from 145€ per adult.* ***Amenities*** *A/C, buffet restaurant, bar, free entry to Hurricanes disco in Disney Village.* ***In room*** *bunk-beds, cots.* ***Distance from the park*** *20-min walk, free shuttle.*

Disney's Hotel Santa Fe®

Welcome to New Mexico where entertainment is rife, including a karaoke bar where you and the children wow the audience with your musical prowess (or not, as the case may be). Most rooms are family rooms. There's a small video games centre for the children and outside the Totem Circle is a Red Indian-themed playground. Throughout the day, Disney characters come round for photo opportunities with the children.

Rates *from 135€ per adult.* ***Amenities*** *buffet restaurant with children's menus, bar, free entry to Hurricanes disco in Disney Village, outdoor games area.* ***In room*** *ceiling fan, cots on demand, TV.* ***Distance from the park*** *20-min walk, free shuttle.*

FAMILY-FRIENDLY DINING

Dining in the Disneyland® Park

Fast food in Disneyland Paris is practically unavoidable. Sit-down (table-service) restaurants offer the most variety and the healthiest choices (some restaurants are excellent), however, keeping to a budget of 10 to 20€ per person is nearly impossible if it doesn't include a burger, hotdog, fries or something equally unhealthy (though vegetarian options and baby food are always available).

This is a complete list of the main eateries per land or lot. For more information on each, or to reserve in advance (advisable in sit-down restaurants) call ✆ *01 60 30 40 50*).

The price per person is as below:

Prices Key
€ = under 12€
€€ = around 20–25€
€€€ = 30€ and over

Main Street USA

Cable Car Bake Shop €
As its name suggests, this café sells sticky cakes, cookies, and buns throughout the day.

Casey's Corner €
This is your first (or last) chance to grab a hotdog, on your way in or out of the park.

Cookie Kitchen €
This place specialises in cookies, but it also sells muffins, donuts, and cream-cakes.

Market House Deli €
Disguised as an old New York deli, this take-away sells generously filled sandwiches.

Plaza Gardens Restaurant €€
Your family can choose what they'd like from the hot-and-cold buffet inside this Victorian-style restaurant near Sleeping Beauty's castle.

The Coffee Grinder ★ €
Follow your nose for a quick coffee, ice cream or a cake.

The Gibson Girl Ice-Cream Parlour €
Choose which sauce you'd like to have drizzled over your ice cream.

The Ice Cream Company €
If the Gibson Girl's got a queue, try the ices here.

Victoria's Home-Style Restaurant ★ €
Amid 19th-century décor, tuck into pizzas, salads, and *croque-monsieurs*.

Walt's – an American Restaurant ★ €€
Offering decent meat and two veg, fish dishes, or hearty salads, this setting includes a gallery paying tribute to Walt Disney.

Adventureland

Agrabah Café ★ €€
Mediterranean and North African-inspired buffets.

Blue Lagoon Restaurant ★ €€€
If you're into seafood, this Caribbean restaurant in the heart of pirate country looks out over a lagoon. Try the gambas prawns, roasted in basil.

Colonel Hathi's Pizza Outpost ★ €€
From the veranda overlooking the park, or in front of a roaring fire, families can enjoy pizzas, pastas, and salads.

Coolpost €
For hotdogs, burgers, and fries, this place is handily situated in Adventureland.

Restaurant Hakuna Matata €
Inspired by the Lion King, this themed restaurant serves plates of spiced chicken wings to share, and a few other spicy specialities.

Fantasyland

Auberge de Cendrillon ★★ €€€
This fairytale restaurant is not just the most expensive, it's the best. Inside Cinderella's swish-looking mansion, enjoy French specialities.

Au Chalet de la Marionnette €
This fast-food restaurant, reminiscent of a McDonalds, is Pinocchio's favourite hang-out. On the menu there's roast chicken, soups, and apple strudel as well as burgers and fries.

Fantasia Gelati €
Real Italian ice cream on the go.

March Hare Refreshments €
A very happy 'un-birthday' awaits you in this snack bar that sells cakes and refreshments.

Pizzeria Bella Notte €
This place looks like a medieval castle and specialises in pastas, pizzas, and Italian desserts.

The Old Mill ★ €
A Dutch-style windmill serving lots of chicken and vegetable wraps, nuggets, cakes, and drinks.

Toad Hall Restaurant ★ €
Join Toad of Toad Hall for some British comfort food such as fish and chips.

Frontierland

Cowboy Cookout Barbecue ★ €
For big, hungry cowboys, you need some of this place's big smoked BBQ chicken, burgers and ribs.

Fuente del Oro Restaurante €
Mexican chillis, tacos, and fajitas are served in this 'cantina'-themed eatery.

Last Chance Café €
Before you dance with the dead inside the Haunted Manor, this café fills you up with chicken nuggets, burgers and fries.

Silver Spur Steakhouse ★ €€
This is the best place in the Disneyland park for a real, juicy all-American steak. Apple crumble is a popular dessert.

The Lucky Nugget Saloon ★★ €€€
Children love this 19th-century Wild West saloon, where Disney characters parade between tables as you tuck into dishes like salmon or lamb and veg kebabs from the all-you-can-eat Tex-Mex buffet.

Discoveryland

Buzz Lightyear's Pizza Planet Restaurant ★ €
When Buzz isn't saving the planet he's tucking into pizzas here, inside a 1950s' rocket. The house speciality is the Pizzaburger – a hamburger topped with a mini pizza.

Café Hyperion ★ €
If you didn't make it into the Lion King show in Vidéopolis, you can watch it live on screen here, while munching on burgers, fries and salads.

Cool Station €
Grab a quick hotdog here while you wait for a ride.

Rocket Café €
This is a second fast-food cabin selling hotdogs and ice creams.

Dining in the Walt Disney Studios® Park

Prices Key
€ = under 12€

€€ = around 20–25€

€€€ = 30€ and over

The main fast-food joints selling sweets, ice cream, pizzas, hotdogs and burgers (all under 12€ in Walt Disney Studios® Park) are **Kiosque Studio Catering Co** in the Backlot, Production Courtyard, and Toon Studio and the **Backlot Express Restaurant** (Backlot).

Café des Cascadeurs ★ €
Choose this place if you want to take your family to an authentically recreated 50s' American diner where everything (hotdogs, nachos and chilli con carne) is giant size.
Backlot.

La Terrasse €
This place entices you to devour yet more junk food on a shaded garden terrace.

Rendez-Vous des Stars €€
This self-service restaurant has more choice than other restaurants in the park with a range of hot and cold all-you-can-eat buffet items.

Restaurant en Coulisse €
Dine like you're part of a film crew in this movie-themed eatery (pizza, burgers, and a wide choice of desserts).

Dining in the Disney® Village

Prices Key
€ = under 12€

€€ = around 20–25€

€€€ = 30€ and over

The golden arches of **McDonalds** (€) beckon in the Disney Village, or for something more novel (only slightly) try **New York Style Sandwiches** (€) that, true to its name, prepares sandwiches and bagels on request to eat in or take out.

Annette's Diner ★ €€
This fun eatery tries to recreate the diner in the famous *Happy Days* TV series (your children probably aren't old enough to remember it). Waitresses serve the burgers, fries and milkshakes on roller-skates.

Café Mickey ★★ €€€
Gourmet French food like foie gras or pork chops with rosemary and honey is served alongside pizzas and pastas. Look out

Café Mickey. ©Disney

for Mickey Mouse, Minnie and friends while you dine.

King Ludwig's Castle ★ €€
The setting for your beers (mums and dads) and Bavarian specialities is a fairytale castle.

La Grange €€
On the third floor of this big saloon, where Country and Western music creates a Wild West feel, enjoy an all-you-can-eat Tex-Mex buffet.

Planet Hollywood €€
As with every Planet Hollywood branch across the globe, this restaurant serves traditional American cuisine amid film memorabilia.

Rainforest Café ★★ €€
Young children will love the rainforest atmosphere with Amazonian animals, giant aquariums, and tropical rain (yes, you get a sprinkling) and the call of jungle creatures. Food includes curries, 'rasta pasta' and cheesecakes.

Tip: Reserve to avoid disappointment.

The Steakhouse ★ €€€
Modelled on a Chicago warehouse, this excellent restaurant serves succulent steaks with a selection of sauces and wonderful crispy fries.

HAVING FUN NEARBY

Disneyland® Paris is a short drive from other family attractions and while here, it would be a shame to miss them:

Davy Crockett's Adventure ★★
This is a fun-filled outdoor adventure park for budding Tarzans or Janes, who swing from tree to tree on harnesses. With five levels of difficulty, children as young as 4 can have a go (anyone under 18 has to be accompanied by an adult). It can be booked at the Davy Crockett Ranch (open Apr–early Nov) or ☎ *08 25 30 02 22*. The session lasts for three hours and includes an obligatory 30min initiation course. 25€ adults, 15€ 4–11s.

Note: Min height 1m 10 and max weight 110kg.

Sea Life Aquarium Val d'Europe ★

Aquarium Sea Life Paris – Val d'Europe, 14 cours Danube, 77711 Serris, Marne-la-Vallée. ☎ *01 60 42 33 66;* ***www.sealifeeurope.com****.*

Just a 5-minute drive from Disneyland Paris, in the Val d'Europe shopping centre, more than 50 separate aquariums house wonderful sealife attractions including shrimps, seahorses, sharks, moray eels, and rare turtles. A 360°-tunnel is a hit with children who like to see the fish from all angles. The emphasis is on protecting the environment and children feel involved right through the visit. There are even touch pools where they can stroke the carp and sturgeon.

Open *10am–5.50pm daily.*
Admission *14€ adults, 10€ 3–10s.*

10 Five of the Best: Must-sees in Outer Paris & Île de France

FIVE OF THE BEST

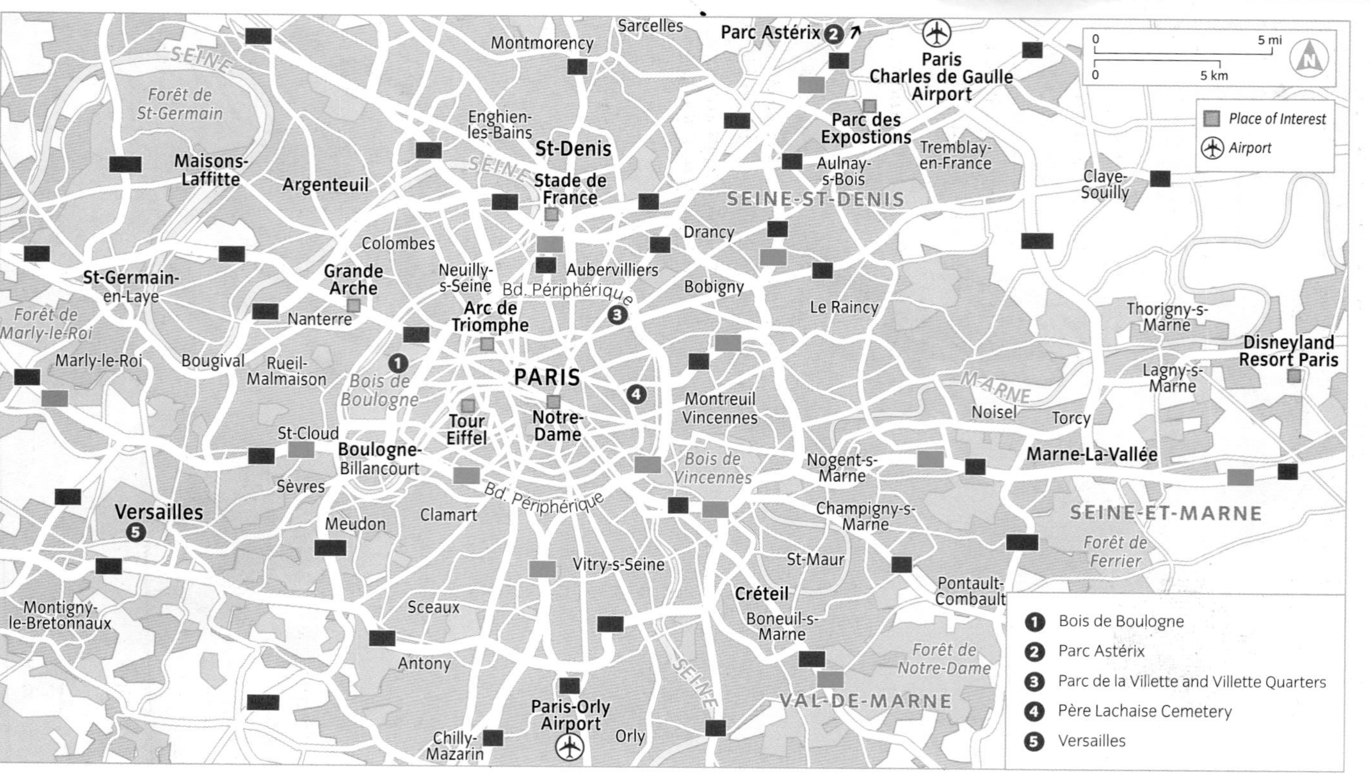

While central Paris is packed with things to do as a family, so too are its suburbs – and I'm not just talking Disneyland Paris. This chapter outlines five of the best things to do with your children around Paris's perimeters and in Île-de-France.

Bois de Boulogne ★★

Bois de Boulogne, 16th arr, ☎ *01 40 67 90 82;* ***www.jardindacclimatation.fr****, M° Porte Maillot, Porte de la Muette, Porte d'Auteuil).*

This 865-hectare green space on the edge of the 16th arrondissement was once the Rouvray hunting grounds and now contains the **Longchamp and Auteuil horse-racing tracks** (see p. 22), woodlands, picnic areas, a children's mini-theme-park (Le Jardin d'Acclimatation) and boating opportunities on the lakes.

On a warm day the **Jardin d'Acclimatation** ★★ is a children's heaven with farm animals to pet, an aviary, bears, two free playgrounds (full of swings, slides, climbing nets, and tunnels), a paddling area with sprinklers to get wet in (La Pateugeoire), a fun-park with small rollercoasters and merry-go-rounds, a radio-control boat centre, puppet shows, and distorting mirrors (prices for each attraction vary). A little train (**Le Petit Train**) transports families from Porte Maillot (M° Porte Maillot), through the Bois to the entrance to the jardin (5.40€/4.05€, including entrance fee). The **Musée en Herbe** ★ (☎ *01 40 67 97-66*, 4€–8€) is entirely devoted to children, with excellent, rotating exhibitions that introduce youngsters aged 0 (in the baby atelier) to 12 to arts and science.

The **Rivière Enchantée** is a narrow man-made river that takes families on a peaceful ride through the park, past ducks, squirrels, and weeping willows. And you and your budding botanists will appreciate the **Jardin de Bagatelle**, famous for the splendour of its roses. From May to September, don't miss the **Jardin de Shakespeare** ★ – a series of Shakespeare-themed gardens (Le Théâtre de Verdure) where the Bard's plays are performed in French and English.

Parc Astérix ★★

Plailly 60128. ☎ *08 26 30 10 40;* ***www.parcasterix.fr****.*

Just 30km from the capital, France's home-grown Astérix the Gaul theme park won't disappoint your children. It is not a wannabe French copy of its US neighbour and, in many ways, is much more charming, defining its attractions with true *Gaulois* spirit, down to the very last wild boar burger.

Split into five historical sections (Ancient Greece, the Roman Empire, Gaul, Vikings and the Middle Ages to 19th-century Paris), it's jam-packed with activities for children of all ages.

Thrillseekers will find bigger stomach-churning rides here than at Disney, with the gravity-defying **Tonnère de Zeus**, the biggest wooden rollercoaster in Europe with a vertical 30m drop; **Goudurix**, with seven nauseating loop-the-loops; and **La Trace du Hourra**, a 900m-long Gaulois bobsleigh. Younger ones will squirm to get wet on **Le Grand Splatch** log-flume, whizz around on revolving cauldrons (**Les Chaudrons**), and take a relaxing cruise through scenes from Astérix's comic books on the **Epidemaïs Croisière**. For some serious handshaking and photo opportunities, star icons, Astérix, Obélix and friends, regularly appear in the **Gaul Village** (an exact replica of Albert Uderzo's village in the original comic book).

A jamboree of quality shows also adds to the experience, with wonderful dancing dolphins in the **Théâtre de Poséidon** and amusing acrobatics and antics inside the **Roman Circus**.

Food in the park is reassuringly French, with the possibility of choosing healthy food. Look out for the **Relais Gaulois** canteen where you can *get-ya-fix* on three *coursixs* for around 13€.

Getting there *RER B Roissy-CDG T1, then shuttle (quay A3 at the airport's bus station; information ☎ 01 48 62 38 33; 9am–7pm every 30 mins, 6.90€ adults, 5€ 3–11s); or direct shuttle from the Louvre (M° Palais Royal, ☎ 01 48 62 38 33, access via staircase in Hall Charles V, on shop-level, 8.45am to park and 6.30pm back to Louvre, 19€ adults, 13€ 3–11s). By car A1 (dir. Lille) exit Parc Astérix between junctions 7 and 8.*

Open *10am–6pm daily Apr–June, 9.30am–7pm July–Aug, 10am–6pm Sat–Sun Sept, Oct and Nov school holidays (usually last week Oct, first wk Nov). Closed Nov–Mar. Call or check the website for details of extra closure dates.* ***Admission*** *37€ adults; 27€ 3–11s; free under-3s. (Disabled tickets 28€ adults, 21€ 3–11s) Handicapped facilities in the park, wheelchair hire and baby-changing spaces in toilets.*

Parc de la Villette and the Villette Quarters ★★

Once classed as the scourge of Paris, the Villette area of the 19th arrondissement along the **Canal de l'Ourcq** (starts at Métro Jaurès or Stalingrad), has undergone extensive redevelopment and is now an activity-packed quarter for families.

The Villette stretch of the canal links with the picturesque **Canal-St Martin** in the south (10th arr, begins at Métro République), lined with cafés and shops, and carries on northwards past Pantin and Bobigny. In the summer, parts of the quays become a **beach** with sand, canoes, and pedalos (part of Paris Plage, see p. 24). **Bikes** can be hired from **Vélo et Chocolat** (75 quai Seine, 19th arr. ☎ *01 46 07 07 87* M° Riquet), which doubles as a café; and **Cyclo Pouce** ★★ (38 quai de Marne, 19th arr., ☎ *01 42 41 76 98;* M° Ourcq.), which offers families seats for small babies and toddlers that can be attached to the bicycle, and options for parents with disabled children. If

Cité des Sciences in Villette

you need refreshments, **Café Zoide** is a child-friendly pitstop with dozens of games for babies up to 16-year-olds (92 bis quai de la Loire, 19th arr., *01 42 38 26 37*; ***www.cafezoide.asso.fr***. M° Jaurès).

At the northeastern extremity of the city, **Parc de la Villette** ★★ (19th arr., *01 40 03 75 75*. ***www.villette.com***. M° Porte de la Villette or Porte de Pantin.) is a retro-futuristic-looking open space with a succession of gardens to kick a ball around in and play areas to explore. There are different zones for 0s to 12s including carousels, ropes, and wacky climbing frames. The canal stretch of the park is dominated by a giant silver sphere, the **Géode Imax cinema** (26 avenue Corentin-Cariou, 19th arr. *08 92 68 45 40*; ***www.lageode.fr***. M° Porte de la Villette) with a huge 3D screen, which takes children and adults through spectacular scenes of nature and animated adventures. The park also has its own open-air cinema festival in August (see p. 24).

No child should leave Villette without seeing the **Cité des Sciences** ★★ (30 avenue Corentin-Cariou, 19th arr., *01 40 05 70 00*; ***www.cite-sciences.fr***. M° Porte de la Villette.), a hi-tech science museum where the main zone, **Explora**, covers Outer Space (including a planetarium), looks at communication (sound and images), and has child-friendly displays on the automobile, energy, and aeronautics industries. It also houses the **Cité des Enfants** ★★ – a museum for 2 to 7s and 5 to 12s with science-themed interactive installations that will amuse children for hours.

If yours are interested in music, the **Cité de la Musique** (221 avenue Jean Jaurès, 19th arr., *01 44 84 44 84*; ***www.cite-musique.fr***. M° Porte de Pantin) has a gleaming collection of restored instruments (many so rare, your children will never have seen them before),

Circus is Coming to Town

The outskirts of Paris are year-round fixtures when it comes to circus. **Cirque Pinder** ★ (Pelouse de Reuilly, Bois de Vincennes, 12th arr, ☎ *01 45 90 21 25*; ***www.cirquepinder.com*** M° Porte Dorée or Porte de Charenton. mid-Nov–mid-Jan) is France's oldest travelling circus with horses, lions, elephants, and monkeys. **Grand Céleste Cirque** (22 rue Paul Meurice, 20th arr, ☎ *01 53 19 99 13*; ***www.grandceleste.com***, M° Porte des Lilas. Nov–end Feb) is a traditional circus. And **Théâtre Equestre Zingaro** (176 avenue Jean-Jaurès, Aubervilliers. ☎ *01 48 39 18 03* or ☎ *08 92 68 18 91*; ***www.zingaro.fr***. M° Fort d'Aubervilliers. Nov–Feb) is a nomadic, equestrian circus with poetic shows that pay homage to the noble creatures and are a must for any horse-crazed child.

commentated by an audio guide in English.

For some clowning around in a big top, **Espace Chapiteaux** ★ (Parc de La Villette, 19th arr. ☎ *01 42 09 01 09;* ***www.villette.com***. M° Porte de la Villette.) hosts shows by avant-garde circus companies with breathtaking acrobatics (for more venues see box right).

Finally, the futuristic, **MK2 Cinema** ★ which straddles the canal (7 quai de Loire and 14 quai de Seine ☎ *08 92 69 84 84*), by Jaurès and Stalingrad Métros, shows films in English (look out for the letters VO) and runs a little canal boat between its two buildings and cafés (free for cinema ticket holders).

Père Lachaise Cemetery ★

16 rue de Repos, 20th arr. ☎ *01 55 25 82 10;* ***www.pere-lachaise.com***. *M° Père-Lachaise or Philippe Auguste.*

Laid out in 1803 on a hill in Ménilmontant (20th arr., M° Père Lachaise), this cemetery offers surprises with its bizarre monuments, unexpected views, and ornate sculpture. The 'grandest address in Paris' is the earthly resting place of some of history's most famous characters. A free map is available at the newsstand across from the main entrance. Everybody from **Sarah Bernhardt** to **Oscar Wilde** is here, along with **Honoré de Balzac**, **Eugène Delacroix**, **Maria Callas**, **Max Ernst**, and **Georges Bizet**, **Edith Piaf**,

Entrance to Père Lachaise cemetery

Frédéric Chopin, and **Molière**. **Marcel Proust's** black tombstone rarely lacks a tiny bunch of violets (he wanted to be buried beside his friend/lover, composer **Maurice Ravel**, but their families wouldn't allow it). Some tombs are sentimental favourites: lovelorn graffiti radiates from the grave of Doors' singer **Jim Morrison**. Poignant monuments also honour Frenchmen who died in the Resistance or in Nazi concentration camps.

***Open** 8am–6pm Mon–Fri; 8.30am–6pm Sat; 9am–6pm Sun (closes at 5.30pm Nov to early Mar).*

Versailles ★★

*Château de Versailles, ☎ 08 10 81 16 14; **www.chateauversailles.fr.** RER C Versailles Rive Gauche station (then 6 min walk). SNCF trains from Gare St-Lazare to Versailles Rive Droite (then 17min walk); and Gare Montparnasse to Versailles Chantiers (then 16 min walk).*

If you're **driving**, exit the *périphérique* (the ring road around Paris) on N10 (Porte de St-Cloud, Avenue du Général-Leclerc), which will take you to Versailles; park on the Place d'Armes in front of the château.

No trip to Paris would be complete without visiting 'Sun King' Louis XIV's sublime château at Versailles; the seat of power between 1682 and 1789, and the home of Louis XVI and Marie-Antoinette before they were beheaded in Paris during the Revolution. It took three architects, two landscape gardeners, and 45,000 workers 50 years to transform Louis XIII's hunting lodge into the envy of Europe.

The highlights to show your family are the magnificent **Grands Appartements** in the Louis XIV style, each bearing the name of the allegorical painting on the ceiling; and the 71m-long **Hall of Mirrors ★★**, begun by Mansart in 1678 and decorated by Le Brun with 17 arched windows faced by bevelled mirrors in simulated arcades.

The German Empire was proclaimed in this corridor in 1871 and on 28 June, 1919, the treaty ending World War I was also signed here. These wonderful royal apartments were, however, for show and to escape the demands of court etiquette, Louis XV and Louis XVI retired to the more manageable **Petits Appartements.**

Outside, nothing can beat a warm day spent as a family ambling through the terraced gardens, admiring the fountains, Marie-Antoinette's hamlet (**Le Petit Trianon**). The gardens cover 100 hectares and can be navigated on foot, or for families with small children or disabled members, on a golf-buggy (hired at the South Terrace, at the top of the gardens nearest the chateau ☎ *01 39 66 97 66*).

Aside from Le Nôtre's ornamental lakes and geometrically designed flowerbeds, and avenues bordered with statuary, don't miss the **Grand Canal**, used by Louis XV for gondola rides (where you can hire bikes and rowing boats; and use the disabled access toilets for a few centimes); the

The château at Versailles

pink-and-white-marble **Grand Trianon**, designed by Hardouin-Mansart for Louis XIV in 1687 and where Madame de Pompadour died; or the **Petit Trianon** (renovated in July 2008), built in 1768 for Louis XV who allowed Marie Antoinette to adopt it as her favourite residence, where she escaped the rigidity of royal life and played at being a peasant girl.

If you are visiting with older children between late August and early September, reserve tickets for the gardens' '**Les Fêtes de Nuit de Versailles**,' festival where onlookers are wooed with an extravaganza of fireworks, pre-recorded classical music, and up to 200 players in period costume.

Audio guides are available in English for 6€ (tour areas) and 10€ (Grandes Eaux Musicale days in high-season).

Open *Palace 9am–6.30pm Tues–Sun Apr–Oct; 9am–5.30pm Tues–Sun Nov–Mar. Trianons noon–6pm daily. Grounds dawn–dusk daily.* ***Admission*** *passport for all attractions 20€ Mon–Fri, 25€ Sat–Sun; palace only: 13.50€–15€; both Trianons 9€; 17s and under free. Gardens free.*

Where to Sleep in Versailles

Fit for a Versailles royal family is the **Trianon Palace** (1 boulevard de la Reine, *01 30 84 50 00;* ***www.starwoodhotels.com***; rooms 200€–600€) right on the edge of the Palace gardens. Aside from swish, modern bedrooms, it offers tennis courts, a swimming pool, sauna, private parking, and a gastronomic restaurant. For somewhere cheaper, with oodles of charm, try the **Hôtel de France** (5 rue Colber, *01 30 83 92 23;* ***www.hotelfrance-versailles.com***; rooms 137€–236€), which is within a two-minute walk of the chateau and decorated in 18th-century style. For a budget option, you won't go wrong with the standard services at **Ibis Versailles Château** (4 avenue du Général de Gaulle, *01 39 53 03 30;* ***www.ibishotel.com***; rooms 69€–105€. On-site parking).

The Insider

It's not essential to speak French when visiting Paris – especially if you go to Disneyland or Parc Astérix – but it will certainly help, even if you only memorise words of politeness like *'bonjour'* (hello), *'merci'* (thank you) and *'parlez-vous anglais?'* (do you speak English?). Being seen to be making an effort will predispose you well to local people. Although, of course, any stay in France is immeasurably enhanced if you all speak decent French; and children, who will be able to mix with French children and join in French-language activities at museums and so on, will get much more out of their trip abroad.

Children pick up new languages much more easily than adults – and if you approach it as a game, learning the lingo can be good fun. On my first family trip to Paris as a child, we used to flip coins to decide who would have to ask for things in French. My six-year-old brother perfectly mastered the ordering of an *'omelette au fromage'* (cheese omelette), whereas my dad managed to say that he 'was a baguette', rather than he wanted to buy one! Capitalise on this facility by introducing your children to a fun language-learning programme: one of the most highly regarded is the award-winning BBC course *Muzzy*, which includes DVDs with cartoons, available at ***www.bbcshop.com*** or ***www.muzzyonline.co.uk***.

Once you're in Paris, stock up at media stores such as Fnac with French-language story books for your child's age group, and song and story CDs or cassettes in French – a great way of making car journeys and even bedtime more entertaining for all the family. *Le Petit Prince* is a classic.

Basic Vocabulary & Greetings

English	French	Pronunciation
Yes/No	**Oui/Non**	wee/nohn
Please	**S'il vous plaît**	seel voo play
Thank you	**Merci**	*mair*-see
You're welcome	**De rien**	duh ree-*ehn*
Hello (daytime)	**Bonjour**	bohn-*jhoor*
Good evening	**Bonsoir**	bohn-*swahr*
Goodbye	**Au revoir**	oruh-*vwahr*
What's your name?	**Comment vous appellez-vous?**	ko-*mohn*-voo-za-pell-ay-*voo*?
My name is	**Je m'appelle**	*jhuh* ma-pell
How are you?	**Comment allez-vous?**	ko-mohn-tahl-ay-*voo*?
I'm sorry/excuse me	**Pardon**	pahr-*dohn*

Getting Around

English	French	Pronunciation
Do you speak English?	**Parlez-vous anglais?**	par-lay-voo-ohn-*glay*?
I don't speak French	**Je ne parle pas français**	jhuh ne parl pah frohn-*say*
I don't understand	**Je ne comprends pas**	jhuh ne kohm-*prohn* pas
Could you speak more loudly/more slowly?	**Pouvez-vous parler plus fort/plus lentement?**	Poo-*vay* voo par-lay ploo for/ploo lon-te-*mon*?
What is it?	**Qu'est-ce que c'est?**	kess-kuh-*say*?
What time is it?	**Qu'elle heure est-il?**	kel uhr eh-*teel*?
How? or What did you say?	**Comment?**	ko-*mohn*?
When?	**Quand?**	kohn?
Where is?	**Où est?**	oo *eh*?
Who?	**Qui?**	kee?
Why?	**Pourquoi?**	poor-*kwah*?
here/there	**ici/là**	ee-*see*/lah
left/right	**à gauche/à droite**	a goash/a dwaht
straight ahead	**tout droit**	too-*dwah*
Fill the tank (of a car), please	**Le plein, s'il vous plaît**	luh plan, seel-voo-*play*
broken down (in car)	**en panne**	*ohn pan*
I want to get off at	**Je voudrais descendre à**	jhe voo-*dray* day-son dr-ah
bus station	**la gare routière**	lah *gar* roo-tee-*air*
bus stop	**l'arrêt de bus**	lah-*ray* duh boohss
by car	**en voiture**	ohn vwa-*toor*
driver's licence	**le permis de conduire**	luh per-*mee* duh con-*dweer*
exit (building or motorway)	**une sortie**	ewn sor-*tee*
luggage storage	**la consigne**	lah kohn-*seen*-yuh
no smoking	**défense de fumer**	day-*fohns* de fu-may
petrol	**du pétrol/de l'essence**	duh pay-*trol*/de lay-*sohns*
one-day pass	**le ticket journalier**	luh tee-*kay* jhoor-nall-ee-*ay*
one-way ticket	**l'aller simple**	lah-*lay sam*-pluh
return ticket	**l'aller-retour**	lah-*lay* re-*toor*
slow down	**ralentir**	rah-lohn-*teer*
underground/Tube/subway	**le Métro**	luh *may*-tro

Shopping

English	French	Pronunciation
How much does it cost?	**C'est combien?/Ça coûte combien?**	say comb-bee-*ahn*?/sah coot comb-bee-*ahn*?
Do you take credit cards?	**Acceptez-vous les cartes de crédit?**	aksep-*tay* voo lay kart duh cray-*dee*?

English	French	Pronunciation
I'd like	**Je voudrais**	jhe voo-*dray*
I'd like to buy	**Je voudrais acheter**	jhe voo-*dray* ahsh-*tay*
aspirin	**des aspirines/des aspros**	deyz ahs-peer-*een*/deyz ahs-*proh*
colouring book	**un livre de coloriage**	uh lee-vr duh colo-ree-*arj*
map of the city	**un plan de ville**	uh plahn de *vee*
swimming trunks	**un slip de bain**	uh sleep duh ban
swimsuit/swimming costume	**un maillot de bain**	uh *my*-o duh ban
suntan lotion/sunscreen	**de la crème solaire**	duh lah krem sol-*air*
toothpaste	**du dentifrice**	doo don-tee-frees
bakery	**la boulangerie**	lah boo-*lohn*-jhe-ree
butcher	**la boucherie**	lah *boosh*-ree
cake shop	**la pâtisserie**	lah pah-tees-ree
grocery	**l'épicerie**	lah *pees*-ree
launderette	**la laverie automatique**	lah la-vairy auto-mah-*teek*
market	**le marché**	luh mar-*shay*
farmers' market	**le marché fermier**	luh mar-*shay* fair-mee-*ay*
shopping trolley	**le caddy**	luh cah-*dee*
shopping bag	**un sac/une poche**	uh sack/ewn posh
till	**la caisse**	lah kess

Children's Stuff

English	French	Pronunciation
babychanging	**une table à langer**	ewn tahb-le a lahn-*jay*
baby equipment	**matériaux de puériculture**	ma-tay-re-o de pu-e-ray-cult-*oor*
bottlewarmer	**une chauffe-biberon**	ewn showf-bee-ber-*on*
buggy/pushchair	**une poussette**	ewn poo-*set*
child seat	**un siege-enfant**	uh see-erj on-*fon*
children's Paracetamol	**Paracétamol à dose pédiatrique**	Pah-ra-say-tam-ol a dos pay-dee-at-reek
dummy	**une sucette**	ewn sue-set
formula milk (newborn–4 months; 4 months–1 year)	**le lait formule (premier âge; deuxième âge)**	luh lay for-mool (pray-mee-ay arge; duh-zee-em arge)
follow-on milk	**le lait de croissance**	luh lay de cwa-sonce
highchair	**une chaise haute**	ewn chez oat
nappies	**les couches**	lay coo-sh
playground	**l'aire de jeux**	lair de jur

English	French	Pronunciation
sterilising tablets	**les comprimés de stérilisation à froid**	lay com-pree-may de stery-lee-za-seon a fwa
wet wipes	**les lingettes**	lay lon-jet

In Your Hotel

English	French	Pronunciation
are taxes included?	**les taxes sont comprises?**	lay taks son com-*preez*?
double room	**une chambre double**	ewn *shawm*-bruh *doo*-bluh
twin room	**une chambre aux lits simples**	ewn*shawm*-bruh o lee *sam*-pluh
family room	**une chambre familiale**	ewn *shawm*-bruh fam-ee-lee-*al*
interconnecting rooms	**des chambres communicantes/ un appartement**	day shawm-bruhs com-oo-ni-*cont*/uhn apart-a-*mon*
extra bed	**un lit supplémentaire**	uh lee sup-lay-mon-*tair*
cot	**un lit bébé**	uh lee bay-bay
shower	**une douche**	ewn doosh
sink	**un lavabo**	uh la-va-*bow*
the key	**la clé (la clef)**	la clay
balcony	**un balcon**	uh *bahl*-cohn
bathtub	**une baignoire**	ewn bayn-*nwar*
bathroom	**une salle de bain**	ewn sal duh *ban*
hot and cold water	**l'eau chaude et froide**	low showed ay fwad
babysitting	**le babysitting/garde d'enfants**	luh bay-bay sitting/gard don-fon

The Calendar

English	French	Pronunciation
Sunday	**dimanche**	dee-*mohnsh*
Monday	**lundi**	lurn-*dee*
Tuesday	**mardi**	mahr-*dee*
Wednesday	**mercredi**	mair-kreh-*dee*
Thursday	**jeudi**	jheu-*dee*
Friday	**vendredi**	vawn-druh-*dee*
Saturday	**samedi**	sahm-*dee*
Yesterday	**hier**	ee-*air*
today	**aujourd'hui**	o-jhoor-*dwee*
this morning/this afternoon	**ce matin/cet après-midi**	suh ma-*tan*/set ah-preh mee-*dee*

English	French	Pronunciation
tonight	**ce soir**	suh *swahr*
tomorrow	**demain**	de-*man*

Eating Out Terms

English	French	Pronunciation
I would like	**Je voudrais**	jhe voo-*dray*
a bottle of	**une bouteille de**	ewn boo-*tay* duh
a cup of	**une tasse de**	ewn tass duh
a glass of	**un verre de**	uh vair duh
breakfast	**du petit-déjeuner**	doo puh-*tee* day-zhuh-*nay*
the bill	**l'addition/la note**	la-dee-see-*ohn*/la not
dinner	**le dîner**	luh dee-*nay*
lunch	**le déjeuner**	luh day-zhuh-*nay*
a knife	**un couteau**	uh koo-*toe*
a napkin	**une serviette**	ewn sair-vee-*et*
a spoon	**une cuillère**	ewn kwee-*air*
a fork	**une fourchette**	ewn four-*shet*
children's menu	**le menu enfant**	luh may-noo *on*-fon
extra plate	**une assiette supplémentaire**	*ewn ay-see-et sup-lay-mon-tayr*
Waiter!/Waitress!	**Monsieur!/Mademoiselle!**	muh-*syuh*/mad-mwa-*zel*
appetiser/starter	**une entrée**	ewn on-*tray*
main course	**un plat principal**	uh plah pran-see-*pahlh*
tip included	**service compris**	ser-*vees* cohm-*pree*

Numbers & Ordinals

nought/zero	**zéro**	eight	**huit**	sixteen	**seize**	sixty	**soixante**
one	**un**	nine	**neuf**	seventeen	**dix-sept**	seventy	**soixante-dix**
two	**deux**	ten	**dix**	eighteen	**dix-huit**	eighty	**quatre-vingts**
three	**trois**	eleven	**onze**	nineteen	**dix-neuf**	ninety	**quatre-vingts-dix**
four	**quatre**	twelve	**douze**	twenty	**vingt**	one hundred	**cent**
five	**cinq**	thirteen	**treize**	thirty	**trente**	one thousand	**mille**
six	**six**	fourteen	**quatorze**	forty	**quarante**		
seven	**sept**	fifteen	**quinze**	fifty	**cinquante**		

Index

See also Accommodations and Restaurant indexes, below.

General

A

B

C

D

E

K

L

M

N

O

P

Q

R

S

T

U

V

W

Z

Accommodations

Restaurants